Reading Curriculum Theory

American University Studies

Series XIV
Education

Vol. 19

PETER LANG
New York • Bern • Frankfurt am Main • Paris

William M. Reynolds

Reading Curriculum Theory

The Development
of a New Hermeneutic

PETER LANG
New York • Bern • Frankfurt am Main • Paris

Library of Congress Cataloging-in-Publication Data

Reynolds, William M.
    Reading curriculum theory : the development of a
new hermeneutic / William M. Reynolds.
    p. cm. — (American university studies.
Series XIV, Education ; vol. 19)
    Bibliography: p.
    1. Curriculum planning—Philosophy.   2. Education—
Curricula—Philosophy.   I. Title.   II. Series.
LB2806.15.R49   1989   375:001—dc19   88-27408
ISBN 0-8204-1001-2   CIP
ISSN 0740-4565

CIP-Titelaufnahme der Deutschen Bibliothek

Reynolds, William M.:
Reading curriculum theory : the development of
a new hermeneutic / William M. Reynolds. —
New York; Bern; Frankfurt am Main; Paris:
Lang, 1989.
  (American University Studies: Ser. 14,
  Education; Vol. 19)
  ISBN 0-8204-1001-2

NE: American University Studies / 14

Dedication

To the memory of my father, Ward B. Reynolds

Contents

Contents

Acknowledgements

I would like to thank the members of my dissertation committee at the University of Rochester. Philip Wexler was supportive and patient. William F. Pinar, currently Chair of the Department of Curriculum and Instruction at Louisiana State University and Madeleine Grumet, currently Dean of the School of Education at Brooklyn College are very special friends and I am indebted to them for their intellectual insight and continuing support.

I wish also to acknowledge the work of my typesetter Sally Krier without whose diligent effort the text would not have appeared and also the support of my colleagues in the Education Department at the University of Wisconsin-Stout. I am also grateful for an understanding wife and son, Jan and Matthew Reynolds.

Foreword

Hermeneutical curriculum studies have enjoyed rapid growth in recent years. Building on a foundation built by seminal theorists such as James B. Macdonald, Dwayne E. Huebner, and later, T. Aoki, contemporary scholars such as Max van Manen, Madeleine R. Grumet, David G. Smith, Margaret Hunsberger, David Jardine, and William Reynolds—among others—have demonstrated the appropriateness and power of the hermeneutical tradition for curriculum theory.

In this major study, William Reynolds has made an important contribution to curriculum theory. Reynolds demonstrates that, in Ricoeur's words, "existence arrives at expression, at meaning, and at reflection only through the continual exegesis of all the significations that come to light in the world of culture." Ricoeur's understanding of the hermeneutical project informs Reynold's reading the major conservative curriculum documents of this decade, i.e., Adler's *Paideia Proposal* and *A Nation at Risk*.

Both Adler's work and that of the National Commisssion on Excellence in Education are read hermeneutically, at once in relation to his own intellectual life history and in relation to "reconceptualist" and "reproductionist" curriculum theory. (Here Reynolds takes seriously the curriculum Marxists' repudiation of the "reconceptualist" characterization, and leaves this category for those who embrace it.) The "arch" is completed as these inter-related readings are linked with Ricoeur"s work, which, not incidentally, is very usefully surveyed in chapter two.

Reynolds moves carefully through these now infamous conservative curriculum documents, reflecting on his reading of them in light of Ricoeur's theory of interpretation. Slowly he is moved to conclude that both sets of documents represent "dungeons." Linking these documents to his own school experience enables him to explicate his own "text" as well. He observes: "By doing the hermeneutic process with the conservative curriculum texts the chief aim of an increased self-understanding has been accomplished."

Reynolds read my own *Sanity, Madness, and the School*, finding its descriptive character in contrast to the prescriptions of *Paideia* and *At Risk*. Here too Reynolds reads conspicuously carefully, moving from point to point, contrasting both the specific curriculum proposals of both as well as their underlying assumptions. Then Reynolds moves to Michael Apple's "Curriculum Form and the Logic of Technical Control: Building the Possessive Individual." Reynolds finds Apple's work neither prescriptive nor descriptive, but rather, "confrontational." He sketches the inter-relationships among all three orders of theory, specifying not only their logical differences, but differences of tone and rhythmn also. Here his work is original, subtle, and pleasing.

> [Adagio]...is the characteristic uniqueness of this Pinar text. It can be compared to the difference between a staccato march tempo, which interestingly enough further ties the style of the conservative curriculum theory texts to the militarism of a "Stars and Stripes Forever" march and an adagio concerto by Bach i.e., "Concerto No. 2 for Violin and Orchestra in E major, S. 1042."

Comparing *Sanity* with "Logic..." Reynolds finds:

> The style of this Apple text, the style of struggle, is like that of the Pinar text in one respect. It possesses that shock quality. Its style is in contrast to the everydayness of the conservative theory texts. ... with the Pinar text, the alienation of the natural is produced. It is also produced in the Apple text. However, it is accomplished in a very different way. It is produced not by an adagio gracefulness, but the language of struggle.

Working with and through both texts Reynolds finds himself working with his own voice, becoming more conscious of his own hisory, and the "biographic functions" of his project. "In a small way this study has shown me a road upon which to continue my journey. It is not Pinar's road. It is not Apple's road. It is my own road." His road is differentiated from others; it becomes what Madeleine Grumet terms the "middle way" between the public and the private, what Jacques Daignault terms the problematics of "translation". It is a process of individuation which conservatives have not undergone and do not understand, but which Reynold's study exemplifies.

We have endured a decade of reactionary curriculum leadership, a decade during which time—perversely it would seem—the curriculum theory field has developed dramatically and progressively. The paths broken by the theorists of the 1950's and 1960's, Huebner, Macdonald, and Paul Klohr as well, have been cleared further, traveled by fine minds who illumine both the course of study and the experience of the course. Those of us who struggled during the 1970's to continue the work of our disciplinary "parents" can take pride in the sophisticated work now being performed by our students. Certainly I take pride in Reynold's achievement, as I know he must. Finally, however, the achievement is a collective and historical one, one in which all of us can share.

William F. Pinar
Professor and Chair
Department of Curriculum and Instruction
Louisiana State University

1
Introduction

> The voyage had begun, and had begun happily
> with a soft blue sky, and a calm sea. The
> sense of untapped resources things to say
> as yet unsaid, made the hour significant
> (Woolf, 1920, p.24)....

A voyage connotes multifarious meanings and images. A voyage is an enterprise, undertaking or adventure of a private character (OED, p. 3660). A written account or book describing a journey (OED, p. 3661), is another meaning connected with the concept of a voyage. The study pursued in these pages is a voyage in both senses. It is a written account of a personal enterprise. A journey toward understanding curriculum theory and understanding that understanding. It is a voyage in progress and it is a voyage with "things to say as yet unsaid" (Woolf, 1920, p. 24).

It is a voyage through various hermeneutic arches with momentary stops throughout the journey. The concept of the hermeneutic arch will be explained in great detail later in this study, but at this point a succinct definition will aid in understanding the explanation of the journey. The hermeneutic arch "replaces explanation and interpretation by a global conception which integrates both explanation and understanding in the reading of a text as the recovery of its sense and meaning" (Bleicher, 1980, p. 267). The journey consists of the movement from the initial reading and naive understanding of texts through the critical reading or explanation to a comprehension and new self-understanding through texts. My personal voyage through understanding of curriculum theory is a long one. It is comprised of many detours. But, it follows through many hermeneutic arches just the same.

Upon completion of one arch I have always proceeded to another one. Often times there has been a pause between the arches. At other times it has been a quick step to the next. It is reminiscent of Brother William's seeking in *The Name of the Rose*.

> I did not then know what Brother William was seeking, and to tell the truth, I still do not know today, and I presume he himself did not know, moved as he was soley by the desire for truth, and by the suspicion — which I could see always harbored — that the truth was not what was appearing to him at any given moment (Eco, 1980, p. 14).

In this selection from Eco's brilliant novel my voyage is nicely summarized. It is the search for an understanding of education through the texts of curriculum theory. Yet, at the same time this journey toward understanding is taking place, there is a problematic. The problematic is one of habitual perception when reading curriculum theory. The possibility exists that many of my own readings of curriculum and philosophy have not moved out of a naive reading as Paul Ricoeur refers to it. They have been readings that only gleen the apparent meanings from texts. A naive reading must be superseded by other ways of explaining and understanding texts. This new way of reading will be the area that this study will cover.

This attitude of habitual perception, which characterizes my early readings as well as others of curriculum theory, philosophy, and other subjects, is a way of looking at the world. According to Martin Heidegger it is an inauthentic way of being in the world. It is the being that belongs to "everydayness".

> This term does not express any negative evaluation, but is is used to signify that Dasein is proximally and for the most part alongside the world of its concern. This "absorption in..." (Aufgchen bei...) has mostly the character of Being-lost in the publicness of the "they". Dasein has, in the first instance, fallen away (abgefallen) from itself as an authentic potentiality for Being its Self, and fallen into the "world". "Falleness" into the "world" means an absorption in Being-with-one-another, in so far as the latter is guided by idle talk, curiosity, and ambiguity. Through the Interpretation of falling, what we have called the "inauthenticity" of Dasein may now be defined more precisely.

On no account, however, do the terms "inauthentic" and "non-authentic" signify "really not", as if in this mode of Being, Dasein were altogether to lose its Being. "Inauthenticity" does not mean anything like Being-no-longer-in-the-world but amounts rather to quite distinctive kind of Being-in-the-world the kind which is completely fascinated with the "world" and by the Dasein-with of Others in the "they". Not-Being-its-self (Das Nicht-es-selbst-sein) functions as a positive possibility of the entity which, in its essential concern, is absorbed in a world. This kind of not-Being has to be conceived as that kind of Being which is closet to Dasein and in which Dasein maintains itself for the most part (Heidegger, 1962, p. 219).

This method of perception or way of being is characterized by a person who is busy, excited and preoccupied. This is a person who lives in the taken for granted world and views the world as it is, or at least as it appears to be. It is a person who is an "undifferentiated self lacking individuality and personal decision" (Sahakin, 1968, p. 350).

Maxine Greene discusses this taken for granted view of the world in her book *Lanscapes of Learning* (1978).

To take the world for granted as predefined or objectively "there" is to be uncritical, submissive and submerged. Obviously, this does not mean that the world is an illusion or that it does not exist independently. It simply means as Merleau-Ponty expressed it that all our knowledge of the world, even our scientific knowledge, is gained from our human point of view, "or from some experience of the world without which the symbols of science would be meaningless." Each of us he said, is a subject "destined to be in the world", our concern is with a disclosure of the world, a clarification of what it means to be (Greene, 1978, p. 44).

Phenomenologically, then, our habitual perception becomes a way of being. It is an inauthentic and a submerged type of being. Our being becomes as if we are in a motion picture. We are so consumed with being-in-the-picture and acting correctly as others in the picture do that we forget it is a motion picture and we can step out of this taken for granted perception. This is the beginning of understanding our involvement with and in the world.

This habitual perception or taken for granted attitude manifests a way of involving ourselves with things. I believe it not only involves our interests in hobbies and novel preoccupations, but also involves our attitudes toward intellectual ventures, in particular reading texts. Before discussing the attitude of "curiosity" (Heidegger, 1962, p. 216), it is necessary to discuss reading in general. Habitual perception and a type or way of reading will be determined to be quite similiar.

What does it mean to read? The original sense of the Teutonic verb raedan are those of taking or giving counsel, taking care or charge of a thing, and having or exercising control over a thing (OED, 1971, p. 2427). In my own intellectual journey I have sought through texts and the reading of those texts, connections. It has been a type of curious reading and a type of inauthentic being. The connections sought were the connections with the "they".

In Heidegger's work *Being and Time*, inauthentic being is contrasted to authentic self by being recognized as the "they-self" that is, as the group self, the public self, or a part of the social existence into which the self is dispersed, "falling" into anonymity and depersonalization. The anonymous individual who has fallen into inauthentic Being is susceptible to what Heidegger refers to as "publicness". Publicness occurs when the anonymous being accepts and conforms to public opinion and socially established standards, thereby withdrawing from responsible independent decisions and commitments based upon his own personal choice (Sahaken, 1968, p. 350). When I begin to perceive my own intellectual journey through reading various philosophies and curriculum theories, it has taken place in this inauthentic publicness it seems. I have lost my own voice at certain points to accept at certain times other "they" voices. Many times I have, in choosing certain arches, given up my responsible independent decisions and followed powerful and attractive other voices. Consequently, I have fallen into voices that were not my own. I will discuss separate incidents of this later in the study.

So, my readings have not only been pursued with an habitual

perception, but also with an attempt to make connections. These connections were not with myself but established standards.

They have also been pursued, I think, with an attitude of what Heidegger calls curiosity.

...it concerns itself with seeing, not in order to understand what is seen (that is, to come into a Being towards it) but just in order to see. It seeks novelty only in order to leap from it anew to another novelty. In this kind of seeing, that which is an issue for care does not lie in grasping something and being knowlingly in the truth; it lies in its possibilities of abandoning itself to the world. Therefore curiosity is characterized by a specific way of not tarrying alongside what is closest. Consequently, it does not seek the leisure of tarrying observently, but rather seeks restlessness and the excitement of continual novelty and changing encounters. In not tarrying, curiosity is concerned with the constant possibilities of distraction...it (curiosity) concerns itself with a kind of knowing, but just in order to have known (Heidegger, 1962, p. 217).

If we substitute reading for seeing, it is possible to understand how my personal journey through various hermeneutic arches has jumped from one arch to another. I prefer to call this characteristic of inauthentic being the loss and search for a personal voice and the constant changing of voice depending on which novelty or idea one is reading or following. The idea of reading as making connections relates when discussing these inauthentic characteristics of "falling" and "curiosity". The connections made in these types of readings are not connections for a unity of the human person or for self-understanding. But, they have been for a type of "publicness". It is a way of running from our own voice and escaping into an accepted voice, one that meets with public approval. It is a voice that stays within the habitual perception because it is a safe place to be. There is no risk involved.

The problems have been, then, this habitual perception in reading curriculum theory and a search for a voice or type of reading that would overcome this habitual perception. Perhaps, it would constitute a possible solution to the problem.

If I set out the itinerary of my various travels throughout the various hermeneutic arches, it will become clear how my readings have been, as described above, a search for a voice to express my experience and understanding of curriculum theory texts. It is the way I have proceeded through these arches that Paul Ricoeur describes as the first moment of the hermeneutic arch. At many points I have simply jumped from one intitial naive reading where I have gleened some apparent meaning to another initial naive reading. I would find the first reading unsatisfying or lacking a type of "publicness" and I would move on to another. I have sometimes even found the "publicness" unsatisfying. I think to a greater or lesser extent we have all experienced this phenomenon. But, at the same time there has always been a single direction, which has led me to the point of this particular study.

HERMENEUTIC ARCHES: A GENERAL PERSPECTIVE

My journey through the various arches of curriculum theory texts can be looked at in two ways. First, from the general perspective of the overall journey it can be outlined. Secondly, a specific deline-ation of each arch with the specific texts can be studied. The two methods of looking at the itinerary of my journeys will demonstrate at least three points: (1) that the problem of habitual perception is a more general problem in reading curriculum theory than in just my own particular case, but that my own case can serve as an example; (2) that the explanation of the various arches will elaborate on the very human phenomenon of striving for "publicness"; (3) that finding one's voice to express these ideas and concepts concerning curriculum theory is, indeed, a hard fought intellectual struggle.

Another major purpose of this explanation of the journeys is to demonstrate the ways in which I arrived at this point of understand-ing my initial reading and understanding of curriculum theory and related matters. I can now express those understandings in a certain voice. It is an introduction to my use of Ricoeur as a new way of hermeneutically interpreting texts, specifically in curriculum theory and a way to foster a comprehension and self-understanding at the same time.

When we have returned home from a long voyage, it is customary to pull out all the photographs, maps, brochures, and the travel log and peruse them. Perhaps, we even make a scrapbook up of the travels we have taken. We remember a certain cafe at which we lingered a little too long. We reminisce about a certain day that was just perfect. We begin to make up our scrapbook. But, the pages must be put in order first so that our scrapbook has coherence and meaning.

Therefore, I wish to put a broad conceptual framework upon my discussion of hermeneutic arches. This framework will be related to curriculum theory and my journey toward understanding that theory.

A CONCEPTUAL SCHEMATA

In *The Age of Structuralism: Levi-Strauss to Foucault*, Edith Kurzweil reports recent French intellectual history. This intellectual history has a direct bearing on the contemporary curriculum theory field and also on my own personal intellectual journey through curriculum theory and its related texts. Perhaps, my coming to these theories is unique to some extent. Most curricular theorists come from in-depth readings of philosophy, sociology, literature and other disciplines to curriculum theory. I have come to curriculum theory from a background of literary study with an emphasis in literary criticism. Before coming to the field of curriculum theory I had not done any extensive reading in philosophy or sociology. Instead, I began to read various curriculum theorists which then led me to read philosophy, sociology, and other related fields. I consider the study of education my primary discipline which has led to the study of other disciplines. Jacques Daignault makes a point quite clearly in a paper entitled "Curriculum Beyond Words with Words" (1984). He discusses the study of education as a second discipline.

Take any journal in education and look at the bibliographies. Almost all the important and interesting works refer to other disciplines than education. And those that refer to education, refer to education works which refer to other disciplines. And my opinion is that writing on education is an obstacle to writing in a first discipline. Because education is essentially a second field (Daignault, 1984, p. 3).

Daignault's comments can refer directly to my own situation. In my readings (journeys) curriculum theory has been a pathway to other disciplines. I have traveled from literary criticism to curriculum theory to philosophy and back to curriculum theorizing. This movement should be explained then understood in the hermeneutic sense. So for me also, in a different way, educational theory has been a means not an end.

When Kurzweil discusses the evolution of modern French intellectual thought, she divides it into significant periods. Although, putting intellectual thought into a specific schematization is a bit artificial, it does aid in the explanation of it. Some comments of Vincent Descombes, from his book *Modern French Philosophy*, serve as an invaluable aid in understanding French intellectual thought. This schemata of Kurzweil and to a certain extent Descombes has a bearing on my journey and hence curriculum thought in general. It is the organizing principle to the "scrapbook".

Descombes divides French thought into two large intellectual periods. The recent philosophical movements in France can be "traced from the generation known after 1945 as that of the three H's to the generation known since 1960 as that of the three masters of suspicion: the three H's being Hegel, Husserl, and Heidegger, and the three masters of suspicion Marx, Nietzsche, and Freud" (Descombes, 1980, p. 3).

Kurzweil, in her study, divides the movement of French thought into four periods. These are the most significant divisions related to this study; they break up Descombes' periods into smaller units. Her divisions include four philosophical periods: (1) The period of the resistance and immediately after liberation when Marxism preoccupied the French intellectuals; (2) The period of growing disillusionment with Soviet Russia and the introduction of Sartre's existential humanism; (3) The period between 1952 and 1956 when Sartre still professed his existential humanism while continuing to support the communists. His theories became suspect; (4) The suspicion of Sartre's theories made it possible for structuralism and the new theories of linguistics and semiotics to gain impetus (Kurzweil, 1980, pp. 1-5). Kurzweil does maintain that all these theories have come to co-exist and that the birth of a new philosophical movement does not indicate the death of another. Three basic strains of thought seem to co-exist in French thought Marxism, existentialism, and structuralism. Although I agree with Ricoeur about the limits of structuralism as philosophy, it is an important mode of thought to discuss.

Current avant-garde curriculum theory can be divided into those same types or categories. It is helpful to break them up in this way for a closer explanation of how I have journeyed through them.

I will delineate the following areas of curriculum theory, which in many respects corresponds to the divisions of French intellectual thought. There are some areas of avant-garde theory I am not going to discuss because those areas are not part of my personal voyage through curriculum theory. A first-rate analysis of the field has been completed by Karen A. Mazza in "Reconceptual Inquiry as an Alternative Mode of Curriculum Theory and Practice: A Critical Study" (Mazza, JCT, 4:2, pp. 5-90).

The field of curriculum theory has been separated into various divisions. These divisions must be discussed both in general and specific terms to situate my own involvement within the field.

THE DIVISIONS OF THE FIELD

There are many divisions in this curriculum theory field. Much has been discussed about the divisions in the field (Pinar, ed., 1974), (Pinar, ed., 1975), (Giroux, Penna, and Pinar, eds., 1981), (Gress and Purpel, eds., 1978), (Giroux and Purpel, eds., 1983). These discussions center on the distinctions among the reconceptualists, the traditionalists and the conceptual-empiricists. These categories of curriculum theory/theorists were created by William Pinar and have been widely used and discussed. It is important for our purposes to review these classifications briefly.

Reconceptualist curriculum theory is "an attempt at a fundamental reconceptualization of what curriculum is, how it functions, and how it might function in emancipatory ways. It is this commitment to a comprehensive critique and theory development that distinguishes the reconceptualist phenomenon" (Giroux, Penna and Pinar eds., 1981, chap. 6).

This group, the reconceptualists, are the theorists whose work is directed toward the individual and his unique educational experiences (Pinar and Grumet, 1974). Their work is based on existential philosophy, phenomenology and Freudian psychoanalysis. It is suggestive of the trend in French thought that was highly influenced by Sartre.

There is another division of this avant-garde curriculum theory and it can be designated by the term, reproductionists. These theories base their work on Marxist and neo-Marxist theory and concentrate on the unmasking of the ideological functions of education. The curricular theories of Apple (1979, 1981, 1982), Giroux (1981, 1983), and Anyon (1979), fall within this category.

The traditionalists or the Tylerites in curriculum theory narrowly define their field and closely allied it with practical concerns of the schools. "What makes this work one territory is its fundamental interest in working with school people and with revising the curricula of schools" (Giroux, Penna and Pinar eds., 1981, p. 90).

The conceptual-empiricists in curriculum theory have closely connected their field with mainstream social science. Their emphasis is in using terminology and methodology borrowed from the canons of social science. "The work of this group can be so characterized, employing the terms conceptual and empirical in the sense social scientists typically employ them. This work is concerned with developing hypotheses to be tested and testing them in methodological ways characteristic of main stream social science (Giroux, Penna and Pinar eds., 1981, p. 91).

That briefly is the curriculum theory field as delineated by Pinar. I have been, however, most interested in the two divisions, the reconceptualists and the reproductionists. I have journeyed through these conceptual areas and would like to analyze them from that point of view.

SPECIFIC HERMENEUTIC ARCHES
THE REPRODUCTIONISTS

The reproductionists' texts are the first set of texts I journeyed through. I will, therefore, begin my look through my intinerary with their texts. These theorists and their texts are linked to a Marxist interpretation and outlook on education. My journey through the first hermeneutic arch is through an arch of neo-Marxist curriculum theory. It is quite like the French intellectuals whose first philosophical bent was toward Marxism. My travels through this hermeneutic arch produced two studies. One entitled "English Teaching and Ideology" (1981). The other was entitled "Freedom from Control: Toward an Abolition of Teacher Materials and Minimum Competency Tests in English Education" (1982). These are patterned on other studies conducted in the Marxist perspective. My initial involvement with curriculum was with a sociology of curriculum. The curriculum was in the area of English education. This can be viewed as an aspect of the "new" sociology of education. I came to this point in the hermeneutic arch after eight years of teaching public school and finding it in many ways both unsatisfying and perplexing. I wanted to understand exactly what was taking place in the institution we call school. I was introduced into a critical perspective by Philip Wexler in an introductory sociology of education course at the University of Rochester. I began to read in the "new" sociology of education. This area can be briefly summarized.

The "new" sociology of education as Karabel and Halsey have called the largely British phenomenon in *Power and Ideology in Education* began to emerge in the early 1970's. It can be viewed as a reaction to or critique of the type of macrostructural analysis that were prevalent in the sociology of education up to that time. These large macrostructural issues of the equality of educational opportunity and the theories of genetic and cultural deprivation were viewed as lacking. They saw the school as a neutral force. The emphasis on research priorities began to be placed on the content of schooling, a type of sociology of the curriculum. The works in which this development can be seen are *Knowledge and Control* edited by Michael F.D. Young (1971) and *Knowledge, Education and Culutral Change* edited by Richard Brown (1973). These two volumes contain collections of papers that focus the study of schooling or the sociology of education on the sociology of knowledge. Young in his introduction to the 1971 volume emphasized that the sociology of education and the sociology of knowledge are, in essence, the same. Knowledge was to be treated as being socially constituted or constructed. This emphasis on a social and historical study of educational forms and school knowledge was a break with the functionalist studies of education. It was precipitated, Karabel and Halsey believe, by the socio-economic historical crisis of the 1960's which brought about the development of strong intellectual critiques in a number of fields of study.

This interpretive or alternative paradigm of the "new" sociology of education and/or curriculum brought about a number of alternative methods of analysis. Some were based on Marxist categories of social analysis. Some of these methods were; conflict theory, action theory, and phenomenology. However, the overall emphasis seems to have been and still for the most part is *reproduction* theory. This emphasis on reproduction theory started one of my journeys through an hermeneutic arch. I began to read all I could find on the literature of reproduction. It led me to one of the spokesmen for the division, Michael Apple. The stress on reproduction theory was far from a united front, however. Michael Apple, editor of *Cultural and Economic Reproduction in Education* (1982), discusses some of the major disputes in the literature of reproduction in education in an essay entitled "Reproduction and Contradiction in Education: An Introduction". This essay puts the disputes into what he calls "ideal types" and although it may be criticized as mechanistic and somewhat superficial it does help put the various studies of the reproductionists and the sociology of curriculum into a perspective that enables explanation. It will also eventually enable me to better understand my infatuation with this specific arch of Marxist theory.

Apple divides the literature on reproduction, which just happens to coincide with most of the important literature in sociology of the curriculum, into two ideal groups. The first group's commitments are in the issues of educational power, economic factors and results. The second group's emphasis lies in culture, power and the effects of that power. It might be helpful to digress for a moment and provide a working definition of reproduction in education which will be referred to repeatedly. Apple, in his book *Education and Power*, gives a brief but adequate definition of reproduction. The theory of both cultural and economic reproduction posits the concept that schools play an important role both in the overt and "hidden" curriculum in reproducing a stratified society that remains basically unequal in many ways (Apple, 1983). Basically, then, the division comes between those that emphasize the economic aspects of reproduction and those that emphasize the cultural aspects. A brief review of the literature I read as part of this hermeneutic is in order.

The first literature I read was in the division of economic reproduction. The economic emphasis could be seen in the following works; *Inequality* (1972) by Christopher Jencks et. al., *Education and the Rise of the Corporate State* (1972) and *The Sorting Machine* (1976) by Joel Spring and most likely one of the most often referred to texts *Schooling in Capitalist America* (1976) by Bowles and Gintis.

The correspondence theory which is defined in the last work forms the basis or is basic to these theories of economic reproduction. This theory basically states that the educational system helps to prepare students to enter the current economic system through a correspondence between its structure and the structure of production. The theory sees school as a factory. The dispositions and skills necessary for various levels of labor are produced by various educational methods such as; tracking, the hidden curriculum (dispositions of various tracks for various kinds of work), and emphasis on accumulation and accreditation. This economic reproduction theory began to view education as part of a larger economic and ideological system. It put education into a broader social context. This was its greatest asset.

The cultural reproductionists are concerned with the sociology of knowledge and this is the division of reproduction theory that was so influential upon me. The field might properly be called the sociology of the curriculum. The works and names most closely associated with this group are Young, Bernstein, and Bourdieu and in America, I feel, Apple and Wexler. Their works are numerous, but I immersed myself in them. They consist of: *Class, Codes and Control Volume 3: Towards a Theory of Educational Transmission* (1975) by Bernstein (he also wrote an interesting article entitled "On Classification and Framing of Educational Knowledge" in Young's *Knowledge and Control* (1971). Bourdieu has several articles. Two extremely important ones it seemed to me were "Cultural Reproduction and Social Reproduction" (1973) and "Systems of Education and System of Thought". Young, the editor of *Knowledge and Control*, has an article entitled "Curriculum as Socially Organized Knowledge" in which he discusses the stratification of knowledge and possible directions for the sociology of education. Apple coming chronologically later has at least three volumes that I read with a naive gleening. *Ideology and Curriculum* (1979), *Cultural and Economic Reproduction in Education* (1982), and *Education and Power* (1982). In the latter work Apple discusses the strengths and weaknesses of the reproduction theory.   Philip Wexler, a strong influence during this particular hermeneutic arch, in an article entitled "Structure, Text and Subject: A Critical Sociology of School Knowledge" (1982) provided not only a penetrating analysis of the field, but also was probably the impetus for leaving this hermeneutic. I began to find it unsatisfactory as well.

These scholars are concerend with studying the specific form and content the curriculum takes and their works were instrumental in my producing works which dealt with the same subject matter. They are interested in terms such as; ideology, hegemony, accumulation, resistance and contestation. Their study is equated with the sociology of knowledge. Besides the continuing emphasis on ideology and culture new concepts were being brought in while I was in this arch. The concepts were/are discourse analysis, textual analysis, signification and others. They are concerned with the cultural capital and its relation to social stratification as part of their studies. The questions that these theorists are asking are many.   What constitutes knowledge? What and whose knowledge are the students learning?   The above are typical questions asked in these studies. Most of these studies seem to stress how the cultural appartuses of society are responsible for the reproduction and maintenance of the ideology of the dominant classes. So, with these cultural reproductionists, the concern becomes an ideological analysis of cultural artifacts.   It analyzes how ideology is maintained through overt and covert practices.

These works held a fascination for me. They were a new way of looking at educational issues. I also began to read works related to this Marxist perspective.   I read portions of Karl Marx's *Capital Volume 1*, Harry Braverman's book *Labor and Monopoly Capital: The Degradation of Work in the Twentieth Century, Contested Terrain: The Transformation of the Workplace in the Twentieth Century* by Richard

Edwards, and a book that was particularly influential *English in America: A Radical View of the Profession* by Richard Ohmann. I began to look at the process of schooling as reproduction. I was reading to make connections. I made the connections based on a naive reading of the texts. In essence, I moved from the initial reading to an application and consequently bypassed the two other components of the interpretational hermeneutic. The sociology of the curriculum that I had read became the sociology of the curriculum I wrote.

The connections I was attempting to make were the connections of the "they". It was a type of knowing in order to know. Although my papers were not written with that particular emphasis in mind at the time, in reflecting on them, they do, indeed, seem this way. I was at the time looking for a voice for my ideas on educational issues and at that particular time the Marxist voice was a novelty for me, therefore, I lingered in that voice for awhile. Marxist theory was looked at with curiosity and then a new novelty or voice was sought. I had gained some recognition for the work I did in the Marxist vein, but the "I" that I was, was not the "I" that I really am (Klemm, 1983, p. 108). I had not found the voice to clearly express my ideas. I was expressing some ideas in a voice that was not my own. Consequently it was very easy to move on to some new and untried voice. It is important to note that these works in neo-Marxist curriculum theory must be looked at once again in the context of a new reading that employs the hermeneutic arch. This will be discussed in Chapter 4 of this study. Since the movement away from these works was in a falling toward "publicness" and after only the naive reading, a new reading must be done of them to see if they open up possible horizons that can fuse with my own horizon.

THE RECONCEPTUALISTS

The next phase in my study of curriculum theory that can be compared with the progress of French intellectual thought is the movement toward existentialism and phenomenology. This phase of my work in curriculum theory produced two papers. It included; "The Self and The Curriculum" (1982), and "The Prose and the Passion: What Does it Mean for a Man to Read" (1983). This phase of my study of curriculum was begun after meeting and reading the works of William Pinar and Madeleine Grumet. Both of these scholars opened the world of existential and phenomenological thought to me. I read, however, naively not only their works on curriculum theory, autobiography and gender, but also works of philosophy that their works led me to. The works of Sartre began to interest me. I read *Search for a Method*, *The Words*, and portions of his magnum opus *Being and Nothingness: A Phenomenological Essay on Ontology*. I then turned to reading about the autobiographical method. I read *The Autobiographical Consciousness: A Philosophical Inquiry into Existence* by William Earle. I also read *Metaphors of The Self: The Meaning of Autobiography* by James Olney. These works led me to read the works of "existential" psychology including: *On Becoming a Person: A Therapist's View of Psychotherapy* by Carl R. Rogers, and *Toward a Psychology of Being* by Abraham Maslow. These works led me to read works by and about Freud. These works included: *The Ego and The Id* and *The Interpretation of Dreams*. These readings lead to the first paper I wrote in this area entitled "The Self and The Curriculum" where I used both the autobiographical method and the works just stated. This work led me to read Martin Heidegger's *Being and Time*. This text has had a great influence on my work and it was especially evident in the paper I wrote entitled "The Prose and the Passion: What Does it Mean for a Man to Read". All of these works held me in their grip for a time.

The works of Pinar and Grumet are part of the curriculum theory field known as reconceptualism. This area of curriculum theory can also be briefly examined.

In her study entitled: "Reconceptual Inquiry as an Alternative Mode of Curriculum Theory and Practice: A Critical Study" Karen Mazza presents a very good overview of the literature in reconceptual theory. She mentions the major works of the reconceptualists. I would like to put these works into a historical perspective also, however, my listing is not nearly as extensive as Mazza's.

The specific texts begin with Maxine Greene and William Pinar's papers from a conference and text both entitled: *Heightened Consciousness, Cultural Revolution, and Curriculum Theory*. The conference was held in 1973 at the University of Rochester. The texts that follow this initial one are also extremely important for any study of the phenomenon of reconceptualism. The initial text is followed by Pinar and Grumet's text *Toward a Poor Curriculum* (1976), which can be seen as a seminal work in existential curriculum theory. This group of texts also includes two texts that are crucial to the understanding of reconceptualism: *Curriculum Theorizing: The Reconceptualists* (1975) and *Curriculum and Instruction: Alternatives in Education* (1981). These works should be purused by those interested in reconceptualist curriculum theory. The periodical of the reconceptualists, *The Journal of Curriculum Theorizing*, also contains many articles of interest to those researching the field.

These works were very important for me and led me to write papers that were very meaningful and at the same time very personal. They were, therefore, not presented in any public way. This meant that I did not receive "recognition" for them in the sense of any kind of academic currency. I still needed that "publicness". I began to get restless in this particular area and I began to search for another area or novelty. Again, my reading (journey) had not completed the hermeneutic arch. It stayed in the naive reading and attempted to make some profound insights with just the gleened apparent meanings from the texts.

I did not take long to find that new area. I became intrigued with the work of Jacques Daignault after hearing and reading a paper of his presented at the Fourth Conference of Curriculum Theory and Practice entitled: "To Make Some One Know as We Make Some Laugh: A Perverse Analysis of Promise and Desire in Curriculum" (1983). In order to understand Daignault's work I began to read the philosophy of Nietzsche. I read *Beyond Good and Evil*, and *Thus Spoke Zarathustra: A Book for Everyone and No One*. I also read several books about Nietzschean philosophy. One of the most outstanding was *Nietzsche: Philosopher, Psychologist, Antichrist* by Walter Kaufman. These works of Nietzsche enabled me to read other works by Daignault and Clermont Gauthier.

Their work entitled "The Indecent Curriculum Machine: Who's Afraid of Sisyphe?" (1982) was particularly important to my studies. "Analogy in Education: An Archeology Without Subsoil" (1983) by Daignault was also very influential to my reading in this period. In order to understand more clearly this work I began as the French intellectuals did to become interested in structuralism.

Structuralism was a very new way to look at the world. It was based on the linguistic theory of Saussure (a detail analysis of the synchronic study of language by Saussure will be done in Chapter 2 of this study). Structuralism allowed me to pursue a long time interest in literary criticism. I began to read as much on structuralist literary theory as I could find. Several studies were read in preparation for a paper entitled "Reconceptualist Curriculum Theory, Epistemes, Formula and Familiarity: A Critique of the Present Discourse in Curriculum Theory". These readings never left that naive reading with its corresponding skimming of meaning. Several methodologies were blended together for the position arrived at in my study. These studies were sometimes blended together when there were large discrepencies among the various philosophical standpoints taken by the respective authors. The works used in the study were of the structuralist mode, but took various interpretations of it. There was the structuralism and semiotics demonstrated in the writings of Roland Barthes, specifically: *Mythologies* (1972), *The Pleasure of The Text* (1751), and *Roland Barthes* (1977). Jonathan Culler's works on literature, specifically: *Structuralist Poetics: Structuralism, Linquistics and the Study of Literature* (1978), *The Pursuit of Signs: Semiotics, Literature, Deconstruction* (1981), and *On Deconstruction: Theory and Criticism After Structuralism* (1982) were also naively read. Ferdinand de Saussure's *Course in General Linguistics* (1968) was also used as a basic source for the study. Two works by Robert Scholes were read in this way. They are *Structuralism in Literature: An Introduction* (1974), and *Semiotics and Interpretation* (1982). Michel Foucault's *The Archeology of Knowledge* and *The Discourse on Language* (1972) was also used in the study. The paper that resulted from these works was presented at the Fifth Annual Conference of Curriculum Theory and Practice. It was seen as an iconoclastic blasting of the various reconceptualist positions. That was not what was intended, but what was perceived. I reworked the paper but it still lacked the ability to go beyond the critical stage.

This study also included reference to the work of Derrida. I began to read Derrida with the conviction that in his writings I would find the answer to the problematic of habitual perception. I read several of Derrida's works and various works on deconstruction the "method" of Derrida.

This reading was also a naive type of reading of deconstruction. I read *Of Grammatology* (1976), *Speech and Phenomena and Other Essays on Husserl's Theory of Signs* (1973), *Writing and Difference* (1978), and *Margins of Philosophy* (1982). After reading these works by Derrida I began to investigate the topic of deconstruction. I began reading various works on the subject including: *Modern French Philosophy* (1980) by Vincent Descombes, *Reconstruction Theory and Practice* (1983) by Christopher Norris, and *Marxism and Reconstruction: A Critical Articulation* (1982) by Michael Ryan. These studies resulted in a newly revised paper on the subject of the interpretation of curriculum theory called "Reading Curriculum Theory: A Deconstruction" (1984).

But, this study did not escape the naive readings and habitual perceptions either. I was still searching for the "they" voice. During a rather restless night at the Sixth Annual Conference of Curriculum Theory and Practice I finally realized that the search I had been on was a search to escape the habitual perception and its consequent attributes; the "fallness" and the "curious" attitude that attends it. It was in actuality a search for interpreting curriculum theory texts with my own voice and what I had been pursuing was not my own voice but for the voice of the "they" and its result of approval.

I began to read again the works of Paul Ricoeur and his "hermeneutic phenomenology" (Ihde, 1971). Not only did I pursue this hermeneutic phenomenology, but also the reflective philosophy that Ricoeur discusses in his works. It is with this reflective attitude that I have approached this present study. I have not attempted to prescribe the works of Ricoeur but perform his reflective mode of thought on the works that I have read and the journeys I have taken through partial hermeneutic arches. It is in the works of Ricoeur that I find the fusion of horizons that many of the phenomenologists discuss. But, it is as Ricoeur states not the fusion of horizons between the author and the reader; it is the fusion of the horizon of the reader and the possible worlds the text opens.

The works of Ricoeur, especially those of his hermeneutic turn, will be discussed extensively in the second chapter of this study.

Those works include *The Conflict of Interpretations: Essays in Herme-neutics* (1974), "Creativity in Language: Word, Polysemy, Metaphor" (1973), *Freud and Philosophy: An Essay on Interpretation* (1970), "The Hermeneutic Function of Distanciation" (1973), *History and Truth* (1965), "The Model of The Text: Meaningful Action Considered as Text" (1973), *The Rule of Metaphor: Multi-Disciplinary Studies of the Creation of Meaning in Language* (1977), *Political and Social Essays* (1974), and "The Task of Hermeneutics" (1973). There are also many excellent studies of Ricoeur, which are discussed in the second study.

The itinerary of my journey has been accomplished. It has been a reflective moment to pause and look at the way I have come to this present point. It has been an attempt to demonstrate in the specific a general problem with the reading of curriculum theory texts and other texts as well. The journey continues, however, in the attempt to overcome this habitual perception problem. The problem of interpretation will be taken up next and its relationship will be shown to this problem.

It is not a totalizing iconclastic answer that I am searching for. It is with a journey toward a method that this study is thoroughly concerned. A search for text worlds where we do not search for the "they-self", but a search for curriculum text worlds that open places where we can become our "own-self".

2

Ricoeur and the Hermeneutical Arch: Toward Understanding Curriculum Theory

The journey through the various hermeneutic arches of curriculum theory has brought me to the present moment and this present study. It has been an intellectual journey fraught with detours. These detours could be looked at as roundabout ways temporarily replacing part of the route or as journeys through a continuous series of hermeneutical arches, the end moment of one being at the same time the starting place of another. In order to understand and appreciate the arch I currently find myself in it has been necessary to examine all the previous arches traveled through. These travels were a search for a voice. The first phase of this study will be an attempt at explaining some of Paul Ricoeur's hermeneutical theory. This will facilitate the understanding of the voyage toward understanding curriculum.

PAUL RICOEUR: HERMENEUTIC THEORY AND TEXTUAL INTERPRETATION

In this portion of the study I wish to analyze and explain the work of Paul Ricoeur especially his interest in hermeneutical theory and the theory of the text. I would like to extend Ricoeur's work on the field of curriculum theory text analysis or at least construct that possibility. It is not an unquestioning allegiance to Ricoeur's work but a critical acceptance and explanation of the major precepts and some insights that hopefully will extend his theories. It is a moment of comprehension of Paul Ricoeur's work and an initial moment for its application to the works of curriculum theory. It will attempt to produce a new hermeneutic way of reading curriculum texts.

DEFINITIONS AND EXPLANATION

A total systematic explanation and critique of Paul Ricoeur's work is beyond the scope of this study. I am, therefore, limiting my contemplation of Ricoeur to his latest important "detour" into hermeneutics, the philosophy of language and the theory of the text. In his essay "From Existentialism to the Philosophy of Language", Ricoeur discusses his intellectual journey and comments on this new aspect of study.

> It is the function of general hermeneutics to answer problems such as: What is a text? i.e., what is the relation between spoken and written language? What is the relation between explanation and understanding within the encompassing act of reading? What is the relation between a structural analysis and an existential appropriation? Such are the general problems of hermeneutics (Ricoeur, 1977, p. 321).

These questions that Ricoeur poses are answered in a number of his writings. I will attempt to explain how these questions are answered and how those answers have direct bearing on the understanding of curriculum theory and its texts.

In order to facilitate a better understanding of Ricoeur's present position concerning philosophy and politics it is helpful to give some historical and biographical information about Ricoeur. This will help to explain his seemingly apolitical position at the moment.

Paul Ricoeur was born of Protestant tradition in Provence in 1913. He now divides his time between the Divinity School at the University of Chicago and the University of Paris (Kurzweil, 1980, p. 87). He said in his "Preface to the First Edition" of his collected essays entitled *History and Truth* (1965):

> I believe in the efficacy of reflection because I believe that man's greatness lies in the dialectic of work and the spoken word. Saying and doing, signifying and making are intermingled to such an extent that it is impossible to set up lasting and deep opposition between "theoria" and "praxis". The word is my kingdom and I am not ashamed of it. To be more precise, I am ashamed of it to the extent that my speaking shares in the unjust society which exploits work. I am not ashamed of it primordially, that is, with respect to its destination. As a university professor, I believe in the efficacity of instructive speech; in teaching the history of philosophy, I believe in the enlightening

power, even for a system of politics, of speaking devoted to elaborating our philosophical memory. As a member of the team *Esprit*, I believe the efficacity of speech which thoughtfully elucidates the generating themes of advancing civilization. As a listener to the Christian message, I believe that the words the "heart" that is, the refulgent core of our preferences and the positions we embrace (Ricoeur, 1965, p. 5)...

In this Preface we have the four functions which Ricoeur sees as being his primary interests. He is a university professor, a student of the history of philosophy, a member of the left-Catholic journal *Esprit* and bearer of the Christian message (Kurzweil, 1980, p. 87). In her book *The Age of Structuralism: Levi-Strauss to Foucault*, Kurzweil offers a most succinct and lucid account of Ricoeur's development. I am indebted to her for much of the information presented below. I think the study of Ricoeur's biography is best analyzed by dividing it up into decades.

1930s

Ricoeur, in this phase of his life, pursued the Christian aspects of his career. Much of his theological interest came from studying with Gabriel Marcel. Ricoeur says that Marcel was the "decisive philosophical shock" in his early career. He dedicated his work, *Freedom and Nature: The Voluntary and the Involuntary* to Marcel. Ricoeur stated that "meditation on the work of Gabriel Marcel is in fact at the root of the analysis of this work" (Spiegelberg, 1982, p. 590).

The other major facet of this period came in 1932 when he joined the left-Catholic group centering on Emmanuel Mounier, who formed *Esprit* (Kurzweil, 1980, p. 82). Ricoeur, in his collection of essays,dedicates one to Mounier entitled: "Emmanuel Mounier: A Personalist Philosopher". Ricoeur concludes his essay by explaining his reason for his attachment to Mounier. It is:

> the rare accord between two tonalities of thought and life; what he (Mounier) himself called strength (la force), following the ancient Christian moralists, or the virtue of confrontation, and the generosity or abundance of heart, which retifies the hardness of the virtue of strength by means of something forgiving and graceful. It is this subtle alliance of a noble "ethical" virtue

with a noble "poetic" virtue which made Emmanuel Mounier the man at once indomitable and selfless (Ricoeur, 1965, p. 161).

This relationship with Mounier and *Esprit* has been very influential on Ricoeur's life and work. One can see many of Ricoeur's political views receiving some basis in Mounier's work and the latter's philosophy of personalism. What Ricoeur found most attractive in Mounier he comments on in the same essay. He discusses Mounier's personalism. Ricoeur states:

> Its main contribution to contemporary thought has been to offer a *philosophical matrix* to professional philosophers, to propose tonalities to them, theoretical and practical holding notes containing one or several philosophies, pregnant with one or several philosophical systemizations. For many of us, this is our true debt to our friend (Ricoeur, 1965, p. 136).

In the translator's introduction to the *History and Truth* (1965) collection, the translator comments on the relationship of Ricoeur, Mounier and the *Esprit* movement.

> Ricoeur a friend and collaborator of Mounier until the latter's death in 1950, is a frequent contributor to Esprit...Ricoeur's association with the *Esprit* movement, however, by no means indicates that he broke with traditional philosophy in the name of more pressing problems of contemporary civilization (Ricoeur, 1965, p. xii).

Although this was only one influence in a broad philosophical horizon, it did have an affect on Ricoeur as demonstrated in essays in the collection, *Political and Social Essays*. His concern with both theology and the Christian message are obvious. Some of these essays are "Ye Are the Salt of the Earth", "Faith and Culture" and "The Project of a Social Ethic". Ricoeur envisions a Christianity that is ecumenical in nature and is not limited to concerns over personal piety, but open to a social commitment as well. His concept seems to be for an ethical and moral commitment to be based upon the unity of the human person and that those persons may make a difference in the world. Ricoeur refers to this dual nature of Christians in his essay, "Faith and Culture". In this essay he discusses the idea of the unity of the person.

The Gospel is in every respect a ministry of reconciliation: of man with man, of Greek with Jew, and finally of oneself with oneself. It is neither possible nor desirable that man should remain divided and torn (Ricoeur in Stewart and Bien, 1974, p. 130).

Ricoeur discusses the task of Christians in his essay "Ye Are the Salt of the Earth".

Being the salt of the earth in politics means maintaining the constant pressure of moral conviction upon the politician's sense of responsibility, maintaining the pressure of non-violence upon legitimate violence (Ricoeur in Stewart and Bien, 1974, p. 122).

The other aspect of this concept is that this be a type of global commitment on the part of Christians. The influences of the 1930s period still play a role in Ricoeur's four areas of interest. His message is carried through in some of his overtly political essays of the 1950s period which will be discussed later in the study.

1940s

This period in Ricoeur's life has an ironic twist. Although physically confined for several years as a prisoner of war in Germany, his mind was free to search for meaning. He devoted his time to studying two philosophers, Jaspers and Husserl. In fact, Ricoeur (with his co-author, Mikel Dufrenne) devoted his first book size publication to Jasper's philosophy of existence, *Karl Jaspers et la Philosophie de l'existence* (1974) (Speigelberg, 1982, p. 591). During this period Ricoeur was concerned, as he still is, with the unity of man or "reconciling the broken unity of man". Jasper's answer to the reconcilment of this broken unity was for Ricoeur not adequate. Speigelberg, in his book *The Phenomenological Movement: An Historical Introduction* (1980), finds another phase of Ricoeur's study of Jaspers more important than the one just mentioned. It centers on the confrontation between Gabriel Marcel and Jaspers. The evidence is found in Ricoeur's *Gabriel Marcel et Karl Jaspers* (1948). It is apparent from this study that Ricoeur sides with Marcel but:

Not much explicit criticism is offered in Ricoeur's highly illuminating cross sections of the two "Christian existentialists". Nevertheless, even in this book one can find indications of Ricoeur's reservation with regard to Marcel's existential philosophy (Speigelberg, 1980, p. 591).

It is apparent that there was a more influential study done during this period in Ricoeur's life. This study was of Husserl's phenomenology. Ricoeur's interpretation of Husserl has affected Ricoeur's life and his life's work. The purposes of the study do not necessitate the explicit analysis of Ricoeur's outlook on Husserl, but some explanation of it is in order. Some scholars believe that Ricouer's work on Husserl and his individual interpretation of Husserl are what distinguish him from the others who also use Husserl, specifically Sartre and Merleau-Ponty. Ricoeur's phenomenology was quite different. Sartre and Merleau-Ponty emphasized Husserl's notion of Lebenswelt (life-world) along with the later Husserl's and Heidegger's being-in-the-world, by stressing the primacy of thought as related existence and to subject-object relations (Kurzweil, 1980, p. 87). Ricoeur discusses Sartre and Merleau-Ponty in his *Husserl: An Analysis of his Phenomenology in a section entitled "Existential Phenomenology"* (1967).

Ricoeur's concept of phenomenology is distinguishable from the primacy of thought and other ideas of Husserl's phenomenology. In *Husserl: An Anlaysis of his Phenomenology* Ricoeur discusses his view of the primacy of thought and other matters.

> ...not from what is most silent in the operation of consciousness, but from its relationship to things mediated by signs as these are elaborated in a spoken culture. The first of consciousness is meaning. (Meinin...) and the act of signifying is intentionality (Ricoeur, 1967, p. 6).

This concept or basis of phenomenology in intentionality of consciousness can be later viewed as fitting in very comfortably with existence and hermeneutics. It leads, as Don Ihde states in *Hermeneutic phenomenology: The Philosophy of Paul Ricoeur* (1971), to hermeneutic phenomenology. Ricoeur states:

> This is why philosophy remains a hermeneutic, that is, a reading of the hidden meaning inside the text of apparent

meaning. It is the task of hermeneutics to show that existence arrives at expression, at meaning, and at reflection only through the continual exegesis of all the significations that come to light in the world of culture. Existence becomes a self-human and adult-only by appropriating this meaning, which first resides "outside", in works, institutions and cultural monuments in which life of the spirit is objectified (Ricoeur in Reagan and Stewart, 1978, p. 106).

But, I am getting ahead of myself. The period of the 40s was an important one for Ricoeur. A period that would, I posit, have affect on the rest of his life's work.

1950s

This period for Ricoeur was perhaps his most politically prodigious. He had two teaching positions during this period. He taught philosophy until 1956 at Stasbourg. He taught from 1956 to 1966 at the Sorbonne. Ricoeur, during this period, was against Sartre's pro Marxist politics and his praxis orientation. Many of Ricoeur's essays of this period I have previously alluded to. They stress not praxis but non-violent commitment to pressing forward with an ethical, moral and globally concerned emphasis. The way to influence the political arena is by stressing moral convictions in a non-violent manner. It is easy to see, therefore, that Gandhi was a type of hero for Ricoeur. The essays where this type of political philosophy is expressed are: "Ye Are the Salt of the Earth" (1958), "Faith and Culture" (1957), "What Does Humanism Mean" (1956), "Adventures of the State and the Task of Christians" (1958), and "From Marxism to Contemporary Communism" (1959). Because of his stance on political matters, his colleagues on the left could always respect him for his sincerity. But, they dismissed even his most radical ideas as being politically conservative (Kurzweil, 1980, p. 88).

1966 - 1970

I have delineated this period in this way to bring to a close this phase of the study primarily because after 1970 Ricoeur concentrates on the philosophy of language and his writings become less politically oriented than they were previous to 1970. This period is significant since it encompasses his appointment to the leftist university of Naterre. He hoped that at this university he could put into practice a pedagogy which would reflect his political philosophy. Apparently while at Naterre he alienated the students on both the right and the left, but especially the students on the political left. He was appointed rector in 1970. He was soon forced to resign his position because of the atagonism he generated while at Naterre. This period seems to have violently ripped Ricoeur away from political concerns, at least overt manifestations of such and propelled him into a period of language study, hermeneutics and textual theory. Perhaps, Ricoeur has discovered that to accomplish his goals, he does not necessarily have to continue the overtly political or it may be just an important detour for him. The other explanation could be that he is just progressing on his own hermeneutic arch and that the "end" of his political period, is the arrival at the beginning of a new hermeneutic arch.

EXPLANATION

The best examples of Ricouer's new interest in the philosophy of language and related matters are found in: *The Rule of Metaphor: Multi-Disciplinary Studies in the Creation of Meaning* (1977), *The Conflict of Interpretations* (1974), and *Interpretation Theory: Discourse and the Surplus of Meaning* (1976). In these works that are extremely well written and meticulously researched, Ricoeur describes the theory of rhetoric and metaphor from the classic work of Aristotle to the work of Frege, Benveniste, I. A. Richards, and Saussure. Ricoeur differentiates semiotics from semantics. He traces this difference in *The Rule of Metaphor* (1977) by using metaphor as the example to distinguish between a semiotic or word definition of metaphor and a semantic or predicative definition of metaphor. This leads to a theory of discourse which according to Ricoeur is necessarily dialectic. It will facilitate an explanation of Ricoeur's theory of discourse to carefully distinguish between the bases of these two concepts of language, that of a semiotically based theory and that of a semantically based theory. Ricoeur's own theory relates the two views in a dialectical theory of discourse.

Ricoeur refers to the differentiation as a crucial aspect in the investigation of language.

> For me, the distinction between semantics and semiotics is the
> key to the whole problem of language...this distinction of the
> argument of Plato in the *Cratylus* and the *Theaetelus* according
> to which the logos relies on the intertwining of at least two
> different entities, the noun and the verb. But, in another sense,
> this distinction today requires more sophistication because of
> the existence of semiotices as the modern counterpart of seman-
> tics (Ricoeur, 1976, p. 8).

This differentiation forms the cornerstone of Ricoeur's theory of
discourse. Ricoeur's hermeneutical theory is based upon his theory
of discourse. It is a building process. The process in *Interpretation
Theory* (1976) proceeds from language as discourse to discourse as
written to a theory of texts and finally arrives at the interpretation of
texts. In *The Rule of Metaphor* the concept of metaphor is through this
process. *The Rule of Metaphor* is directly related to *Interpretation
Theory* and many of the essays in *The Conflict of Interpretations*. It is
sensible, then, to proceed with an explanation of Ricoeur's theory of
discourse and its consequential arrival at interpretation theory to
investigate the possibilities for a new way of reading and interpreting curriculum texts.

The first step in a theory of discourse is to distinguish between the
semiotic concepts and the semantic concepts of language and meaning.

THE STRUCTURAL MODEL—SEMIOTICS

This model of language was given its most crucial beginnings
with Ferdinan de Saussure in *Cours de Linguistique General*. Saussure
considers language as a system or structure. In order to achieve a
complete explanation of Saussure some of his basic terminology
must be elaborated upon.

The most fundamental concept in Saussure is the distinction
between langue and parole. Langue is the system of language, the
code or the system of codes. Parole is the utterance or the choice a
speaker makes from this code. We have, then, the system and the
message. Saussure chose to concentrate in his study on the langue
not on the parole.

For Saussure the linguists profer job was to study not speech but language, because it was only by doing so that he could grasp the principles on which language functions in practice (Sturrock, 1979, p. 8).

This choice to give langue the predominate place in the study of language has a number of consequences. The first consequence is that the method of study necessitates a certain view of time. The first distinction between langue and parole produces a further dichotomy. Parole or the message is language that is "intentional and is meant by someone" (Ricoeur, 1976, p. 9). It is an event in a series of events constituted over time. It demands a diachronic concept of time. The langue or system of language is outside of time. It has no intention. It exists unconsciously as Ricoeur states. It is unconscious in the sense "of a nonlibinal structural and cultural unconscious" (Ricoeur, 1976, p. 9). It is a code for a given linguistic community. A different community would necessarily have a different code. Different language systems have different codes. But, the primary characteristic is that it is a systematic code. Since it is systematic and necessary, its study can be "scientific" and synchronic. The study of parole necessitates numerous scientific categories whereas the study of langue can be reduced to one synchronic study of a system. It is the study of the sign or the system of signs.

Before tracing the consequences of this choice, more explicitly in Ricoeur's postulates concerning structuralist linguistics, a connection must be made. Earlier in this section of the study I referred to Ricoeur's nexus between Aristotle's work on language and Saussure's work on language. It is at this point I would like to clarify that link. Ricoeur demonstrates this connection in his study on metaphor. He explains that Saussure's emphasis on the sign is not a break, but a unique continuation of Aristotle's bond between meaning and the word. The word is viewed as being the basic unit of meaning. This primacy of the word in Aristotle's theory brings about a correlation with idea. Word and idea, therefore, have a close correlation. Ricoeur discusses Aristotle's use of the word. He is discussing metaphor, but for our purposes the emphasis on the primacy of the word is most important.

If, then, Aristotle is the father of this model, it is not at all because of his definition of the field of rhetoric, and thus the place of lexis in it, but solely because of the central position accorded the noun in the enumeration of the parts of lexis and the reference to noun in the definition of metaphor (Ricoeur, 1977, p. 47).

If it was the word as the kernel of meaning, then it is the sign for Saussure and semiotics. It is a "semiotic monism". For Saussure the primary unit is the sign. The basic intent of Saussure's *Cours de Linguistique General* is "to identify, define, demarcate the fundamental linguistic unity, the sign" (Godel in Ricoeur, 1977, p. 102). Ricoeur, then, astutely points out that not only is Saussure's study of signs a "rupture" but a continuation of a tendency begun with the primacy of the word with Aristotle. Saussure has obviously brought about some drastic changes, but the monism of the sign is also a:

stage within a discipline whose contours had already been sketched before Saussure, and whose fundamentally lexical preoccupations it reinforces (Ricoeur, 1977, p. 103).

Although the monism of the sign in structural thought has not limited the structural model to linguistical concerns as demonstrated by the work of Levi-Strauss and V. Propp, it still has the overriding concern with a system or sign system.

Ricoeur in *Interpretation Theory* gives four postulates that define and describe semiology in general and structural linguistics in particular (Ricoeur, 1976, pp. 4-6). I would like to point these out and elaborate on some of them. They result in a demarcation of the structural model.

The first postulate Ricoeur explains is that synchronic approaches must precede any type of diachronic study in this model (Ricoeur, 1976, p. 5). In other words the study of the system is more decisive than changes. Langue takes preference over parole. This type of study is "directly opposed to the historicism of the nineteenth century" (Ricoeur, 1976, p. 5).

The second postulate is that the structural model gives us a finite set of discrete entities, signs. "The paradigmatic position of systems constituted of finite sets of discrete entities lies in the combinatory capacity and the quasi-algebraic possibilities pertaining to such sets" (Ricoeur, 1976, p. 5).   This postulate reinforces the type of synchronic understanding emphasized in the first postulate.

Postulate three is pivotal. It, in essence, says that no sign has meaning outside the system. It is a system of differences, but not substantial existence. "Language is form not substance" is Saussure's famous maxim. Therefore, without difference there is no meaning. This leads to the fourth postulate.

The fourth postulate of the structural model is that all these relationships are linked to the system. Ricoeur points out that "in this sense semiotic systems are closed, i.e., without relations to external, non-semiotic reality" (Ricoeur, 1976, pp. 5-6). This aspect of not having external relations can be seen in the very definition of the sign and its constitutive elements, the signifier and the signified. The signifier is the utterance, a spoken word etc... The signified is the "differential value in the lexical system" (Ricoeur, 1976, p. 6). If we wish to reprent this formulaically it would be represented as S:S:S... A concrete example can be given. As Ricoeur correctly states the two constitutive elements of the sign allow for two different types of analysis. The signifier can be anlayzed phonetically and the signi-fied semantically. If we take the word lock, for example, a phonetic study would compare it with other words which are near it in the system. The words lack and luck would be anlayzed. This is, of course, the process differentiation. The other process would be constrict the meaning by differentiating lock from words (signs) which approximate it semantically. Fasten, and secure would be studied. But, there would not be any mention of or to an external referent (Klemm, 1983).

Ricoeur feels that there are drawbacks to the structural model in general and I agree with his tenet. It must be kept in mind that Ricoeur does not flatly reject this mode. In fact, he uses it to some extent in his hermeneutical theory. However, his use of the struc-tural model is not in the eclectic manner. It is in the dialectical manner. Ricoeur believes the structural model is unidemensional.

Language no longer appears as a mediation between minds and things. It constitutes a world of its own, within which each item only refers to other items of the same system, thanks to the interplay of oppositions and differences constitutive of the system. In a word language is no longer treated as a form of "life", Wittgenstein would call it, but as a self-sufficient system of inner relationships (Ricoeur, 1976, p. 6).

It seems this is a sufficient point of departure from structural-semiotics. We must, therefore, proceed to semantics.

SEMANTICS

Ricoeur in both *The Rule of Metaphor* and *Interpretation Theory* established the counterpoint to semiotics in semantics. The major emphasis in semiotics is the word. In semantics the focus is on the sentence as the core of meaning. Ricoeur gives a concrete definition of semantics. Semantics is "the theory that relates the inner or immanent constitution of the sense to the outer or transcendent intention of the reference" (Ricoeur, 1976, p. 229). This definition can be grasped more adequately after some terminology and conceptual matters are clarified. The focus of Ricoeur's discussion of semantics is his theory of discourse. This automatically differentiates his theory from structuralist theory. Saussure abated the focus on discourse by focusing on langue instead of parole. Ricoeur wants to return to discourse and theories about it. It is a necessary first step to hermeneutics or the eventual goal of interpretation. Hence, it is a first step toward an interpretation of curriculum theory.

The first step in this return is to focus on the sentence rather than the word or sign. Ricoeur feels that these two entities, the sign and the sentence, need two distinct sciences. The sentence is not simply a larger category. It is a different category. The sentence is a "whole irreducible to the sum of its parts. It is made up of words but it is not a derivative function of its words. A sentence is made up of signs but is not itself a sign" (Ricoeur, 1976, p. 7). The focus of study is switched from langue to parole (discourse).

Important questions arise from this distinction. In order for a clear answer to these fermenting questions to be established, the postulates or aspects of discourse must be explained and developed. Ricoeur speaks specifically to the point of language as discourse but these concepts all have bearing on hermeneutical theory and as a result they have a bearing on my analysis on curriculum theory. Ricoeur calls these facets, criteria to differentiate.

Ricoeur synthesizes a number of approaches in his theory of discourse. They are: (1) linguistics of the sentence (semantics), (2) phenomenology of meaning from Husserl's *Logical Investigations*, and (3) Anglo-American linguistic analysis that deals with "ordinary language" (Ricoeur, 1976, p. 8). As a result of this synthesis two dialectics are set up for Ricoeur's theory of discourse. The first dialectic is between event and meaning. The second dialectic is between sense and reference. There are a number of good studies concerning this dialectical theory of discourse, but two are first rate. One which I have relied on for this study is *The Hermeneutical Theory of Paul Ricoeur* (1983) by David E. Klemm and another is an article "The Significance of the Text in Paul Ricoeur's Hermeneutical Theory" by David Pellauer in a collection of essays entitled *Studies in the Philosophy of Paul Ricoeur* (1978) by Reagan. Two other books of interest in this area are *Extension of Ricoeur's Hermeneutic* (1973) by Bourgeois and *The Question of Belief in Literary Criticism: An Introduction to the Hermeneutical Theory of Paul Ricoeur* (1979) by Mary Gerhart. The primary sources are *Interpretation Theory* (1976), *The Rule of Metaphor* (1977), and *The Conflict of Interpretations* (1974).

EVENT AND MEANING

Much of the way Ricoeur establishes the difference between semiotics and semantics, which eventually leads to his discourse theory, relies on the concepts of the French sanskritist, Emile Benveniste. Ricoeur uses Benveniste's theories and elaborates on them in the third study of *The Rule of Metaphor*. The first trait of discourse which Benveniste discusses, according to Ricoeur, is event and meaning. "Discourse always occurs as an event, but is to be understood as meaning" (Ricoeur, 1977, p. 70).

The event side of the dialectic can be called the "instance of discourse" as Benveniste labels it in *Problems in General Linguistics* (1971). This alludes to the fact that the event of discourse is transitory and fleeting. A speaker is saying something. Immediately we have a difference between semiotics and semantics. Ricoeur, along with others, is establishing the "ontological priority of discourse resulting from the actuality of event as opposed to the mere virtuality of the system" (Ricoeur, 1976, p. 9). So, the actual events of discourse establish the code, therefore parole takes precedence over the language. However, the act of discourse is more than a transitory moment. It may be "identified and reidentified as the same, so that we may say it again or in other words" (Ricoeur, 1976, p. 9). This identity that is preserved is defined as the propositional content. The event, therefore, has both a subjective and an objective side. The subjective side of the event is the actualization of the code of discourse. A person intends something and says something.

The objective side of the event of discourse deals with this propositional content. The objective side is the "what is said". The sentence has basically two functions, identification and predication. Identification calls into use the grammatical devices which identify one item. Nouns, proper nouns, and pronouns are among the identifiers. The predicate "designates a kind of quality, a class of things, a type of relation or a type of action" (Ricoeur, 1976, p. 11). Discourse, then, is more than just a transitory moment. It is "a structure in the synthetic sense, i.e., as the intertwining and interplay of functions of identification and predication in one and the same sentence" (Ricouer, 1976, p. 11). So, as event discourse is fleeting and transcient but as meaning it endures in the propositional content. Hence, Ricoeur's axiom; "If all discourse is actualized as event, all discourse is understood as meaning" (Ricoeur, 1976, p. 12).

Ricoeur in explaining the dialectic between event and meaning does not stop at this point, but presents some additional aspects to this dialectic in discussing the subjective and objective aspects of the self-reference of discourse. He believes that: to mean is both what the speaker means, i.e., what he intends to say, and what the sentence means, i.e., what the conjunction between the identification function and the predicative function yields (Ricoeur, 1976, p. 12). There is self-referential aspect to discourse. This self-reference is or can be determined by grammatical devices known as "shifters". Therefore, the self-reference does not become reduced to mere psychological intention. The meaning can be found in the discourse itself through personal pronouns. A pronoun such as "I" only has one function. "Its only function is to refer the whole sentence to the subject of the speech event" (Ricoeur, 1976, p. 13). There are other "shifters" Ricoeur lists, but the important point he emphasizes is that discourse has many suitable ways of referring back to the speaker.

Ricoeur states two advantages to this emphasis on grammatical devices and the self-reference of discourse.

> On the one hand, we get a new criterion of the difference between discourse and linguistic codes. On the other hand, we are able to give a nonpsychological, but purely semantic, definition of the utterer's meaning. No mental entity need be hypothesized or hypostasized. The utterence meaning points back to the utterer's meaning thanks to the self-reference of discourse to itself as an event (Ricoeur, 1976, p. 13).

Ricoeur adds other dimensions to this dialectic of event and meaning. He discusses J. L. Austin's theories as well as those of Roman Jakobson. Austin's *How to Do Things With Words* (1963), is discussed in *Interpretation Theory* and in greater detail in *The Rule of Metaphor*. Ricoeur posits that the traits Austin analyzes concern the structure of the acts of discourse. Every act of discourse or speech act has three aspects and each has a specific definition. The structure of the speech act is brought to bear upon the event and meaning dialectic and its subjective and objective aspects. In performative discourse the model is the promise. "In the promise I *do* the very thing (illocutionary act) which is *said* (locutionary act) in the promise: by saying I commit myself under the obligation of doing (Ricoeur, 1977, p. 33). The doing of the discourse is the event of discourse—the subjective side. This event side or this doing also follows semantic rules which are exhibited by the structure of the sentence; the verb must be that of the first person indicative. Here, too, a specific "grammar" supports the performative force of the discourse (Ricoeur, 1977, p. 14). This subjective side has an objective correlative in the prelocutionary act. This act is what I yield in the doing of saying (Klemm, 1983, p. 78). Ricoeur adds that there is also an interlocutionary act because all discourse is communication:

> One important aspect of discourse is that it is addressed to someone. There is another speaker who is the addressee of the discourse. The presence of the pair, speaker, hearer constitutes language as communication (Ricouer, 1976, p. 14).

In the event and meaning dialectic the event or what is communicated, first of all, Ricoeur states, is the propositional content of the discourse, the private becomes public.

Something is transferred from one sphere of life to another. This something is not the experience as experienced, but its meaning. Here is the miracle. The experience as experienced, as lived, remains private, but its sense, its meaning, becomes public. Communication in this way is the overcoming of the radical noncommunicability of the lived experience (Ricoeur, 1976, p. 16).

Communication, then, involves what is transferred from the speaker to the hearer in the event of discourse. The sense of the discourse is transferred. This is possible because the sense of the sentence is external to the event. "This exteriority of discourse to itself - which is synonymous with the self-transcendence of the event in its meaning — opens discourse to the other. The message has the ground of its communicability in the structure of its meaning" (Ricoeur, 1976, p. 15), (Klemm, 1983, p. 78).

In order to further develop the event and meaning dialectic, Ricoeur discusses the concept of exteriority of meaning and its relationship to the various constitutive parts of the speech act. Propositional content best survives the exteriorization of meaning from event, but the illocutionary act is also indicated objectively through grammatical moods, use of imperatives or optatives, and the like. The prelocutionary dimension is the least exteriorizable of the three, and points out the potential ambiguity of all discourse in that it always relies on context to screen the multiple sense of the words combined in sentences (Klemm, 1983, p. 78). Ricoeur's event and meaning dialectic, then, leaves us with the subjective side of the dialectic and the objective or propositional side in the meaning. However, there is also a dialectic of meaning and that will be discussed next.

SENSE AND REFERENCE - - SINN AND BEDEUTUNG

Ricoeur credits in both *Interpretation Theory* and *The Rule of Metaphor* the introduction of the terms sense and reference to Gottlob Frege in *Uber Sinn und Bedeutung (On Sense and Reference)* (1952).

This dialectic serves to further the distanciation between semiotics and semantics. The sentence is what makes the dialectic possible. "Only at the level of the sentence, taken as a whole, can what is said be distinguished from that of which one speaks" (Ricoeur, 1977, p. 74). In semiotics where signs relate only in a differential way to other signs the problem of reference is nonexistent. In the sentence, as was previously stated, language passes outside itself. Reference becomes an important part of a new dialectic for Ricoeur.

Sense, then, is the "what" of discourse and the "about what" is the reference. Whereas, the sense is immanent to the discourse, and objective in the sense of ideal, the reference expresses the movement in which language transcends itself. Discourse is pointed to something a world, or the referent. The sense of the discourse brings together the identification and predicative functions. It is another name for discourse's claim to be true.

The dialectic of sense and reference can be related to the dialectic of event and meaning.

> That someone refers to something at a certain time is an event, a speech event. But this event receives its structure from the meaning as sense. The speaker refers to something on the basis of, or through, the ideal structure of sense. The sense, so to speak, is traversed by the referring intention of the speaker. In this way the dialectic of event and meaning receives a new development from the dialectic of sense and reference (Ricoeur, 1976, p. 20).

This dialectic has, Ricoeur states, ontological significance. Since as has been implied in the distinction between semiotics and semantics language is not a world of its own, it must have referential character. "Only this dialectic says something about the relation between language and the ontological condition of being in the world" (Ricoeur, 1976, p. 20).

Language points toward the extra-linguistic as an end result. But, this is only part of the movement that begins in the experience of being in the world and its movement toward expression in language. It is first, because that there is something to say, because we have an experience to bring to language, that conversely language is not only directed towards ideal meanings but also refers to what is

(Ricoeur, 1976, p. 21). Language i.e., discourse refers to the world and back to the speaker.

The difference from semiotic analysis has been established by the two interrelated dialectics of event and meaning and sense and reference. Since the latter dialectic is a stage in the development of interpretation (hermeneutic) theory, there is a distinction made. Ricoeur emphasizes that the task of his eventual hermeneutics will be different than the Romanticist hermeneutics of Schleiermacher and Dilthey. These writers equated understanding, which was the major intent of hermeneutics, with the investigation of the author's intention. In fact, their romanticist hermeneutics was attempting a psychological reconstruction of the author's intention. Ricoeur attempts to call into question this hermeneutic from the point of view of a philosophy of discourse in order to release hermeneutics from its psychologizing and existential prejudices (Ricoeur, 1976, p. 23). There is a double misunderstanding in this hermeneutic of the event and meaning dialectic and the sense and reference dialectic. The double misunderstanding leads to the concept of interpretation as psychological reconstruction.

We have been discussing these dialectics in terms of speech. In order for these theories of discourse to become part of a theory of the text the differences and similiarities between speech and writing must be clarified. Ricoeur does this in "Study Two: Speaking and Writing" of *Interpretation Theory* and to some extent in *The Rule of Metaphor*.

WRITING

What happens in writing is the inscription or fixation of the intentional exteriorization of speaking. The inscription substitutes for the immediate spoken expression. This is the event pole of the event and meaning dialectic. However, the inscription does not fix the event but the said of discourse. This is not the end to the question of writing, however. The differentiation of speech and writing is not simply a matter of a "change of medium" (Ricoeur, 1976, p. 24).

The process of thought to writing is not an indirect process via human speech. Writing substitutes for speaking. Writing is not simply the fixation of oral discourse. Ricoeur uses Roman Jakobson's "factors" and "functions" of discourse to establish the changes that take place between speech and writing in the communication process. Ricoeur also considers texts when considering writing. His definition of texts in "What is a Text? Explanation and Interpretation" (1971) equates the two.

Let us call a text every utterance or set of utterances fixed by writing. According to this definition the fixation by writing is constitutive of the text itself (Ricoeur, 1971, p. 1).

The first change as a result of writing taking the place of speaking is that the relations message and speaker and hearer are changed. This is replaced with the writing-reading relationship. It is not "a particular case of the speaking-hearing relationship" (Ricoeur, 1976, p. 29). This change brings out a crucial differentiation. Because of the immediacy of the dialogical situation the speaker is present during interlocution. Therefore, the speaker's intention and the discourse's meaning are the same. When thoughts are inscribed the author's intention and the meaning of the text cease to coincide. The text has "semantic autonomy" (Ricoeur, 1971, pp. 21-30). The text's career escapes the finite horizon lived by its author. What the text means now matters more than what the author meant when he wrote it (Ricoeur, 1976, p. 30). It is an opposition, but a dialectical relationship between intentional fallacy and the fallacy of the absolute text.

Another characteristic of written or textual language is that the limited hearer becomes a potentially unlimited universal audience (reader). However, in actuality the text only reaches a particular audience. Therefore, reading does "suffer from limitations" (Ricoeur, 1971, p. 30). There is the opportunity for many interpretations. Hermeneutics, Ricoeur states, begins where dialogue ends. The use of codes and reference in relation to the writing and text phenomenon will be discussed later in this study. It appears that the fact of inscription heightens the polarity between the event and meaning dialectic. But, the new process of writing and reading produces a new dialectic. The dialectic is between distanciation and appropriation.

Distanciation is not a quantitative phenomenon. It is the

dynamic counterpart of our need to, our interest, and our effort to overcome cultural estrangement. Writing and reading take place in this cultural struggle. Reading is the pharmakon, the "remedy" by which the meaning of the text is "rescued" from the estrangement of distanciation and put in a new proximity, a proximity which suppresses and preserves the cultural distance and includes the otherness within the ownness (Ricoeur, 1977, p. 43).

This distanciation is apparent in three areas. There is: (1) distanciation from the author, (2) distanciation from the situation, and (3) distanciation from the original audience (Ricoeur, 1973, p. 135). It is distanciation of meaning and event, which is emphasized in writing. It takes on a virtual state. Appropriation is "to make one's own what was foreign and alien" (Ricoeur, 1976, p. 31). Appropriation is in a struggle with distanciation in the writing and reading process. We will return to this dialectic later in the study when we consider Ricoeur's theory of textual understanding.

THE TEXT AS A WORK

When we begin to explain the text, the necessity for the inclusion of Ricoeur's discourse theory in this particular study becomes obvious. The text (inscribed discourse) evinces both the dialectic of event and meaning and the dialectic of sense and references as does spoken language. In order that the relationship between the dialectics and texts can be explained, Ricoeur's notion of a text must be made intelligible.

Ricoeur, in a number of his works, most notably in "The Hermeneutical Function of Distanciation" (1973), discusses the concept of the text as work. This structuring of discourse as work or discourse as a structured work refers to the sense pole of the sense and reference dialectic. It is a work because it is in a process of production. Ricoeur says that there are three characteristics of discourse as work: (1) A work is a sequence longer than the sentence, which gives rise to a new problem of understanding relative to the final and closed totality which constitutes the word itself; (2) The work is submitted to a form of codification that is applied to the composition itself and which makes the discourse into a poem, an essay or a story;

(3) A work receives a unique configuration that assimilates it to an individual and which we call its style (Ricoeur, 1973, p. 134). The concept of work implies the imposition of form on matter, hence a unique message is given over to rules of production. According to Ricoeur these rules consist of composition, genre, and individual style. In this analysis it is the individual's message that is of the utmost importance, and that the forms of production are secondary. They are made so that the message may be communicated. While structural anlaysis of the forms of production is made possible by this process of work, i.e., the submitting of the message to the codes of production, the message is what is ultimately important.

In "The Hermeneutic Function of Distanciation" (1973), Ricoeur delineates each aspect of discourse as work. It is necessary for our understanding to briefly summarize these explanations of composition, genre, and style. They will be used in the explanation of curriculum theory so it is imperative that we understand their implications.

As composition, discourse as a work is distinguished from a sentence as a "second order organization" over the sentence as the minimal unit of discourse.

> The text as a whole has to be "constructed" as a hierarchy of topics. The very word "topics" suggests that the production of discourse as a whole implies more than a semantics of the sentence, it implies, say, a "topology" of discourse, which would be the proper semantics of discourse, with the notion of one or more "isotopics" interwoven in the text (Ricoeur, 1973, p. 135).

The second aspect, Ricoeur highlights, is the necessity of submitting discourse as a work to a process of codification, specifically a production code of literary genres. He compares this process to the way in which sentences are submitted to grammatical and lexical rules to produce messages. Compositions are submitted to larger codes such as poems, novels or essays. However, we should look at these genres not so much as classifications but as means of production. "Literary genres contribute to produce discourse as work. To master a genre is to master a "competence" which offers practical guidelines for "performing" an individual work" (Ricoeur, 1973, p.

135). The reader also must achieve competence for the particular genre. This function allows the writer to encode the message and the reader to decode the message with some common rules. Of course, since these rules govern the form of the discourse they also govern thought. They are a "dynamics of thought" (Ricoeur, 1973, p. 136).

Finally, in the sense pole of the dialectic, works of discourse are viewed as products of individual style. These are the "aspects of the work that make it a unique configuration" (Ricoeur, 1973, p. 136).

> ...we define the task of stylistics as the theory devoted to the general conditions ruling the insertion of structure into an individual practice (Ricoeur, 1973, p. 137).

This, then, is the sense pole of the dialectic of sense and reference. The discourse (work) as a structured entity. It is the fixation of the meaning of discourse. The structure of discourse, however, does not end the dialectic. The work of discourse points to (refers) to the "world of the text".

THE WORLD OF THE TEXT

The world of the text centers on the reference pole of the dialectic of sense and reference. This is, according to most analyses of Ricoeur, the pivotal point of his hermeneutical theory (Klemm, 1983, Pellauer, 1979). It is the world of the text that can be understood in the moment of comprehension and interpreted. The structure of the work, the sense, is what the work says. The reference of the work is what it is about. "Hermeneutics is the theory that regulates the transition from structure of the work to the world of the work (Klemm, 1983, p. 85). Ricoeur distinguishes between two types of work, the descriptive or scientific and the literary. Each type has a specific type of reference.

The scientific work's reference is not problematic according to Ricoeur. It contains a type of "first order reference" (Ricoeur, 1973, p. 141). By use of what is called univocal language, scientific and descriptive works refer to the given reality. These works give us reference to our everyday world. They exhibit the power of "showing a reality common to the interlocutors" (Ricoeur, 1973, p. 140). It is referred to in *The Rule of Metaphor* as the "first-level denotation of discourse" (Ricoeur, 1977, p. 221). Denotation is the case referring to a literal definition of reality. Consequently, this case of reference is hermeneutically unproblematic.

The second type of text, the literary, poses a different type of reference. A reference that is hermeneutically problematic. Ricoeur combines his ideas with Heidegger's project of our utmost possibilities and applies it to the text. "What is to be interpreted in a text is a proposed world, a world that I might inhabit and wherein I might project my ownmost possibilities" (Ricoeur, 1973, p. 140). This second order denotation is only possible when the first order denotation is suspended or destroyed, only when this primary reference is surpassed.

> But it is essentially with the appearence of certain literary genres, generally tied to writing but not necessarily so that this abolition of reference to a given world is led to its most extreme conditions. It is the role of most of our literature, it would seem to destroy this world. This is true of fictional literature...but also of literature which we can call poetic literature...(Ricoeur, 1973, p. 140).

It seems, then, that the world constructed in the imagination is the world of the text. It is according to Ricoeur in fictional literature and poetic literature where this phenomenon is most likely to take place. I will posit later in this study that in certain theoretical texts this possible world reference is also a possibility. In fact, most theoretical texts point in both directions of reference. They contain a first order reference to the world as it is, but they also point toward a second order reference to a world of possibility.

RICOEUR'S INTERPRETATION THEORY

Ricoeur's interpretation theory encompasses both hermeneutics and structuralism in an hermeneutic arch, which seems somewhat more linear in character than arched, however. It would appear as:

NAIVE READING — EXPLANATION — UNDERSTANDING

It is essential to discuss each phase in the hermeneutic arch. The process can be seen as the working out of the problematics between explanation and understanding, writing and reading and distanciation and appropriation.

For Ricoeur, textual interpretation is a process of dialectical movement between distanciation and appropriation, between the objectifying stance that enables us to identify the otherness of the text and the self-examination which takes place as we struggle to relate to our own situation (Schwartz, 1983, p. 299).

THE THREE STAGES OF RICOEUR'S HERMENEUTIC

The three stages of Ricoeur's hermeneutic are very succinctly explained in Mary Gerhart's *The Question of Belief in Literary Criticism: An Introduction to the Hermeneutical Theory of Paul Ricoeur*. I would like to delineate the three stages and then explain them in greater detail. Stage one has been called a naive reading (Klemm, 1983, p. 92), or as determining the apparent meaning of the literary text (Gerhart, 1979, p. 250). The second stage has been dubbed structural analysis, or as verifying the meaningfulness of the text (Gerhart, 1979, p. 250). The last stage has been referred to as the dialectic between distanciation and appropriation and hermeneutic comprehension (Ricoeur, 1976, p. 61). These three stages must be looked at most carefully.

Stage one consists in reading a text and guessing and grasping the apparent meaning (Klemm, 1983, p. 92), (Gerhart, 1979, p. 256). Klemm in *The Hermeneutical Theory of Paul Ricoeur* (1983) is clear in pointing out that with scientific or descriptive texts this is not problematic because of their single-literal meaning. It is in the case of literary texts that the figurative meaning presents a problem. It seems that the reader moves "from an uncritical involvement with the text to a reflective awareness of its effects. After an initial reading of the text the reader will recall those particularly meaningful passages and construct them, first descriptively, then in formal critical terms" (Gerhart, 1979, pp. 266-267). It is a description of our initial reaction to a text. There is one facet that must be remembered. There is brought to this initial reading what Heidegger calls the fore-structure of understanding and Gadamer calls prejudice in interpretation.

the important thing is to be aware of one's own bias, so that the text may present itself in all its newness and thus be able to assert its own truth against one's own fore-meanings (Gadamer, 1975, p. 258).

The first stage is this initial reading and reaction to the text and the attempts at stating the apparent.

Stage two is the point at which these hypotheses are submitted to a type of critical reading. The best model for this explanation process is the structural model. It is discussed in *Interpretation Theory: Discourse and the Surplus of Meaning* (1976), *"What is a Text?: Explanation and Interpretation"* (1971), *The Conflict of Interpretations* (1974), and *The Rule of Metaphor* (1977). He invariably discusses it in terms of the dialectic of explanation and understanding with structural analysis taking on the explanatory role. The process of reading consists in the dialectic interplay of these two attitudes (Ricoeur, 1971, p. 139). They are not opposed but in a dialectical relationship.

If, on the contrary, one considers structural analysis as a stage—and a necessary one—between a naive interpretation and a critical interpretaion, between a superficial interpretation and a depth interpretation, then it would seem possible to locate explanation and interpretation at two different stages of the hermeneutical arch and to integrate the opposed attitudes of explanation and understanding within the unique concrete act of reading (Ricoeur, 1971, p. 148).

This structural analysis comprises the analysis of the sense in the sense and reference dialectic. The text as work, as previously discussed, was divided into three categories or classes; composition, genre and style. It would be in the analysis of these three categories that this structural analysis would be efficacious. Ricoeur's example of structural analysis is Levi-Strauss's investigation of myths. Specifically one would deal with the areas of composition, genre and style in specific texts as they relate to a generic system and their differences of individual style from that system. The analysis would never venture beyond that system, but always stay within the system. Ricoeur's ideal of structural anlaysis refers to:

the results of the French school of structuralism in literary criticism in setting forth the method of structural analysis...the aim is to uncover the deep-structure or specific generative code that generates the surface structure or message. The deep-structure is often expressed as a set of relations between binary combinations (Klemm, 1983, p. 93).

Ricoeur, however, disconnects structural analysis from any philosophical implications. Structuralism is not a philosophy.

It seems to me suspect when it sets itself up as a philosophy. An order posited as unconscious can never to my mind, be more than a stage abstractly separated from an understanding of the self by itself; order in itself; order in itself is thought located outside itself (Ricoeur, 1974, p. 51).

With a structural analysis (explanation) a work is analyzed by its form (genre) and its individual difference (style) to other works of the same type. It is also analyzed by the basic binary oppositions within the work itself. It actually analyzes the major episteme (paradigmatic assumption) in the individual work. This explains the sense of the work. But, we have not interpreted it. Ricoeur gives us examples of structural studies in his own work. He includes Levi-Strauss, Propp, Roland Barthes and A. J. Greimas.

These studies not only categorize the forms, but they also perform these functions in a synchronic way as to make clear the functioning of the specific logic of the various genres.

Today the concept of explanation is no longer borrowed from the natural sciences and transferred into a different field, that of written documents. It proceeds from the common sphere of language thanks to the analogical transference from the smaller units of language (phonemes and lexemes) to larger units of discourse beyond the sentence, including narrative, folklore and myth (Ricoeur, 1977, p. 86).

We have up to this point only dealt with the sense of the text. It is not something hidden but something disclosed (Ricoeur, 1977, p. 87). Comprehension, the next point on the arch, is concerned with the reference of the text. The hermeneutic arch is not, as previously alluded to, concerned with the author, his intentions or his situation. But, is concerned with the possible worlds the text points to. We are following the movement in a text from "what it says (sense) to what it talks about (reference)" (Ricoeur, 1977, p. 88).

What is the referential character of the text? By clarifying through objective procedures the sense of meaning of the text, we are able to move on to its referential aspects. This reference, Ricoeur believes, is possible when the literary text refers to possible worlds rather than using ostensive reference. I posit that some theoretical texts posses this same quality. This is given a thorough treatment in *The Rule of Metaphor* (1977), especially in Study 7. The relationship between explanation and understanding is elaborated upon in an article entitled "Explanation and Understanding: On Some Remarkable Connections Among the Theory of the Text, Theory of Action and Theory of History" (1978). The movement from explanation to understanding is elucidated.

> Understanding is rather the nonmethodic moment which, in the sciences of interpretation, comes together with the methodic moment of explanation. Understanding precedes, accompanies, closes and thus envelopes explanation. In return, explanation develops understanding analytically (Ricoeur in Reagan and Stewart, 1978, p. 165).

The last phase of Ricoeur's hermeneutic arch or interpretation theory deals with comprehension or understanding. This understanding is comprehension i.e., appropriation. The concept of appropriation receives attention in Ricoeur's essay "What is a Text? Explanation and Interpretation" (1971). He discusses three characteristics of appropriation.

The first characteristic of appropriation occurs when a reader interprets a text and the interpretation ends in self-interpretation with the consequence that the interpreter understands himself better as a result of doing the interpretation. The emphasis is mine.

> Hermeneutics and reflective philosophy are here correlative and reciprocal: on the one hand, self-understanding provided a round-about way of understanding of the cultural signs in which the self contemplates himself and forms himself, on the other hand, *the understanding of the text is not an end in itself and for itself*; it mediates the relation to himself of a subject who, in the short circuit of immediate relfection, would not find the meaning of his own life...reflection is nothing without media-

tion by means of signs and cultural works and that explanation is nothing if incorporated as an intermediary stage (Ricoeur, 1971, p. 145).

Ricoeur feels that the constitution of the self and meaning are simultaneous. I have found through my personal journeys that what has been said about self-understanding is true.

A second characteristic of appropriation is the overcoming of cultural distance. The distance means *any* distance between the time period of the text and the reader. In addition to that distance can be from "the system of values or cultural milieu to which the text belongs (Ricoeur, 1971, p. 145). It does not necessarily need to be a distant period of time, but can be a matter of perspective that is foreign to our own. Appropriation is the attempt to make that which is foreign, one's own.

The third characteristic of appropriation relates to the world of the reader and the world of the text.

> Reading is like the performance of a musical score: it betokens the fulfillment, the actualization of the semantic virtualities of the text (Ricoeur, 1971, p. 145).

In interpretation writing is given a quality of speech. We cannot, of course, talk to the author or even reconstruct his intentions. It is not a dialogue with the author. The text, then, is freed from its author, its originary anudience and the dialogical situation and this allows the text to project a world.

Again, Ricoeur is not referring to texts that have an ostensive reference, but texts with the ability to abolish this reference and present another level of reference. Since it not the dialogical situation with the author, it becomes a fusion of horizons. The fusion is between the horizon of the reader and the horizon of the text.

This fusion is made possible because of the abolition of the real. The world of the text "constitutes a new kind of distanciation which we call a distanciation of the real from itself" (Ricoeur, 1973, p. 41).

> It proposes a kind of being in the world which is unfolded in front of the text which my interpretation seeks to explicate (Pellauer in Reagan, 1979, p. 108).

By doing this kind of interpretation, we can see the possibilities for our own being, in the possible world a text opens up by the "metaphoric process" (Ricoeur, 1977, p. 188).

> I would say that interpretation is the process by which the disclosure of new modes of being-or if you prefer Wittgenstein to Heidegger, of new "forms of life" -gives to the subject a new capacity of knowing himself. If there is somewhere a project and a projection, it is the reference of the work which is of a world, the reader is consequently in his capacity of self-projection by receiving a new mode of being from the text itself (Ricoeur in Reagan and Stewart, 1978, p. 145).

The text cannot refer to the text world or referent exactly (Klemm, 1983, p. 102). It must be referred to in the language of existential analysis. This is when hermeneutical reflection truly begins.

Klemm, in his study of Ricoeur, presents an interesting outlook on this last phase of the hermeneutic arch. He discusses the subject as a "finite floating subject" (Klemm, 1983, p. 107). "It recognizes that what is presented to structural anlaysis represents a second dimension of the total meaning there. As for itself, it can either participate directly or step back for critical distance, or it can relate the results of either of those with the other. As a floating subject, the "I" recognizes that the meaning there includes all the dimensions: the naive meaning, the critical dissolution of meaning to a design of immanent signs and the meaning opened up by comparison of the two" (Klemm, 1983, p. 109).

There is another possibility for the "I" according to Ricoeur and Klemm. That possibility is that the "I", the hidden and elusive self of self-consciousness, can find itself represented and displayed in the self-world relations presented in the text (Klemm, 1983, pp. 108-110). We can discover ourselves through texts.

> The "I" is free to judge, of the self-understanding that ultimately surfaces as the Sache of the text, whether that self-understanding is one for me in the sense that the text-world presented there provides a context of meaning in which "I" can be the one "I" really am (Klemm, 1983, p. 108).

There is one text in which Ricoeur applies his hermeneutics. It is "Listening to the Parables of Jesus". He follows his hermeneutic arch from the intital "naive" reading in the shock of the parables through the structural analysis of the parables to the listing for "new possibilities disclosed by the extravagance of these short dramas" (Ricoeur in Reagan and Stewart, 1978, p. 245). An interpretation of this essay is not necessary, but it is important to note that Ricoeur does use his own hermeneutic arch.

THE HERMENEUTIC ARCH AND CURRICULUM THEORY

The explanation of Ricoeur's theoretical work has opened up a possible world for understanding curriculum texts in a new way. We must remember, however, that the curriculum texts to which I refer are theoretical texts. This presents a problematic on the referential nature of theoretical texts.

Ricoeur in his texts distinguishes between scientific texts and literary texts. The basic difference being their referents. The scientific text has ostensive reference or reference to concrete reality. On the other hand, the literary text has by nature of the metaphoric process abolished the ostensive reference and opened up possible worlds. I would like to construct the possibility that certain curriculum theory texts possess aspects of both the scientific text in that they refer to the concrete reality of schools and education and yet, since they are critical in some cases of this reality, they in a sense abolish it and open up the possibility of moving people to see other possible worlds. Perhaps the closer one moves to a metaphorical (poetical) curriculum discourse the more enhanced are the possiblities of opening up these possible worlds. Since there would be an improved possibility of opening up possible worlds, the possibility of discovering ourselves through curriculum theory texts will be improved. The study of specific curriculum texts will determine to a great extent whether Ricoeur's interpretation theory is applicable to curriculum theory texts. It is a theoretical assumption that needs to be analyzed to see if it is a viable one. The only way to test its viability is to use it. To test Ricoeur's theories and their application to curriculum theory, we must do Ricoeur.

This is not a prescriptive methodology. I certainly would not posit the hermeneutical reading of curriculum texts as a type of totalizing methodology. Rather, it is my own reading of curriculum texts. It

is, as Ricoeur has demonstrated in "Listening to the Parables of
Jesus", a hermeneutic reading of certain texts. It is a movement
opened up by reading Ricoeur's texts. I have passed through the
hermeneutic arch with Ricoeur's theoretical works and they themselves have opened up new possibilities for understanding curriculum texts and understanding my own understanding of these texts.
It becomes less and less imperative to explain Ricoeur and more and
more important to do what Ricoeur suggests and demonstrates. It
must be pursued with curriculum theory texts.

I believe it is important, therefore, to read certain texts within this
hermeneutic arch. I hope to go through the entire process with these
texts.

The process will start with an intitial reading and reaction to each
of the texts. Establishing the pre-understanding or prejudicial
aspects of this understanding will be the first step. Trying to situate
what tradition I am bringing to the text is the first stage of the first
reading. It will also be a chance to react to significant passages which
appear to be especially significant and to "reconstruct them in
critical terms" (Gerhart, 1979, pp. 266-267). So, the first step will be
an attempt to give an initial reaction in descriptive and critical terms
to certain curriculum theory texts. The attempt will be made to
assess their apparent meaning also.

The second stage will be the explanation of curriculum texts using
the methods of structural literary analysis. A synchronic study of
certain curriculum texts will be attempted. Each curriculum text will
be studied as representative of composition, genre and style within
a specific system of these categories. The category of essay, manifesto, letter and academic writing will be discussed in this part of the
hermeneutic arch. Some of the works of Barthes will be considered:
Mythodologies (1972), *The Pleasure of the Text* (1975), and *Roland
Barthes* (1977). Jonathan Culler's works on literature, specifically:
*Structuralist Poetics: Structuralism, Linguistics and the Study of Litera-
ture* (1978), *The Pursuit of Signs: Semiotics, Literature, Deconstruction*
(1961) and *On Deconstruction: Theory and Criticism After Structuralism*
(1982) will be used. Ferdinand de Saussure's *Course in General
Linguistics* (1968) will also be a basic source for this phase. Two
excellent works by Robert Scholes will be used. They are *Structural-*

ism in Literature: An Introduction (1974) and *Semiotics and Interpretation* (1982). A final work that will be referred to is *Semiotics and the Philosophy of Language* by Umberto Eco. Their concepts of codes, binary oppositions, systems and isotopics will be explained and used to explain the sense aspects of curriculum theory texts. This use of structuralism will model itself according to Ricoeur's inclusion of it in the hermeneutic arch.

The final post on the hermeneutic arch will be the reflexive comprehension of the possible worlds that individual texts open up to this reader. Through this reading it is hoped that certain curriculum texts will provide a certain context in which "I can be the one I really am" (Klemm, 1983, p. 108). This will be discussed in the language of being in the world. It will, indeed, make it a hermeneutic phenomenology.

The study of these texts can be divided up into the various groups of texts I well read in this hermeneutic way.

The study will read, in this hermeneutic way, Mortimer Adler's *Paideia Proposal: An Educational Manifesto* (1982) and *Paideia Problems and Possibilities* (1983). It will be an attempt to look for possible worlds this discourse opens. This type of reading will also be performed upon The Commission on Excellence in Education's report entitled *A Nation At Risk: The Imperative for Educational Reform* (1983). These texts will be read, explained and understood using Ricoeur's interpretation theory.

Another study will read reconceptualist curriculum theory texts and reproductionist theory texts. William Pinar's *Sanity,Madness and the School* (1976) will be read within the hermeneutic arch. The reproductionist theory that will be read is contained in Michael Apple's "Curricular Form and the Logic of Technical Control: Building the Possesive Individual". This work apperars in *Cultural and Economic Reproduction in Education: Essays on Class, Ideology and the State* (1982). This text will be analyzed in this section.

The hermeneutic reading of these theoretical texts will hopefully lead to an understanding and self-understanding which will enable a new way for curriculum theory texts to be read. A way that will enable the reference of these texts to be read less ostensively and increasingly pointed toward a level of second reference, which includes self-understanding.

These studies will hopefully contain "the sense of untapped resources, of things to say as yet unsaid" (Woolf, 1920, p. 24). Therefore, let us proceed.

3
Listening to Conservative Curriculum Theory

To listen anew to conservative curriculum theory is the journey that this study takes. It is the initial stage of the hermeneutic process that Ricoeur discusses in his various texts. It asks the same questions about conservative curriculum theory that Ricoeur asks about the "Parables of Jesus". Is it possible to listen to the "Parables of Jesus" or conservative curriculum theory "in such a way that we are once more astonished, struck, renewed, and put in motion" (Ricoeur in Reagan and Stewart, 1978, p. 213). Does contemporary conservative curriculum theory have these attributes? Treating conservative curriculum theory as a "text among other texts" (Ricoeur in Reagan and Stewart, 1978, p. 213), is one way to answer this question.

Three texts will be read in this study. They are *The Paideia Proposal: An Educational Manifesto* (1982), *Paideia Problems and Possibilities* (1983) and *A Nation At Risk: The Imperative For Educational Reform* (1983). These texts do not represent an exhaustive review of contemporary conservative curriculum theory, but they do represent the main and perhaps best known examples of this trend.

The first step in this process of understanding this theory is to give these texts an initial reading. The first step to my initial reading of these particular texts is to delineate those pre-understandings or prejudicial understandings I bring to these texts. According to Gadamer in *Truth and Method*, it is practically impossible to eliminate this type of prejudicial understandings, yet it is essential to situate myself and this study before attempting any initial readings. So, we are not eliminating but situating.

These readings are pursued by a thirty-five year old, white, male who has been in the educational field as a practitioner for fourteen years and has been concerned with understanding the present moment in educational theory. My disciplinary background has been in reconceptualist curriculum theory. This puts my views of curriculum theory at odds with what Pinar in many of his articles refers to as traditionalist curriculum theory and what I am calling for the most part conservative curriculum theory. I come to this work, therefore, with an attitude of suspicion and at the same moment with a willingness to listen to what is being said. This attitude of suspicion is an interesting one. *The Oxford English Dictionary* gives as a denotative meaning for suspicion: "the imagination of something possible (not necessarily evil) as possible or likely; a slight belief or idea of something, or that something is the case; a surmise; a notion or inkling. (Chiefly in the negative sense)" (OED, 1971, p. 3180). My suspicion is that this conservative curriculum theory will be unproductive and will not put anything into motion in an emancipatory sense. I will not allow myself, however, to succumb immediately and intensely to my suspicions. This would not be at all productive and would amount to dismissing these texts as worthless without giving them at the very least an initial reading. These initial readings will take the form of reading and replying to what are the significant passages for this author. These same passages may not be significant for other readers, but this is not a prescriptive methodology. It is an attempt to exemplify a hermeneutic-phenomenological analysis of certain texts based on various concepts discussed by Paul Ricoeur in *The Conflict of Interpretations, The Rule of Metaphor* and numerous articles. These intitial readings/reactions will be in descriptive as well as critical terms. The critical aspect of these terms will be supplied by knowledge of the contemporary curriculum field and its concepts, history and terminology. In Ricoeur's works he suggests the use of the terms and concepts of literary criticism. These will also be used when the need arises.

AN INITIAL READING

The first point we begin to notice when beginning to read *The Paideia Proposal: An Educational Manifesto* is best characterized as an attitude. The attitude is a prescriptive one. The proposal is telling us what is best for us and what we should do to reform education. It has the characteristics of a traditional sermon. Adler, as the spokesperson for the Paideia group, states rather emphatically:

> We should have a one-track system of schooling, not a system
> with two or more tracks, only one of which goes straight ahead
> while others shunt the young off onto sidetracks not headed

toward the goals our society opens to all. The innermost meaning of social equality is: substantially the same quality of life for all. That calls for the same quality of schooling for all (Adler, 1982, p. 6).

This seems to be the essence of a prescriptive type of theory. It is in keeping with the goals of the traditionalist and conservative curriculum theorists. Their goal is the goal of the Paideia group, yet the Paideia group's agenda is different in many respects as will be pointed out in this study. "Its intent is clearly to guide, to be of assistance to those in institutional positions who are concerned with curriculum" (Pinar in Giroux, Penna and Pinar, 1981, p. 90). It appears, then, that by its inherent nature this curriculum theory is prescriptive. It is focused on improving the system of public schooling by dealing with the present system as it is and rearranging curricula within the present system of public education. It can be seen as a prescriptive external force for change.

The next important aspect that strikes me as I read through the text is the objectives that are set out to achieve this goal of a one track system with quality education for all. Adler enumerates three main objectives. They are: 1. There should be improved opportunities for personal growth and self-improvement. 2. There should be preparation for the duties and responsibilities of citizenship. 3. There should be basic skills given that are common to all work in our society (Adler, 1982, pp. 16-18). These are noble goals. Almost every practitioner in the field would no doubt agree with these goals. We as curriculum theorists would probably agree with some of them. But, a question arises. How are these objectives to be met? It is interesting to note that when we read a text produced by a traditional/conservative type of theorist we ourselves begin to slip into their language by using terms like objectives. The meeting of these objectives is made possible first by the removal of much of the present curriculum (content) and the insertion of a "three column program". What is to be taken out?

All sidetracks, specialized courses, or elective choices must be eliminated. Allowing them will always lead a certain number of students to voluntarily downgrade their own education...Electives and specialization are entirely proper at the level of advanced schooling - in our colleges, universities, and technical schools.

The curriculum that is instituted to replace all of this is completely required. The only option it presents is the choice of a second langauge. My initial reaction to these points is negative. If we are concerned with letting people become proficient in making decisions, then how is this to be achieved when the program is making all the meaningful decisions for them.

Adler delineates his three column curriculum with a diagram. It is not necessary to include the diagram in this study, but a summary of the proposal is necessary. His three columns correspond to his three major goals. They are: 1. The acquisition of organized knowledge; 2. The development of intellectual skills - the skills of learning; and 3. The enlarged understanding of ideas and values (Adler, 1982, p. 23). These basic goals are arrived at according to Adler because:

> They comprise the most fundamental branches of learning. No one can claim to be educated who is not reasonably well acquainted with all three. They provide the learner with indispensible knowledge about nature and culture, the world in which we live, our social institutions, and ourselves (Adler, 1982, p. 24).

Even during this initial reading and reaction, some assumptions of Adler stand out quite clearly. Adler's theory of knowledge itself is evidently that knowledge is a neutral black box and the more educated we become the more of the black box we are required to possess. It appears at this point that even though Adler from the outset is discussing the democratic nature of education, his system is edging toward elitism. He may have to answer to this charge later in this study. But, at this point the shades of elitism are present. Basically, his assumption that all children can handle this classical material are erroneous. I will discuss the specific components of the curriculum later in this study. There are other views of knowledge and knowledge acquisition that Adler either rejects or forgets. Knowledge as a social construct is a concept that Adler misses. It also appears that Adler and the rest of the Paideia group accepts the current system (form) with the taken for granted attitude that is prevelant in much of contemporary curriculum theory and curriculum plans. The present study is an effort to eliminate or at the very least to bracket this type of attitude from curriculum discussions. So, it is rather ironic, that despite the noble efforts of Adler and his associates to erect a "quality of democratic education" (Adler, 1982, p. 16), upon this initial reading of his theory or proposal my suspicion of a tendency toward elitism cannot be put aside.

Martin Carnoy discusses Adler's work in his article entitled "Education, Democracy, and Social Conflict" (1983). This article is part of a Symposium on the *Paideia Proposal: An Educational Manifesto for the Harvard Educational Review*.

> The Paideia Group, however, carefully avoids the whole issue of democracy in the schools; curriculum is specifically set by educational professionals and is based on rigid classical criteria. In such a curriculum, democracy is not experienced but taught through civic education (Carnoy, 1983, p. 399).

Carnoy, in this article, is comparing the Paideia Group's theory with that of John Dewey. He experiences in his reading also the inkling that this democratic education offered by the Paideia Group is not quite as democratic as is advertised.

Adler's second column discusses the development of intellectual skills. These include "reading, writing, speaking, listening, observing, measuring, estimating, and calculating. They are the linguistic, mathematical and scientific skills" (Adler, 1982, p. 26). The area of skill acquisition is a moment where I can find agreement with Adler. He does not rest with only a passing reference to the development of basic skills. As we have seen in recent years the emphasis on back to the basics has led to many programs and tests which only emphasize minimum competencies. This results in a plethora of drilling and teaching to externally devised state mandated tests. Adler's approach to this skills question is quite reasonable at this initial reading stage.

> Since what is learned here is skill in performance, not knowledge of the facts and formulas, the mode of teaching cannot be didactic. It cannot consist of the teacher telling, demonstrating

or lecturing. Instead, it must be akin to the coaching that is done to impart athletic skills. A coach does not teach simply by telling or giving the learner a rule book to follow. A coach trains by helping the learner to do, to go through the right motions, and to organize a sequence of acts in a correct fashion. He corrects faulty performance again and again and insists on repetition of the performance until it reaches a measure of perfection (Adler, 1982, p. 27).

My initial reaction to this idea of coaching skills is a positive one. Before we develop any type of critical thinking skills, a basic grasp of these areas that Adler discusses are crucial. To some degree my inkling that Adler and I would disagree on everything seems to have been a bit premature. Although at this point in the initial reading I disagree with Adler and the Paideia Group's major tenets. There are some small points where I do agree. The idea Ricoeur emphasizes of a willingness to listen through our suspicions is a point well taken.

But, with Adler and the Paideia Group's third column the negative suspicions return again. The third column—the enlarged understanding of ideas and values takes Adler back to his classical curriculum. It is the curriculum of "great" books. It is again a democratic education that is imposed and not experienced. Maxine Greene in an article entitled "Opening to Possibility: The Common World and The Public School" included in a collection of essays entitled *Bad Times, Good Schools* discusses the idea of choice, the kind of choice that is obviously lacking in the Paideia Proposal. The empahsis is mine.

> To take an initiative, to feel that one has a choice to make, is to break the limits of what exists at any given moment; it is to try to bring something into being, something that is not yet. There is no choosing *if there is no awareness of alternatives*, no sense that one mode of action is to be preferred over another (Greene, 1983, pp. 82-83).

Despite Adler's admirable call for the use of the Socratic method to develop the critical capacity in students through the use of classics, the freedom is lost. He feels that through the use of this Socratic method of "coaching" the classics the student will develop this critical capacity. The classics are included.

> ...careful reading and discussion of the following documents:
> the Declaration of Independence, the Constitution, selections
> from the *Federalist Papers* and the Gettysburg Address. Other
> books will fill this purpose out, but these few are basic to
> understanding our democracy (Adler, 1982, p. 30).

We come, therefore, to the end of the explanation of the purposes
and methods of the three columns with the plea for a better understanding of our democracy. It is ironic that this is brought about in
this proposal in such an undemocratic way. There is no choice
allowed.

Adler next discusses the integration of the three columns. He
compares his proposed innovation to what exists currently in the
schools. He explains that there is little joy in "most of the learning
that they are now compelled to do" (Adler, 1982, p. 32). Adler feels
that neither the teachers nor the students are interested or have
much enthusiasm for the curriculum of the contemporary schools. I
would concur with him on this point. The point that I have difficulty
with, in this proposal, is the replacement of one required curriculum
for another no matter how innovative. Although the method of
instruction would change, it is still imposed. Perhaps the fact of that
imposition is what lies at the center of the lack of interest or
enthusiasm that Adler correctly perceives in today's schools.

The Paideia Group with Adler as its spokesperson does advocate
some "auxiliary studies". There should be some training for manual
activities and for choosing and obtaining a career. But, any specific
training for the world of work should be pursued after the years of
basic schooling. Most of the rest of this proposal section discusses
the elimination of many programs present in the schools. Two of the
most significant eliminations would be in the areas of specific job
training and extracurricular activities.

The last few paragraphs of this section on the proposal I find quite
significant. It appears that Adler and the Paideia Group are trying
to create a panacea with the Paideia Proposal.

> Worse evils than ignorance, lack of discipline, deficiency in
> rudimentary skills, and the impoverished understanding re-

sult from most of the existing programs of instruction in our public schools. The absence of intellectual stimulation and the failure to challenge students by expecting the most of them leads to boredom, delinquency, lawless violence, drug dependence, alcoholism, and other forms of undesirable conduct (Adler, 1982, p. 36).

Not only is the Paideia Group proposing to change the basic curriculum of the schools, but also to solve many of our social ills as well. I find these ideas somewhat superficial.

The remainder of *The Paideia Proposal: An Educational Manifesto and Paideia Problems and Possibilities* discusses the implementation and use of the proposed curriculum. I will, therefore, discuss both of these works together. Even though the Paideia Proposal has what Ronald Gwiazda in an article in *The Harvard Educational Review* entitled "The Peter Pan Proposal" called "a certain Peter Pan quality" (Gwiazda, 1983, p. 388), it does contain some comments I find positive and can agree with. This Peter Pan quality is discussed by Gwiazda:

> We are told that if we believe strongly enough we can fly. We are also told that this idea is gift enough and that all mundane questions concerning gravity and wings should be answered by the aspiring Icaruses themselves. Yet some of the practical questions point back to the inherent weaknesses in the Proposal. Many questions will have to be answered before *The Paideia Proposal* can stand as a legitimate blueprint for educational reform (Gwiazda, 1983, p. 388).

This quality is in evidence in the work, but there are some positive qualities that deserve attention. In the third part of *The Paideia Proposal: An Educational Manifesto*, Adler begins discussing the problems of implementing his program. He begins by discussing teaching. The Socratic model is the basis for his conception of good teaching. Adler discusses three ways of learning. They are: "1. by the acquisition of information and organized knowledge; 2. by the development of intellectual skills; 3. by the enlargement of the understanding" (Adler, 1982, p. 51). These types of learning necessitate, Adler insists, the different modes of teaching. Teaching should become less and less a single mode or method. There should be various methods employed for the various types of learning. Students are at some points empty vessels that need to be filled according to Adler. This would be the first stage of learning. The acquisition stage would demand the methods of drilling, memorizing and lecturing. The use of textbooks would also be necessary at this phase. Even though I have a fairly negative reaction to this proposal, it seems to me that at this point of the initial reading that these points make some good sense. The other two methods, that of coaching the learner and class discussions, I have already discussed and found to be fairly positive. However, Adler and the Paideia Group's proposal does have a Peter Pan quality. Classroom size, class size, facilities and many other external conditions that are a necessity are magically going to orient themselves to this program!

Adler covers an immense area in his Proposal. He next covers "The Preparation of Teachers" (Adler, 1982, pp. 57-61). His comments here are significant. Having been a teacher in high school for ten years I do appreciate a number of his comments. His comments about pay, respect, and status all ring true. He adds a comment about other negative conditions which I find piercing and incisive.

> Add to this the many administrative, public relations, and quasi-menial duties that teachers are asked to perform, duties that take mind and energy away from teaching, and it is easy to understand why our educational system is not able to attract many of the ablest young into the teaching profession, or to turn those who do join the ranks into adequate teachers (Adler, 1982, p. 58).

Adler leaves, however, an important question out. The critical question of the reasons for this dilemma are left unasked and unanswered. Adler accepts it as a necssary given and proceeds from that point. This taken for granted assumption is a crucial mistake. It makes Adler's concern with the state of education a concern not with radical or fundamental questions but with the symptoms resulting from those major questions. He also discusses the current teacher-training programs. He states what they are turning out.

> ...persons who are not sufficiently equipped with the knowl-

edge, the intellectual skills, or the developed understanding needed to guide and help the young in the course of study we have recommended (Adler, 1982, p. 60).

What does Adler recommend as a remedy to this situation? These prospective teachers need to be brought rigorously through a Paideia curriculum themselves. Since I have already discussed my initial reactions to the basic Paideia curriculum, it is not necessary to make further negative or positive comments about teachers brought up in this system. He does recommend a Socratic type of teacher who is proficient in the "cooperative art" of teaching.

The cooperative art of the teacher depends on the teacher's understanding of how the mind learns by the exercise of its own powers, and on his or her use of this understanding to help the minds of others to learn (Adler, 1982, p. 61).

As I stated previously I do appreciate this call for a more guiding type of teacher, but despite Adler's disclaimers, this would be difficult to achieve if the teachers themselves were never given the opportunity to exercise freedom of choice. Teachers who are brought up in an undemocratic system of education will most likely not generate a democratic system themselves.

The Paideia Group's next target is the school administrator. Adler indicates that the effectiveness of any curriculum and any teacher effectiveness is enhanced or harmed by the specific building administrator.

What is important is that the principal provide the educational leadership that the school community needs. It has been shown in repeated studies that the quality of teaching and learning that goes on in a school is largely determined by the quality of such leadership (Adler, 1982, p. 64).

I agree with this statement. After teaching in a school district with a highly ineffective educational leader, Adler's remarks ring true. In a school with a highly ineffective administrator the teachers' responsibilities are overwhelming. They not only become responsible for their own teaching responsibilities, but they also become responsible for many of the educational decisions that should be the task of the administrator. Adler's comments about effective administrators are useful for any curriculum theory whether it be Paideia or reconceptualist theory.

The final chapter of the original *Paideia Proposal: An Educational Manifesto* that this initial reading will cover is entitled "Higher Learning". In this chapter Adler discusses college curriculum. He views negatively the idea of intense specialization.

> But we can and should do something to mitigate the barbarism of intense specialization, which threatens to be as destructive in its own way as the abandonment of specialization would be. We can reconceive the role and offerings of our colleges and universities, made possible by the time saved and skills acquired that reformed basic schooling will provide (Adler, 1982, p. 72).

It reads like the proposal will solve even some of the problems that plague our institutions of higher learning. Again, like the solution to the problems of adolescence the solution of the problem(s) of higher education tend toward the superficial. It is the Peter Pan answer.

The initial reading of the first Paideia text completed I would like to move on to its sequal, *Paideia Problems and Possibilities* (1983). The first twenty-four pages of the sequal is basically a review of the first Paideia text. There is some clarification made about the program in these twenty-four pages which I will discuss in this initial reading. Adler does say that this particular text is not for those who object to the Paideia Proposal, but for those who have questions about the proposal.

> The present statement, therefore, confines itself to the questions raised by those whose response is favorable—those who approve of the ends to be served and generally concur in the choice of means for establishing a truly democratic system of basic schooling in this country (Adler, 1983, p. 1).

According to Adler, the prime inspiration for the Paideia Proposal is John Dewey's *Democracy and Education*, he and the Paideia Group hope to make a truly democratic program of education. The group hopes that this type of education will "promote the general welfare of this country in a number of ways" (Adler, 1983, p. 9). It is quite important to note the ways that this program will benefit the nation. It appears at this initial reading that this program is tied into the corporate interests in America. The benefits discussed appear to be an appeal not only to the citizens of this country but to those interests as well.

There are five benefits and they can be summarized. The first benefit is the distribution of the same quality of education to all, which is a right of the people. The second benefit is that this program will contribute to the prosperity of this country by educating people for new jobs resulting from the technological revolution. This program will also supply the military with educated people who can adapt to technological changes in weaponry. The fourth benefit would be that the people educated under this program would preserve and add to our cultural heritage. The final benefit would be that people educated under this program would have an increased ability to pursue happiness (Adler, 1983, pp. 9-11). The area of supplying the military machine as one of the primary goals and benefits of the educational system is one that confirms my early suspicions of conservative curriculum theory. Where in this program is the opportunity to question the forms and types of education, educational systems and political systems that we have? The Paideia Group is not questioning in any critical sense the basic system, but it is adapting a classical education to the demands of the modern industrial and military complex. They make this quite clear and are evidently proud of it. This is certainly a suspicion confirming facet for me.

Adler next discusses the specific curriculum and clarifies some points made in the original work. The sameness of the curriculum rests on a particular point.

> ...solely in the sameness of this recommended framework, not in any sameness of detail as to the materials used, the precise organization of the curriculum, and other particular measures and methods to be devised. These will be inevitably and desirably different in different school districts (Adler, 1983, p. 15).

After this defense of the curriculum, Adler goes on to explain the three column chart from the Paideia Proposal. The rest of the text deals with questions raised by the original text *The Paideia Proposal: An Educational Manifesto*. The answers to some of these questions are significant enough to deal with at this stage of an initial reading.

The first set of questions deals with principles associated with the Paideia Proposal. This series of questions is subdivided into certain sets of questions. The first set of questions deal directly with the "Curricular Framework". In this initial reaction stage I will deal with what strikes me as the most significant questions and answers.

Question number two asks if this proposal is a "call for the restoration of a classical education, its only novelty being that it advocates giving such an education to all children instead of only some" (Adler, 1983, p. 28). Adler's answer to this question is quite interesting. He believes that this curriculum should be a curriculum of great books. He writes about the recommended curriculum.

> The Paideia program recommends the reading and discussion of classics—that is, any works of lasting value—only in the sense that the books and other artifacts chosen have this lasting value and only for the sake of their relevance to problems that anyone must face in today's world (Adler, 1983, pp. 28-29).

Again, this imposition of a specific curriculum framework of lasting value leaves little choice to the student. Despite the call for discussion generated by these specific works, there is no mention made of discussing the basis and logic of the choice of these specific works. There is discussion of whether or not these works merit classic status, but there is little discussion of that concept of status. Rather than having a truly democratic community of learners, who make decisions about programs that directly affect them, this program or proposal calls for a framework imposed on that community. It would give a type of limited freedom and a type of false consciousness. The students would feel that they were making important decisions, but the most significant decisions which affect them are made for them. Questions concerning the nature of such matters as lasting value are left unanswered by this program.

Problem number four, concerning the curricular program, is another significant point in this sequal to the original proposal. This question addresses a charge I have made in this initial reading. Adler deals with the question of whether or not this program is elitist.

> How, then are we to understand the perversity of the question
> whether our proposal is elitist? Only in this way; where the
> term elitist is used to mean a concern with excellence, then the
> Paideia program—a program designed to provide a high quality
> of schooling—can be labelled elitist; but only when it is also
> understood that its elitism is applicable to all, not just a privi-
> leged few. It is concerned with excellence as a democratic goal.
> The word elitist thus amounts to no more than name calling
> (Adler, 1983, p. 31).

This answer possesses a type of "Peter Pan" quality. It leaves out
or ignores entire sectors of the student population. The learning
disabled, the problem student and many other portions of the
student population are not discussed. It appears, despite all the
positive intentions of the Paideia Group, their program leaves the
actual issue of true elitism unaddressed. It is dismissed quickly with
a passing shot. The program begins to take on the qualities of a magic
lamp. The program will work for all children in almost every
situation if we just wish it to be that way. I think the charge of elitism
is a serious one. It amounts to more than just name calling. It
confirms some of my early impressions about this conservative
curriculum theory.

The Paideia Group, with Adler as its spokesperson, answers the
question concerning the elimination of all electives from the curriculum and the consequent ramifications. There are several sections of
the answer to this particular issue that are enlightening. There are
five significant sections to address. The reason cited for the elimination of electives is that the Paideia curriculum, if used effectively,
would consume the entire school day. There would be no time for
anything else.

> Many of the electives thereby eliminated have no educational
> value at all; some have value that can be realized in one or
> another form of extracurricular activity (Adler, 1983, p. 36).

The point that Adler and his associates miss is that the value of
some of these electives may not lie specifically in the course content,
but in the value of letting the student make a decision that directly

affects his educational progress and consequently his future. This is a democratic decision.

Adler believes that "neither regimentation nor deprivation result from the same required course of study for all" (Adler, 1983, p. 36).

> The great merit in eliminating the present plethora of electives is that it will keep students from wasting their time in courses that are of low instructional value and that fit in no coherent scheme of progressive learning (Adler, 1983, p. 37).

In this passage there is evidence that once again the determination of course value is made by an external group and not by members of the community of learners. Adler next addresses the major charge of an undemocratic imposition of a specific curriculum. The answer is long but provides some insight into this Paideia Proposal.

> Finally, the charge that a required course of study is authoritarian and anti-democratic is groundless. One might just as well say that requiring children to be vaccinated or otherwise rendered immune, or requiring them to have balanced diets, take certain amount of physical exercise, have a certain amount of sleep at regular intervals, and submit to medications they need for the cure of ailments they suffer, is authoritarian and anti-democratic. At a higher level, the requirements for a job or for a profession are and will remain uniform without being on that account any infringement on liberty. There is plenty of room left for the exercise of freedom of choice in other matters (Adler, 1983, p. 37).

When does this choice in other matters occur? According to Adler it happens after one becomes a specialist. But, this only happens after one has become a generalist. The Paideia Proposal is an education for or toward the generalist. The charge of authoritarianism is not actually answered. It is simply put aside and dismissed with mixed metaphors. Apparently by magic when one leaves the World of Paideia, where there was little choice in matters affecting a student's education, the choices are made for them, one donnes the cap of the specialist and is able to make these types of choices very easily. Where or how a student achieves this ability or desire to make choices is never answered. Adler leaves no answer or an ambiguous one. He constantly refers to the point that the Paideia Proposal is "only a framework of ends and general means that is prescribed" (Adler, 1983, p. 37). Still, one does not need the specific to read and criticize the basic intent of the framework.

At this point I must interject that my comments and initial reactions to this proposal are sounding quite negative. I am sure that some of that is due to my prejudicial understandings. It is difficult to eliminate them completely. In listening to this proposal I have had hopes that there would be a chord or two that would be in harmony with my thought and opinions. At this point of an initial reading those, indeed, have been very few.

There is one section of the sequal text *Paideia Problems and Possibilities* that is worth considering in this section of initial reading. The section is entitled "The Possibilities". The few sections before this portion of the text concern logistical problems of implementation and need not concern this initial reading.

Adler in this section reiterates his disregard for those who disagree with the basic intent of the Paideia program. He is only concerned with those who agree with his basic concept.

A substantial majority of the comments we have received—in reviews, conferences, and public discussions of *The Paideia Proposal*—do not regard the reform proposed as being aimed in the wrong direction and do not reject the recommendation of the means as not the right prescription for achieving the appointed goals. Our discussion in these pages has therefore been an attempt to answer the questions raised by those who approve the Paideia principles (Adler, 1983, p. 80).

Adler does not want a dialogue with those who oppose the principles of his theory. This is another problem I find with the prescriptive format of his theory. If a theorist never engages in debate as to the relative merit of his theoretical position, then we can expect that his theory will stagnate. It will no longer be a question of the political and social ramifications of the theory; it will evolve into questions of efficiency and results. From the first initial reading of the volumes of the Paideia Proposal it appears that the Paidiea Group is headed in this direction with its outright refusal to engage in constructive debate. We can see this view emerge in the closing comments in the sequal to the first Paideia volume.

> We think it is now sufficiently clear that The Paideia Proposal has persuaded a large number of administrators, teachers, school boards, and others concerned with basic schooling in this country—persuaded them of the rightness and the soundness and indispensibility of the general means recommended. We believe that such persuaded practitioners will eventually achieve a substantial measure of success if they do not despair because of all the obstacles to be surmounted and all the difficult problems to be solved (Adler, 1983, p. 82).

It is not a question of engagement, but a question of implementation.

A NATION AT RISK: THE IMPERATIVE FOR EDUCATIONAL REFORM

The next text to be read is produced by The National Commission on Excellence in Education. The text is entitled *A Nation at Risk:The Imperative for Educational Reform*. This commission was created by T. H. Bell, the Secretary of Education. Bell created the commission and gave it the responsibility of presenting a report on the "quality of education in America" (National Commission on Excellence in Education (NCEE), 1983, p. iii). The result was the text read for this study.

The text of the NCEE is closely tied to major thrust of the traditional and conservative purposes for curriculum theory. The major impetus for conservative curriculum theory is to be practical and applicable to school implementation and to work closely with the school practitioners. On the first page of this text there is a comment made to this effect.

> In accordance with the Secretary's instructions, this report contains practical recommendations for educational improvement and fulfills the Commission's responsibilities under the terms of its charter (NCEE, 1983, p. 1).

Again, we find in this text the close tie conservative curriculum theory has with the status quo or the current ideological structure. In this particular example we have a piece of theory produced by an agency which is a direct part of that structure. Theory produced in this manner is important to listen to. It is especially interesting in the beginning of the text to see the traditional tie between educational theory and its practical orientation toward the competitive market place. The commission states its reasons for supporting new educational reforms.

If only to keep and improve on the slim competitive edge we still retain in the world markets, we must dedicate ourselves to the reform of our educational system for the benefit of all—old and young alike, affluent and poor, majority and minority. Our concern, however, goes well beyond matters such as industry and commerce. It also includes the intellectual, moral, and spiritual strengths of our people which knit together the very fabric of our society (NCEE, 1983, p. 7).

Once again the connection between the traditional/conservative outlook on the curriculum and this report's outlook is evident. After the opening remarks about the purposes of this text and its possible ramifications, the authors indicate that there are several warning signs of risk. Perhaps, the one that appears most significant is the risk seen by business and the military.

Business and military leaders complain that they are required to spend millions of dollars on costly remedial education and training programs in such basic skills as reading, writing, spelling and computation. The Department of the Navy, for example, reported that one-quarter of its recent recruits cannot read at the ninth grade level, the minimum needed simply to understand written safety instructions. Without remedial work they cannot even begin much less complete, the sophisticated training essential in much of the modern military (NCEE, 1983, p. 9).

This interest in securing more efficient workers for the industrial and military complex in the United States is consistent with the outlooks of typical conservative curriculum theory. As I read this document for the first time that lingering suspicion that my prejudicial understandings bring to this material comes vibrating back strongly. Although this suspicion does continue, there are some points made in this text that bear attention. It is the connections that are made with this information that I cannot possibly view as opening up any movement in emancipatory directions. But, some of the comments made in this text are important for all curriculum theorists to recognize.

Many 17-year-olds do not possess the 'high order' intellectual skills we should expect of them. Nearly 40 percent cannot draw inferences from written material; only one-fifth can write a persuasive essay; and only one-third can solve a mathematics problem requiring several steps (NCEE, 1983, p. 9).

These facts are important to consider when theorizing about the potential for a liberating type of education that requires sophisticated thinking skills on the part of the students involved.

I begin to hear the fear of this commission; it is the fear of the "Evil Empire" beating us at last by the poor quality of our educational system. It is the cold war rhetoric returning.

If an unfriendly foreign power had attempted to impose on America the mediocre educational performance that exists today, we might well have viewed it as an act of war (NCEE, 1983, p. 5).

As I read this text visions of the 1950s and early 1960s come rushing into my mind. In fact, the image of Admiral Rickover and his text *Education and Freedom* looms distinctly in the background. The text produced by the Bell Commission discusses developments in education at this point.

On the positive side is the significant movement by political and educational leaders to search for solutions—so far centering largely on the nearly desperate need for increased support for the teaching of mathematics and science. This movement is but a start on what we believe is a larger and more educationally encompassing need to improve teaching and learning in fields such as English, history, geography, economics, and foreign languages. We believe this movement must be broadened and directed toward reform and excellence throughout education (NCEE, 1983, p. 12).

This emphasis especially on mathematics and science is quite like the emphasis Rickover urged in the late 1950s. According to Joel Spring in his text, *The Sorting Machine: National Educational Policy Since 1945*, Rickover was supporting the same type of statements as this 1983 commission.

> Admiral Rickover's basic message was that the United States was losing the technological and military race with the Soviet Union because America's public schools were failing to iden- tify and adequately educate talented youth as future scientists and engineers (Spring, 1976, p. 12).

It is evident then that the goal of conservative curriculum theory has remained fairly constant for the last thirty-five years. The emphasis on practical solutions to curriculum problems and the concern with the practitioner still exists. The commitment to the progress of the corporate and military structure are also still in evidence in this report.

The report next discusses the commitment on the part of the public to this reform of education. The report quotes many statistical proofs including Gallop Polls and numerous surveys that indicate beliefs concerning education.

> People are steadfast in their belief that education is the major foundation for the future strength of this country. They even considered education more important than developing the best industrial system or the strongest military force, perhaps be- cause they understood education as the cornerstone of both. They also held that education is "extremely important" to one's future success, and that public education should be the top priority for additional Federal funds (NCEE, 1983, pp. 16-17).

With this commitment of the American people stated, the report proceeds to discuss its findings. The findings are broken up into four aspects of the educational process: content, expectations, time and teaching. The NCEE believes that the crisis in American education result from "disturbing inadequacies" in these four areas of the educational process. The text delineates the four areas and the findings in each area. A summary of these findings is enlightening and significant.

The basic problem in the content (curriculum) aspect of education is the relative weakness of the specific credits and courses accumulated during high school years.

Secondary school curricula have been homogenized, diluted, and diffused to the point that they no longer have a central purpose. In effect, we have a cafeteria-style curriculum in which the appetizers and desserts can easily be mistaken for the main courses (NCEE, 1983, p. 18).

The text explains that there has been and continues to be a flocking toward the mediocre. Students are opting for the "general track", giving up the more strenuous academic track or the vocational track. This explains, according to the commission, the phenomena of having good academic courses with few students taking them.

The fact that escapes the Commission is that the students may not be taking these simply because they are not committed to them. The important question that arises at this initial reading stage is not simply the fact that the students are not opting for these courses but the far more important question as to why the students feel no commitment to these courses. This report is revealing some important negative aspects of education. But, it is significant that for this reader at this first reading the most important revelations are not overtly stated by the commission. This may be the greatest asset of conservative curriculum theory. The fact is that it does reveal problems that it doesn't realize it is revealing. To dismiss this theory simply because of its connections and orientations, is a mistake that curriculum theorists with different orientations should not make. There should be a willingness to listen despite our suspicions. This type of reading and listening may lead to productive avenues of research, which will be discussed later in this study.

The next group of findings concern expectations in education. The commission defines expectations.

...levels of knowledge, abilities, and skills school and college graduates should possess. They also refer to the time, hard work, behavior, self discipline, and motivation that are essential for student achievement (NCEE, 1983, p. 19).

The commission explains several deficiencies that they noted during their research. Since there are numerous ways that expectations are conveyed to the students, there are several deficiencies in those areas. Four of the deficiencies strike me as being rather significant for a number of reasons.

The first "notable deficiency" is in the area of homework assignments. The commission found significant not the type or quality of homework assigned but the quantity of homework assigned. Their findings indicate that the average high school student (66%) spends less than one hour a night on homework. The question is important because it raises several issues that all curriculum theorists can address. In my own case it raises a question about the commitment on the part of teachers and students to the type, purpose, and methods of assigned homework.

The second deficiency concerns minimum competency examinations. The commission feels that these examinations fall short of the needed minimum competencies. A second phenomena they found was that by instituting minimum competencies the "minimum tends to become the maximum, thus lowering the educational standards for all" (NCEE, 1983, p. 20). After having done research on minimum competency tests in writing (Reynolds, 1988), I agree with this finding. The questions that arise from this problem are, however, multifaceted and speak to a number of separate issues. Questions about the purposes and functions of minimum competency tests and their effect both on teachers and students need to be addressed.

A third deficiency noted by the commission concerns the continuing decline in the general level of selectivity on the part of colleges and universities and their respective admission requirements.

> About 23 percent of our more selective colleges and universities reported that their general level of selectivity declined during the 1970s, and 29 percent reported reducing the number of specific high school courses required for admission (NCEE, 1983, pp. 20-21).

Listening to this deficiency brings forth various why questions that apparently escape the commission. It appears that they are not concerned again with these why questions, but with dealing with the situation as a given and offering some practical suggestions.

The final finding regarding expectations deals with the material of some textbooks. Apparently the commission discovered that the texts used in some courses are too simplistic.

A recent study by Education Products Information Exchange revealed that a majority of students were able to master 80 percent of the material in some of their subject-matter texts before they had even opened the books. Many books do not challenge the students to whom they are assigned (NCEE, 1983, p. 21).

Again the problem stems from low expectations on the part of the texts used in schools. This raises varied issues also. Why questions arise from everywhere. Listening to this curriculum theory reveals them.

The next category of findings discuss time. The text states that the findings about time utilization are disturbing.

Evidence presented to the Commission demonstrates three disturbing facts about the use that American schools and students make of time: (1) compared to other nations, American students spend much less time on school work; (2) time spent in the classroom and on homework is often used ineffectively; and (3) schools are not doing enough to help students develop either the study skills required to use time well or the willingness to spend more time on school (NCEE, 1983, p. 21).

Listening to this problem, it appears that the solution to it and many other of these problems could be solved by using a business mentality.

The final category of findings concern teaching. The Commission found that there are serious deficiencies and problems in this area also.

The Commission found that not enough of the academically able students are being attracted to teaching; that teacher preparation programs need substantial improvement; that the professional working life of teachers is on the whole unacceptable; and that a serious shortage of teachers exists in key fields (NCEE, 1983, p. 22).

The Commission has shown through its investigation what Adler and the Paideia Group were discussing. Teaching is in trouble in America. The questions as to why teaching is in trouble, basically in this report are questions related to salaries. There is also one comment that is made in this section that I find could create some positive motion. The emphasis is mine.

> The average salary after 12 years of teaching is only $17,000 per year, and many teachers are required to supplement their income with part-time and summer employment. In addition, *individual teachers have little influence in such critical professional decisions as, for example, textbook selection* (NCEE, 1983, pp. 22-23).

There is a positive note in this section worth listening to for a moment. The idea that teachers should exercise decisions concerning matters of course content is a comment that could initiate a serious look at how teachers have become deskilled.

The Commission gives next its recommendations for improving the state of American education. These recommendations are based on the findings I have just discussed. There are five comprehensive recommendations and subsequent "implementing recommendations". The basic recommendations are divided into the same four areas of concentration that the Commission divided its findings.

The first recommendation concerns the content of schooling and the course of study to be pursued by the students during the high school years. The Commission suggest that graduation requirements be "strengthen". What is meant by that strengthening is significant. The recommendation emphasizes that present requirements be reinforced. The significant aspect is that it seems the logic behind the stiffer requirements is to give more of the same kind of courses and thereby the educational system will improve. My reaction is a negative one. The rationale that simply requiring more of the same will enhance the soundness of education is certainly questionable. The new program would consist of:

> All students seeking a diploma be required to lay the foundations in the Five New Basics by taking the following curriculum during their 4 years of high school: (a) 4 years of English; (b) 3 years of mathematics; (c) 3 years of science; (d) 3 years of social studies; and (e) one-half year of computer science. For the college bound, 2 years of foreign language in high school are

strongly recommended in addition to those taken earlier (NCEE, 1983, p. 24).

We are given a prescriptive answer to the problems of content in the schools by this Commission. The answer appears to be give more course work to the student and that will improve the curriculum. I know this has caused several states in the country to begin to add to their graduation requirements, but I question the rationale behind simply adding more of the same to the curriculum.

The second recommendation is in the area of standards and expectations. Here in this recommendation is evidenced the same rationale. The requirements for entering colleges and universities should be increased. There are eight implementing recommendations. The second recommendation shows a similarity to the prescriptive answers about content.

> Four year colleges and universities should raise their admission requirements and advise all potential applicants of the standards for admission in terms of specific courses required, performance in these areas, and levels of achievement on standardized achievement tests in each of the five Basics and, where applicable, foreign languages (NCEE, 1983, p. 27).

Although I agree that standards and expectations should be raised, I am not convinced that this method of increasing them will lead to any positive motion.

The recommendations about time usage are the ones that I find most significant. I find that they raise in me the suspicions of my prejudicial understandings. I can foresee that these recommendations could result in some motion. But, the motion would not be toward emancipatory education. It would be a move toward using business and management techniques and applying them to education. This movement toward a business mentality for education will be under the guise of the quest for effectiveness.

> We recommend that significantly more time be devoted to learning the New Basics. This will require more effective use of the existing school day, a longer school day, or a lengthened school year (NCEE, 1983, p. 29).

This is the overall recommendation. This shift toward the corporate mentality is also seen in the implementing recommendations. The recommendations concern the efficient use of time through more efficient organization and management. This emphasis has given rise I believe to much of the current research concerning teaching effectiveness. This is a movement that I think will inevitably continue. It is set in motion by a text such as this. This text does set up motion, but it is not motion that renews or astonishes. It is motion that repeats or retrenches the present course. It is motion and questions that accept the taken for granted.

The fourth set of recommendations concern the area of teaching. It contains seven parts. Some of these recommendations I can listen to and find positive, but within the same recommendation find some negative suspicions at this initial reading. The question of better pay for teachers is a sensitive one. The Commission states:

> Salaries for the teaching profession should be increased and should be professionally competitive, market sensitive, and performance-based. Salary, promotion, tenure, and retention decisions should be tied to an effective evaluation system that includes peer review so that superior teachers can be rewarded, average ones encouraged, and poor ones improved or terminated (NCEE, 1983, p. 30).

The idea of raising teacher salaries is, indeed, a good one. This is motion in a positive direction. My suspicions arise when I read the terms effective evaluation system. This needs to be explained in greater detail or salaries of teachers might become hinged on any number of arbitrary factors. This I find a negative possibility. One other recommendation concerns the possibility of teachers obtaining grants and loans. This becomes difficult to comprehend in a job that might become even more taxing because of longer school days and years.

The final comprehensive recommendation concerns the political leadership and the exercise of citizens rights.

> We recommend that citizens across the Nation hold educators and elected officials responsible for providing the leadership necessary to achieve these reforms, and that citizens provide

fiscal support and stability required to bring about the reforms we propose (NCEE, 1983, p. 32).

Perhaps the issue of holding elected officials responsible for education is a positive one. It is one that might bring about some positive motion. In this particular case it is tied to the Commission's program and although I wouldn't push the elected officials to stress this particular program, it is a strategy well worth considering for other agendas.

In the Commission's closing remarks we have a call or plea for attention. It is a plea that all curriculum theorists should listen to. It is a plea for commitment to the Commission's recommendations, but it could serve to be a call for commitment to any specific curriculum theory program.

Our final word, perhaps better characterized as a plea, is that all segments of our population give attention to our recommendations. Our present plight did not appear overnight, and the responsibility for our current situations is widespread. Reform of our educational system will take time and unwavering commitment. It will require equally widespread, energetic, and dedicated action (NCEE, 1983, p. 36).

This section on the initial readings of the texts of conservative curriculum theory leads to questions and analysis of the texts based on a structural analysis. The process has gone from reading to explanation. This area of explanation of what Ricoeur defines as the sense of the texts is the next step in the hermeneutic process.

EXPLANATION: THE STRUCTURAL ANALYSIS OF CONSERVATIVE CURRICULUM DISCOURSE

The next phase of the hermeneutic arch is the explanation aspect. This is the position of the arch that includes structural analysis. This phase is best explained in texts by Paul Ricoeur including: *Interpretation Theory: Discourse and the Surplus of Meaning* (1976), "What is a Text?: Explanation and Interpretation" (1971), *The Conflict of Interpretations* (1974), and *The Rule of Metaphor* (1977). This is a necessary stage or phase between the initial reading and the in depth understanding concerned within the sense and reference dialectic that Ricoeur discusses.

This explanation phase of the hermeneutic journey through curriculum theory discusses the sense pole of the sense/reference dialectic. Succinctly, the sense pole deals with the "what" of discourse. The sense is immanent to the discourse and objective in the sense of ideal. The explanation phase or structural analysis of a text has three aspects. Ricoeur delineates these in "The Hermeneutic Function of Distanciation" (1973). These three aspects include: (a) the text as composition, (b) the text as genre, and (c) the text as style. In this specific study of curriculum theory texts the three texts *The Paideia Proposal: An Educational Manifesto* (1982), *Paideia Problems and Possibilities* (1983), and *A Nation at Risk: The Imperative for Educational Reform* (1983) will be structurally analyzed with these concepts in mind. The two Paideia texts will be analyzed together with the National Commission on Excellence in Education's text dealt with separately.

The structural analysis of these curriculum texts is a necessary step between a naive reading of the texts and an in depth understanding. Ricoeur states in "Structure and Hermeneutics":

It is not at all my intention to oppose hermeneutics to structuralism, the historicity of the one to the diachrony of the other. Structuralism is part of science, and I do not at present see anymore rigorous or more fruitful approach than the structuralist method at the level of comprehension which is its own. The interpretation of symbols is worthy of being called hermeneutics only insofar as it is a part of self-understanding and the understanding of being; outside this effort of appropriating meaning, it is nothing. In this sense hermeneutics is a philosophical discipline to the extent to which the aim of interpretation is to put at a distance, to objectify, to separate out from the personal equation of the investigator the structure of an institution, a myth, or rite, to the same extent hermeneutics buries itself in what could be called 'the hermeneutic circle' of understanding and of believing, which disqualifies it as a science and qualifies it as mediating thought. There is no reason to juxtapose two ways of understanding; the question is rather to link them together as the objective and the existential (or existentiell). It is this objective examination, put to work in the concept of synchrony and diachrony, that I want to perform in the hope of leading hermeneutics, through the discipline of objectivity, from a naive to a mature comprehension (Ricoeur, 1974, p. 30).

The explanation phase of the hermeneutic journey, then, involves the use of structural analysis.

So, our naive reading/understanding of texts is basically a guess at the meaning of those texts. Ricoeur explains that we must guess at the meaning of the text because the author's intention isn't beyond our reach. This guess is the primary function of the pre-hermeneutical reading. Our first understanding or our pre-hermeneutical understanding is a guessing. The second phase, that of explanation, can be seen as validation.

> ...as concerns the procedures for validation by which we test our guesses, I agree with E. D. Hirsch that they are closer to a logic of probability than to a logic of empirical verification. To show that an interpretation is more probable in the light of what we know is something other than showing that a conclusion is true. So, in the relevant sense, validation is not verification (Ricoeur, 1976, p. 76).

Structural analysis becomes our objective validation procedure. Structuralism deals with the objective explanation of the sense of the text in discourse.

Ricoeur emphasizes the importance of viewing the text as a work before considering it as an example of composition, genre and style.

> Even the term 'work' reveals the nature of these new categories, which are those of production and of labor. To impose a form upon material, to subject a production to genres, and to produce an individual style are ways of considering language as a material to be worked and formed. They are ways in which discourse becomes the object of a praxis and a technique (Ricoeur, 1973b. p. 134).

The first portion of the discourse as work is to impose form upon material. The first distinctive feature of discourse as a work is that of composition.

COMPOSITION

Before proceeding with the structural analysis of conservative curriculum theory tests the explanation of the categories of that analysis must be undertaken. The explanation and procedures of the structural analysis will be drawn from various methods, techniques and investigations in the structuralist field.

The first of the three categories of analysis of the text as a work is that of composition. Ricoeur discusses in "The Hermeneutical Function of Distanciation" that the discourse as a work is a "sequence longer than a sentence presenting a second-order kind of organization, as compared to the sentence taken as the minimal unit of discourse" (Ricoeur, 1973b, p. 134). Ricoeur is referring to the way that a sentence as a semantic unit must follow a specific logic of order and organization. This is true of the text also, but at a second-order level of form. His concept bears reiteration.

> The text as a whole has to be 'construed' as a hierarchy of topics, of primary and subsidiary topics. This very word topics suggests that the production of discourse as a whole implies more than a semantics of the sentence, it implies say, a 'topology' of discourse, which would be the proper semantics of discourse, with the notion of one or more 'isotopics' interwoven in a text (Ricoeur, 1973b, p. 135).

The concept of this hierarchy of topics and especially this concept of isotopics bears some explanation.

The concept of isotopics and consequently a hierarchy of topics is discussed by Greimas in his work *Semantique Structurale, Recherche de Methode* and explained and elaborated upon in a brilliant text by Umberto Eco entitled *Semiotics and the Philosophy of Language*. I will use both texts and their ideas to delineate the concept of text as composition. According to Eco, Greimas originally defines isotopy as a "complex of manifold semantic categories making possible the uniform reading of a story" (Greimas in Eco, 1984, p. 189). This would serve, Eco suggests, as a method of "disambiguation". But, it appears that this original definition of isotopics has been modified to the extent that a cogent definition of isotopics is not as appropriate as using isotopics or isotopy as umbrella terms (Eco, 1984, p. 190).

It is, therefore, fair to assume that isotopy has become an umbrella term covering diverse semiotic phenomena generically definable as coherence at various textual levels (Eco, 1984, p. 190).

I have included Eco's chart from *Semiotics and the Philosophy of Language* of the various textual levels to aid in the understanding of this concept of isotopics. I will refer to this as Figure 3.1 (Eco, 1984, p. 191). If we examine figure 3.1.4, we can begin to enumerate possible meanings of the term isotopy. Eco feels and I concur with him that our aim should be not so much to arrive at a definitive definition, but to "distinguish different meanings of the concept" (Eco, 1984, p. 192). Since the concept does, indeed, have a multitude of meanings, it is best for the purposes of this study to appropriate the specific meaning of most use in explaining curriculum theory texts.

Again, if we look at Figure 3.1.4 (Eco, 1984, p. 192), we can see a connection among Ricoeur, Greimas and Eco's concepts of isotopics. The isolation and explication of the major topics or isotopics interwoven in a text is the first step in the process of a structural explanation of the conservative curriculum theory texts that I have initially read and made guesses at concerning possible meanings.

It is, therefore, the task of isolating and enumerating these isotopics and their relative status in the hierarchy of topics and the hierarchy itself that is the first step in the explanation of a text as a work. This is the conceptual definition of isotopics I am using. Isotopics are these organizing topics, which assume the highest level in the hierarchy and give the text its coherence and cohesiveness. They achieve the status of isotopics by the fact that they are the topics reinforced by constant repetition within a specific text. They are significant because they not only give a type of metatopic analysis, but also can provide insight into the philosophic nature of the text being analyzed. By explaining this organization of topics and interwoven isotopics, we are dealing with Ricoeur's concept of composition as he delineates it in "The Hermeneutical Function of Distanciation".

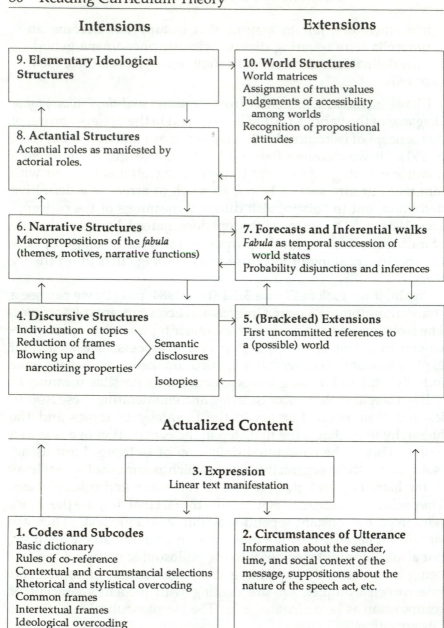

Figure 3.1

GENRE

Ricoeur discusses genres not so much as a classification schemeta, but as a means of production. "Works are submitted to rules of specific kinds of coidification which are traditionally called literary genres" (Ricoeur, 1973b, p. 135). These genres allow for mastery on the part of the writer as he encodes and the reader as he decodes.

> ...in other words a literary genre has a genetic function, rather than a taxonomic function. Just as 'grammaticality' according to Noam Chomsky, expresses the 'generative function of grammar i.e., it provides the speaker and the hearer with common rules for encoding and decoding individual messages, that is, for uttering and understanding isolated sentences, so the function of literary genres is to mediate between speaker and hearer by establishing a common dynamics capable of ruling both the production of a certain kind and its interpretation according to the rules provided by the genre (Ricoeur, 1973b, p. 136).

According to Ricoeur this generative function of literary genres has two consequences. The first consequence is that as this is a dynamics of form it is also a dynamics of thought (Ricoeur, 1973b) so that content and form are generated together. The second consequence is a provocative one. Ricoeur states that a "certain confession of faith is expressed in the form of the narrative, or of a prophecy, or a hymn, etc." (Ricoeur, 1973b, p. 136). There is a commitment to the specific form used. A type of recognition that the form chosen is the best to convey the message.

> The function of genre conventions is essentially to establish a contrast between writer and reader so as to make certain relevant expectations operative and thus to permit both compliance with and deviation from accepted modes of intelligibility. A statement will be taken differently if found in an ode and in a comedy. The reader attends to characters in a different way if he is reading a tragedy or if he is reading a comedy which he expects to end in multiple marriages (Ricoeur, 1978, p. 147).

Our analysis of the generative literary genre will proceed with Ricoeur's two assumptions regarding genres and will analyze curriculum theory texts in terms of the generative function of their genre form. The genres that will most closely be analyzed are: 1. the manifesto, 2. the letter, and 3. the academic essay. Each of these has the dual role of generating form and thought. We may find that the content produced is "in harmony with the corresponding literary genre" (Ricoeur, 1973b, p. 136).

Applying these concepts to conservative curriculum theory will facilitate: 1. The analysis of the specific genre code used and its generative functions. 2. The explication of the ways in which this generative function is also a dynamics of thought in any discourse, but most specifically in conservative curriculum theory discourse. 3. The connections to be made between the content and the form in a specific genre. The methods of explicating codes will be based on structural literary analysis.

STYLE

The third aspect of this concept of text as work or in the structural explanation of a text is that of its style. Ricoeur believes that this is the aspect of the work that makes it a "unique configuration" (Ricoeur, 1973b, p. 136).

> At first sight, this trait seems to contradict the preceeding one: how is it possible to treat discourse as a work, first under the concept of genre, then under that of style? But this twofold description would constitute a descrepency only if by genre we should have to understand a class. If genre is a competence, i.e., a set of generating rules, in the way that grammatical rules generate individual sentences, then it belongs to the function of "genre" to be directed toward the production of those individuals which we call works. Genre is a generative process ending in the performance of singular discourse (Ricoeur, 1973b, p. 137).

It is possible to have this unique configuration even if the product is produced within a certain genre. Ricoeur defines stylistics as the intersection of structure into an individual practice. He explains style in more detail. He sees style as a choice from among several strategies.

Stylization appears as a transaction between complex, concrete situation which presents contradictions, indeterminacies and residues of previous unsatisfactory solutions, and an individual project. The transaction between a project and a situation is nothing else than a restructuration within an already structured experience which includes openings as well as obstacles (Ricoeur, 1973b, p. 138).

This restructuration according to Ricoeur is stylization. Our work with sytle and conservative curriculum theory texts will center on this restructuration with a structured experience.

CONSERVATIVE CURRICULUM THEORY TEXTS—AN EXPLANATION

The Paideia Proposal: An Educational Manifesto and Paideia Problems and Possibilities are the first two texts to be explained. The two texts will be dealt with simultaneously. The first area of explanation will be the area of composition.

THE PAIDEIA TEXTS - COMPOSITION

When we begin to isolate the isotopics in the Paideia texts, a pattern of opposition emerges. A set of isotopics in a hierarchy becomes apparent. These isotopics are set up in a type of binary opposition. Binary opposition is a basic concept in structural analysis. The concept is quite adequately defined by Jonathan Culler in his book *Structuralist Poetics: Structuralism, Linguistics and the Study of Literature:*

> Indeed, the relations that are most important in structural analysis are the simplest: binary oppositions. Whatever else the linguistic model may have done, it has undoubtedly encouraged structuralists to think in binary terms, to look for functional oppositions in whatever material they are studying (Culler, 1975, p. 14).

In the Paideia texts, then, we have a hierarchy of preferred concepts laid out against the threatening background of undesirable consequences of the present moment. The Paideia texts present the forces of good education diametrically opposed to the evils of a common and mediocre education. The major isotopocs are listed in chart 3.2. These are presented in a hierarchical order which is developmental.

PAIDEIA TEXTS
CHART 3.2

MAJOR POSITIVE ISOTOPICS
  I.   There is an absolute body of required knowledge.
  II. There is in reality a classless society therefore we need a classless education.
  III. A democratic education is a priority.
  IV. The universal educability of all children is a given.

MAJOR NEGATIVE ISOTOPICS
  I.   There is a chaotic mass of elective knowledge.
  II. There is at present a stratified education which leads to a stratified society.
  III. There exists in schools undemocratic curriculum which results in mediocrity and inequality.
  IV. There are many instances of specialization or training in the schools.

The four major isotopics in Paideia texts allow the writer and consequently the investigator to organize the content of the texts around these intertwined major topics. Since we have with these texts theoretical and not fictional literature, the particular definition used of isotopics as being organizing factors seems relevant. But, we must analyze these isotopics separately to see their organizing principles more clearly.

THE ABSOLUTE AND UNIVERSAL BODY OF REQUIRED KNOWLEDGE
The first and most important principle of the Paideia texts is mentioned countless times and in different ways throughout the texts. The major emphasis of this particular isotopic becomes quite apparent if a list of references to the isotopics from the texts is given.

1. The one track system of public schooling that *The Paideia Proposal* advocates has the same objectives for all without exception (Adler, 1982, p. 15).

2. To give the same quality of schooling to all requires a program of study that is both liberal and general, and that is, in several, crucial, overarching respects, one and the same for every child (Adler, 1982, p. 21).

3. The course of study to be followed in the twelve years of basic schooling should, therefore, be completely required with only one exception. That exceptio   n is the choice of a second language (Adler, 1982, p. 21).

4. The diagram on the opposite page (page 23) depicts in three columns three distinct modes of teaching and learning, rising in succesive gradations of complexity and difficulty from the first to the twelfth year. All three modes are essential to the overall course of study (Adler, 1982, p. 22).

5. (referring to the column diagram) no one can claim to be educated who is not reasonably well acquainted with all three. They provide the learner with indispensible knowledge (Adler, 1982, p. 24).

6. The skills to be acquired are the skills of reading, writing, speaking, listening, observing, measuring, estimating, and calculating. They are the linguistic, mathematical and scientific skills. They are the skills that everyone needs in order to learn anything (Adler, 1982, p. 26).

7. The first thing to be said about the means in general is that there should be a required course of study for all. To this principle there is only one exception, the elective choice of a foreign language. That one choice should itself be mandatory: the study of at least one foreign language should be required for all (Adler, 1983, p. 13).

8. The nationwide sameness for all students resides solely in the sameness of the recommended curriculum (Adler, 1983, p. 15).

9. There may be regional modifications of the required course of study. The only result should be a differentiation of the ways that differing students move along the same track (Adler, 1983, p. 13).

10. The country has tried diversity of aims and means and that has failed. A common aim and a common general means are now imperative (Adler, 1983, p. 15).

These several illusions to a common, universal and required curriculum demonstrate the pervasive nature of this first isotopic. It is the organizing topic for the Paideia texts. It is set up in opposition to the present educational or curricular system which is labelled "an ideal betrayed" (Adler, 1982, p. 5). Schooling is a failure. At best it is a mediocre system according to the major isotopic. This is the primary opposition set up. The positive universal curriculum set against the antiquated, failing and abysmal system that now exists. The most evident source of this opposing isotopic is in a section entitled "To Our Readers". A few of these comments provide a clear and concise picture of the opposition.

1. To Parents who believe that the decline in the quality of public schooling is damaging the future of their children (Adler, 1982, p. xi).

2. To College Educators burdened by the increasing need to provide remedial education which detracts from their ability to offer a meaningful higher education (Adler, 1982, p. xii).

3. To American Citizens alarmed by prospects of a democracy in which a declining proportion of the people vote or endeavor to understand the great issues of our time (Adler, 1982, p. xii).

These three examples demonstrate the fall of education versus the binary opposite of the salvation of *The Paideia Proposal: An Educational Manifesto*. This first isotopic in binary opposition gives us the age old opposition between good and evil. The good and salvation for the American educational system is contained in the same curricular framework for all.

THE CLASSLESS SOCIETY AND THE CLASSLESS EDUCATION

The second isotopic in the Paideia texts concerns the very nature and makeup of our society. The assumption of a classless society is made and commented on directly and implicitly.

1. We are politically a classless society. Our citizenry as a whole is our ruling class. We should, therefore, be an educationally classless society (Adler, 1982, p. 5).

2. The innermost meaning of social equality is: substantially the same quality of life for all. That calls for: the same quality of schooling for all (Adler, 1982, pp. 5-6).

3. We must end that hypocrisy in our national life. We cannot say out of one side of our mouth that we are for democracy and all its free institutions including, preeminently, political and civil liberty for all: and out of the other side of our mouth, say that only some of the children - fewer than half - are educable for full citizenship and a full human life (Adler, 1982, p. 7).

4. Basic schooling is the only institutional education that is compulsory; it is the only schooling that is common to all (Adler, 1983, p. 5).

These few allusions to the text demonstrate the concepts of the second major isotopic of the classless education or curriculum. The opposing isotopic would be that of the present stratified society and thus the present stratified curriculum. There are a few references to this stratified curriculum or educational system in the Paideia texts. Stratified curricular offerings are also known as the tracking system.

1. If once there they are divided into the sheep and the goats,

into those destined solely for toil and those destined for economic and political leadership and for a quality of life to which all should have access, the democratic purpose has been undermined by an inadequate system of public schooling (Adler, 1982, p. 5).

2. It (public schooling) fails because it has achieved only the same quantity of public schooling, not the same quality. The failure is a downright violation of our democratic principle (Adler, 1982, p. 5).

This classless curriculum versus the stratified curriculum is the second major organizing isotopic of the Paideia texts. It is ironic that what is suggested is to remove one ineffective and prescribed system with another. Perhaps what is set up at this point is a false dichotomy or opposition. The choice of options is only two choices from the same area.

THE PRIORITY OF A DEMOCRATIC EDUCATION

The third major isotopic of the Paideia texts concerns the nature of a democratic education. The references to this "new" form are numerous, but only a few examples are to demonstrate its pervasive nature in the texts. Adler and the Paideia Group refer back to John Dewey in this organizing isotopic. The work of Dewey's that is referred to frequently is *Democracy and Education*. The point to keep in mind while taking a look at this concept of democracy is to remember that there are several uses of the term democracy. There is democracy in practice or pratical democracy. There is democracy that is in a sense imposed. It is, indeed, interesting to see the type that the Paideia Group advocates.

1. A democratic society must provide equal educational opportunity not only by giving to all its children the same quantity of public education - the same number of years in school - but also by making sure to give all of them, all with no exceptions, the same quality of education (Adler, 1982, p. 4).

2. Progress toward the fulfillment of democracy by means of our educational system should and can be accelerated (Adler, 1982, p. 6).

3. Robert Maynard Hutchins, as much committed to democracy as Dewey was before him, stated the fundamental principle we must now follow in our efforts to achieve a true equality of educational conditions. 'the best education for the best,' he said, 'is the best education for all' (Adler, 1982, p. 6).

4. A constitutional democracy such as ours does not rest only on the principle of political equality - the equal status of citizenship. It is also committed to the principle of equal educational opportunity - equal in quality, not just quantity. The one without the other makes democracy a sham and a delusion (Adler, 1983, p. 6).

This democratic equality of education both in quantity and quality is opposed to the current system of mediocrity and inequality. Although the educational system is given credit for the achievement of a democratic equality of education in quantity, the evils of the present system are chided for not obtaining equality in terms of quality. The good of a democratic program of quality and quantity becomes a major organizing principle or isotopic of the Paideia texts. There is reference to the cultural deprivation theory of educational inequality in the Paideia texts.

UNIVERSAL EDUCABILITY

The final major isotopic of the Paideia texts is what might be called the universal educability of children. This supports the one track universal curriculum. Evidence of this basic organizing isotopic abound in the Paideia texts.

1. With the exception of a few suffering from irremediable brain damage, every child is educable up to his or her capacity. Educable - not just trainable for jobs! As John Dewey said almost a century ago, vocational training, training for particular jobs, is not the education of free men and women (Adler, 1982, p. 7).

2. There are no unteachable children. There are only schools

and teachers and parents who fail to teach them (Adler, 1982, p. 8).

The opposing view would be the specific specialized training for a vocation. There are many comments concerning this type of education.

1. That kind of specialized or particularized job training at the level of basic schooling is in fact the reverse of something practical and effective in a society that is always changing and progressing (Adler, 1982, p. 18).

2. As the school population rapidly increased in the early decades of this century, educators and teachers turned to something that seemed more appropriate to do with that portion of the school population which they incorrectly and unjustly appraised as being educable - only trainable. In doing this, they violated the fundamental democratic maxim of equal educational opportunity (Adler, 1982, p. 19).

The enumerated isotopics clearly demonstrate that these basic binary oppositions exist as organizing principles or themes in the Paideia texts. It is also obvious that all of the isotopics are intertwined into and through each other. Perhaps the major controlling isotopic could be viewed as the Utopian Paideia Curricular Framework versus the Sad and Stratified Present Curriculum.

GENRE

The generative function of genres that Ricoeur has delineated has many interesting applications to and for the Paideia texts. The function of generating thought as well as form has applicability to these texts.

It has been demonstrated that some clearly discernable isotopics exist in these Paideia texts. It becomes rather evident as well when we discuss the genre form of the Paideia texts, that the form of the genre is generative of these types of isotopics and their language.

The genre of the Paideia texts is clearly enumerated in the title of the first volume, *The Paideia Proposal: An Educational Manifesto*. It becomes important to see if in reality what we have with these texts is a true manifesto. So let us assume for the moment that the genre is the manifesto.

The definition or qualities of a manifesto are crucial to analyze. The genre of manifesto may be defined as: 1. "a proof, or piece of evidence; 2. a public declaration or proclamation usually issued by or with the sanction of a sovereign prince or state or by an individual or body of individuals whose proceedings are of public importance, for the purposes of making known past actions, and explaining the reasons or motives for actions announced as forthcoming" (OED, 1971, p. 1716). This definition clearly fits the Paideia texts. The production of thought and form concerned with these definitions is our next point of major interest.

The salient points of this definition for the structural analysis or explanation of the Paideia texts are three in number. The first is the reference to the manifesto as proof. The second characteristic of relevence is the nature of manifesto as proclamation. The final important category is the purpose of making known past actions and explaining actions that are forthcoming. The Paideia texts (especially volume 1, volume 2 simply elaborates on volume 1) fit all these aspects in a classificatory scheme. But, this is not only a classification schemata but a chance to look at the generative function of the specific genre known as manifesto.

The first step in the explanation of manifesto as a genre is to analyze its classifying function. Therefore, let us look at the manifesto as proof.

The term proof denotes the procedures, statements and data necessary to establish the validity of an argument or hypothesis. This aspect of as proof is evident in the Paideia texts. The entire organization of the text as demonstrated in the analysis of composition explicates the texts as opposing the Paideia curriculum framework against the present curriculum framework. This is accomplished by constantly comparing a new curriculum framework and proving its superiority and validity over the present system. This logical method of proof is the method of comparison and contrast. However, this is not only a classification scheme, but also generative of certain language, ideas and attitudes.

When scientists and researchers are trying to establish the validity of their proposals or proving them, the attempt is made to make the language and thought used as objective and precise as possible. Not only do we observe this objective and fairly precise language in the Paideia texts, but also the language is forceful and distinct. The attempt is made to hammer the point home and in the case of the Paideia texts it is a sledge hammer that is used.

Before discussing the specific statements used, the other aspect, that of proclamation must be explained. In this particular case we have a proclamation issued by a group or body of individuals. The Paideia Group is comprised of twenty-two individuals from the fields of education, research and government. The list of the members is found in the front of each Paideia text. This helps to establish the credence of the document.

If we look at the nature of this manifesto as a proclamation or decree, the texts fit this classification. The nature of these written texts are reminiscient of the edicts issued by kings and rulers of ages past. Each paragraph of the original text and its sequel are in essence small edicts within the larger Paideia proclamation. These small paragraphs or edicts are constantly reassuring the readers that they all hold something to be true, therefore, there are consequences. This concept of small edicts or decrees and its subsequent tie with establishing the validity of the program becomes more obvious if the specific statements from the texts are used as illustrations. I have used the first statement or sentence of each paragraph to demonstrate the point. The language is forceful and staccato-like which is necessary when using declaration -like sentences.

1. We must end that hypocrisy in our national life (Adler, 1982, p. 7).

2. True, children are educable in varying degrees (Adler, 1982, p. 7).

3. There is no acceptable reason why trying to promote equality should have led to the lessening or loss of quality (Adler, 1983, p. 6).

4. The simple fact is that educational institutions, even at their

best, cannot turn out fully educated men and women (Adler, 1982, p. 9).

These decree-like statements fill both of the Paideia texts. In a manifesto, then, readers when they are decoding expect to find these edicts and the writer when encoding the text under the code of the manifesto tends to make these types of statements. The genre as a generative process works not only to generate the form, in this case manifesto, but also that form generates the type and substance of the individual or group's thought.

The third aspect of the genre of manifesto is that it makes known past actions and explains actions that are forthcoming. We have seen that the Paideia texts fulfill this aspect of the genre by the critique of the present system of education (curriculum) or our past actions within that educational system. It also explains many of the actions that the Paideia Group view as forthcoming as a result of *The Paideia Proposal*. In fact, an entire chapter of the sequal text, *Paideia Problems and Possibilities* is devoted to the "Possibilities" (Adler, 1983, pp. 79-82).

Everyone is willing to agree that at least some portion of our school population can be given the high quality of basic school-ing that we recommend. It is only when the recommendation is extended from some to all that anyone becomes skeptical and demurs on the grounds that we are going beyond the bounds of the possible. They are then inclined to turn aside and busy themselves with things much easier for them to do. But these easier things leave unsolved the problem of giving all the children equal educational opportunity. It is these easier things that are really impractical for the stated feasible purpose that we cannot - dare not - abandon (Adler, 1983, p. 81).

The Paideia texts, then, can be categorized within the context of a specific genre, the manifesto. This is only one aspect of the genre area of explanation. There is the other area of the generative function of genres that needs exploration. Ricoeur states that these genre forms have a generative function. They, in essence, give the writer and the reader common rules respectively for both the encoding and decoding of a specific text or number of texts. It must be remembered that Ricoeur considers discourse and consequently texts as works.

> The consideration of discourse as work suggests that we look at literary genres less as means of classification than as means of production. Literary genres contribute to produce discourse as a work. To master a genre is to master a "competence" which offers practical guidelines for "performing" an individual work. We should have to add that the same competence in the reader helps him to perform the corresponding operations of interpretation according to the rules prescribed by the genre for both sending and receiving a certain type of message (Ricoeur, 1973b, pp. 135-36).

On the one hand we have genres being "initially rules of production" (Klemm, 1983, p. 84), and on the other hand the genre functions as rules of decoding. We have then a code that makes this entire process possible.

This has specific meaning for the Paideia texts. It has been demonstrated how the texts fit the classification scheme of the manifesto. But as these concepts are being encoded in this production of a text, the genre takes on another function. Just as the required code of a sentence is a vechile for encoding messages the manifesto is a code for encoding specific messages.

The point that is crucial is that since there is this code of requirements for producing a specific message within a specific genre, the thought and message to be produced in that code is also shaped by that code. When the writer sets down ideas within a certain code or genre the ideas generated are consequently limited to and by that form or code. In the specific case of the manifesto it has been demonstrated that the ideas must: 1. be expressed as proof, 2. be issued as proclamations or decrees and 3. be explanatory of past and future actions. At once the writer is limited to those types of composing. As Ricoeur aptly puts it the writer must achieve a competence in performing in the specific code.

In the particular case of the Paideia texts the code necessitates giving these ideas in a prescriptive and forceful way. The writer has learned competence in the manifesto form and realized that this particular prescriptive thought pattern is necessary in producing an adequate manifesto.

As readers encountering the text of a manifesto we are working, reading or decoding under the same code or constraints as the writer who is encoding. The readers realize that there are certain guidelines or qualities to the manifesto such as its edict-like nature and consequently their decoding of the message is developed within the code.

> The identification of the genre, on the part of the reader, implies the same competence, i.e., the aptitude to interpret a certain category of sayings along the rules of a traditional type of interpretation (Ricoeur, 1973b, p. 136).

As readers recognize the genre of a manifesto and its consequent characteristics they treat this writing as edict-like. They, in essence, expect prescriptive messages and treat those messages as prescriptions or remedies. However, the text as genre is far from a closed text.

> The form ascribed to the work by the genre makes it both "closed" and "open": "closed" in the sense that the kind of circumscription imposed on it preserves it from distortion, "open" in the sense that the same process that keeps it from distortion reserves it for new interpretations. This paradox is only apparent. The genre establishes the first contextualization but, being at the same time a virtual decontextualization of discourse, it makes subsequent recontextualization of the message possible (Ricoeur, 1973b, pp. 137-38).

As a result of studying the Paideia texts as a manifesto, the isotopic of the Utopian Paideia Curriculum has been given by the genre of manifesto a very prescriptive and edict-like nature. The verification of the initial reading or prehermeneutical reading is becoming established.

STYLE

> At first sight, this trait seems to contradict the preceding one: how is it possible to treat discourse as a work, first under the concept of genre, then under that of style? But this twofold description would constitute a descrepency only if by genre we should have to understand a class. If genre is a competence, i.e.,

a set of generating rules, in the way that grammatical rules generate individual sentences, then it belongs to the function of "genres" to be directed toward the production of those individuals we call works. Genre is a generative process ending in the performance of singular discourse (Ricoeur, 1973b, p. 137).

Even within a genre code there is an individual voice or style. Ricoeur elaborates on this concept of style and stylization.

Stylization appears as a transaction between a complex concrete situation which presents contradictions, indeterminacies and residues of previous unsatisfactory solutions and an individual project (Ricoeur, 1973b, p. 128).

How can this concept of style be applied to the Paideia texts and what is their style? The key to the answer lies in the transaction aspect of stylization. The individual or in the case of the Paideia texts the group project invests the genre form of the texts with a specific style. In the specific case of the Paideia texts the two combined and mold very well.

I want to posit that the individual project of the Paideia Group and the transaction between it and the complex concrete situation of the state of American education today allows a certain stylization to emerge. In the case of theoretical texts I believe the stylization derives from the philosophical basis of the theorist. In much the same way as this study emerges from the phenomenological and hermeneutical perspectives of the author. When an author becomes immerse in a certain philosophical tradition the style of his writing and thinking become inextricably mixed with that perspective. This is also true in the case of the Paideia texts. The style of the Paideia texts derives or emerges from its philosophical basis in perennialism. When we begin to analyze the "style" of perennialism the other modes of explanation, i.e., composition and genre become intertwined with this concept of style. The style fits in well with the particular genre, manifesto, which fits in with the particular isotopic identified in the explanation of composition. Style, therefore, when discussing theoretical texts, is a particular world view expressed as an individual tentative solution to a concrete problem. It is somewhat different than the style of literary texts.

Therefore, the analysis of the individual project structured within the genre form is the analysis of the epistemes of perennialism. The style of the perennialist is evident from the outset of the Paideia texts.

The Paideia texts are dedicated to Horace Mann, John Dewey and Robert Hutchins. Robert Hutchins is one of the chief proponents of perennialism. At least in the dedication of this document we find the allusion to an initiator of modern perennialism.

More importantly, however, we find the Paideia texts reiterating and reinforcing many of the major themes of perennialism. There are a number of basic tenents to the philosophical perspective known as perennialism, but for the analysis of the Paideia texts a concise list is sufficient. There are basically four major precepts of rational humanism, which is one strand of the perennial perspective. They are: 1. The belief that the ultimate ends and means of education are universal. "It is the liberal arts that bring out the common human nature in all of us, and since that nature is the same for all men, the liberal arts are for all men" (Wingo, 1974, p. 254). 2. There should be an attempt at the recovery of the classics. The classics are defined by the perennialist as books that have a universal quality - that are "contemporary with every age" (Wingo, 1974, p. 255). 3. There is an attack against vocationalism. 4. The content of education is defined as "permanent studies" and these are found in their "most universal and therefore most valuable form in the great literary products of the West" (Wingo, 1974, p. 258). The last point concerning "permanent studies" has also acquired the title of "Great Books".

Mortimer Adler's association with the perennial movement is a long running one from the text entitled "The Crises in Contemporary Education" (1939) to the Paideia texts in the 1980s. This long running tradition of perennialism and its connection with the Paideia texts surfaces when the individual project of the Paideia texts is connected with several works from the tradition. There are several works worth mentioning. They are: *Liberal Education* (1943) by Mark Van Doren, *The Conflict in Education in A Democratic Society* (1953) and *The Higher Learning in America* (1936) by Robert Maynard Hutchins.

When we discuss the philosophical tenets of the perennialist "style" of the Paideia texts, the voices of Hutchins and Van Doren echo through the years and resound loudly in the texts of the 1980s.

The first area of the Paideia style or voice is its contention that the ultimate ends and means of education are universal. Robert Hutchins discussed this concept in *The Conflict in Education in a Democratic Society* (1953).

This is the education appropriate to free men. It is liberal education. If all men are to be free all men must have this education. It makes no difference how they are to earn their living or what their special interests or aptitudes may be. They can learn to make a living, and they can develop their special interests and aptitudes, after they have laid the foundation of free and responsible manhood through liberal education. It will not do to say that they are incapable of such education. This claim is made by those who are too indolent or unconvinced to make the effort to give such education to the masses (Hutchins, 1953, pp. 72-73).

The perennial voice is in Mark Van Doren's *Liberal Education* (1943). Van Doren discusses the critics of universal ends and means in education. He states about them:

Least of all do they tolerate in him the disposition in him to say that of liberal education what liberal education is, it is the same for everybody; that the training it requires, in addition to being formal, should be homogeneous through four years - if the best is known, there is no student whom it will not fit, and each should have all of it. The search for a curriculum is the search for one that is worthy to be uniform and universal (Van Doren, 1943, p. 110).

Although these two voices of perennialism are speaking about the college curriculum what the contemporary perennial voice is speaking of is using the same type of curriculum for high schools. Adler as spokesman for the Paideia Group echoes this same style.

The one-track system of public schooling that the *Paideia Proposal* advocates has the same objectives for all without exception (Adler, 1982, p. 85).

It has been demonstrated previously through various explanations and examples how this universal curriculum is advocated in the Paideia texts. The explanation of the style links this 1980s style with the ever present voice of perennialism. What Van Doren was expressing in the 1940s and Hutchins in the 1930s, 1940s and 1950s is what in essence Adler is expressing in the 1980s. The tie between the style (individual project) of these perennialists is quite obvious.

The second area of concentration in the perennial style is the attempt at recovering the classics and the scholastic. The currents of this aspect of style run deeply through many perennial texts. This aspect also is a long running one. Van Doren discusses this area:

> The four years of every student will be devoted to two principle and simultaneous activities: learning the arts of investigation, discovery criticism, and communication, and achieving at first hand an acquaintance with the original books, the unkillable classics, in which these miracles happen (Van Doren, 1943, pp. 144-46).

Van Doren goes as far as to list the classics he refers to as the curriculum. The list includes such titles as *The Illiad*, *The Odyssey*, *The Bible*, *The Critique of Pure Reason* and one hundred and six more essential titles. The curriculum, according to Van Doren, is a recovery of the classics.

For Hutchins in *The Higher Learning in America*, the notion of the recovery of the classics is evident.

> Our erroneous notion of progress has thrown the classics and the liberal arts out of the curriculum, overemphasized the empirical sciences, and made education the servent of any contemporary movements in society, no matter how superficial. Our purposes of education is to draw out the elements of our common human nature. These elements are the same in any time or place (Hutchins, 1936, p. 66).

There is, again, this emphasis on a core of classics. Hutchins advocated their return because we had tossed them aside. It is interesting to note here that it appears that Hutchins is trying to remove the concept of the school being part of a social context and views the school as an entity divorced from the society. Adler is advocating in the perennial style the recovery of the classics in the Paideia texts. It must be rememebered that Adler has a long association with the "Great Books" curriculum.

The Paideia program recommends the reading and discussion of classics - that is, any works of lasting value - only in the sense that the books and other artifacts chosen having this lasting value and only for the sake of their relevance to the problems that anyone must face in today's world (Adler, 1983, p. 29).

As our working definition of style as the transaction between complex concrete situations and an individual project suggests, the style of perennialism is evident as a second characteristic in the 1980s Paideia texts.

The third important aspect of the perennialist style is the attack against vocationalism. Van Doren speaks against vocationalism as part of the perennial style.

The most painful single thing about American education is the system of "vocational choice" which extends down as far as the high schools. In college this would be evil and in fact it is; but even the high school student is nagged until he declares what he wants to do when he grows up. The boy who knows that much about himself is one out of a thousand. The rest pretend they know, and from that moment are channeled toward a life which they may not discover to be the wrong one until they are middle aged (Van Doren, 1943, p. 168).

Van Doren believed that there was a time for this type of choice, but the time was not in a person's youth. Hutchins discusses vocationalism in *The Conflict in Education* (1953) as adjusting to the environment. He is against the notion of vocationalism as well.

The whole doctrine of adjustment to the environment seems to me radically erroneous. As I have said, it leads to a curriculum of miscellaneous dead facts. It leads to vocational training, which the schools are not equipped to give and misses the most important contribution that schools can make. But it is far more urgent that we notice that our mission here on earth is to change our environment, not to adjust ourselves to it (Hutchins, 1953, p. 20).

Hutchins, speaking in the voice or style of perennialism, attacks vocationalism and advocates change. He reinforces the standard of perennialism.

Adler discusses vocationalism in the 1980s perennial style. The attack against vocationalism in this case is an attack against its undemocratic nature.

> Why then, was such false vocationalism ever introduced into our schools? As the school population rapidly increased in the early decades of this century, educators and teachers turned to something that seemed more appropriate to do with that portion of the school population which they incorrectly and unjustly appraised as being uneducable - only trainable. In doing this, they violated the fundamental democratic maxim of equal educational opportunity (Adler, 1982, p. 19).

> In appraising the use of computers or other devices, we are not abandoning our opposition to particularized job training of every sort (Adler, 1983, p. 41).

The voice against vocationalism is truly a major component in the style of perennialism and specifically in the style of the 1982 and 1983 texts.

The last aspect of style to be concerned with is the specific curriculum that the perennial voice advocates. It has been known by different appellations. It has been known as permanent studies, the great tradition and great books. This is the most important and fundamental aspect of the style of perennialism. In 1943 Mark Van Doren discussed the great tradition. He was speaking about a college curriculum but the essential idea is in evidence.

> The classics of our world, the great books, ancient and recent, in which the Western mind has worked and played, are more essential to a college than its buildings and its bells, or even perhaps its teachers; for these books are teachers from which every wise and witty man has learned what he knows (Van Doren, 1943, p. 148).

In 1936, Hutchins in *The Higher Learning in America* discussed this notion as permanent studies.

> Such books are then a part, and a large part, of the permanent studies. They are so in the first place because they are the best books we know. How can we call a man educated who has

never read any of the great books in the Western world?

In the second place these books are an essential part of general education because it is impossible to understand any subject or to comprehend the contemporary world without them (Hutchins, 1936, pp. 78-79).

Hutchins is also discussing a college curriculum like his counterpart Van Doren. But, the essential fact that this aspect of the style of perennialism is a major facet is unquestionable.

Adler and the Paideia Group in the 1980s advocate the same perennialist program and its beneficial nature for the high school curriculum.

The Paideia program recommends the reading and discussion of classics - that is, any work of lasting value - only in the sense that the books and other artifacts chosen have this lasting value and only for the sake of their relevance to problems that anyone must face in today's world (Adler, 1983, p. 28).

The style of these Paideia texts, defined as the individual project or an attempted solution to a concrete problem, is the style of perennial philosophy. It has been demonstrated that this is one of the important and long running voices in educational and curriculum theory. Adler and the Paideia Group are the 1980s voice in the perennial style.

A NATION AT RISK: THE IMPERATIVE FOR EDUCATIONAL REFORM

The explanation of the NCEE's "open letter to the American people" begins with the delineation of the major isotopics evident in this text.

COMPOSITION

The structural analysis of *A Nation at Risk* reveals some interesting major isotopics. They also are set up in a binary opposition between good and evil.

MAJOR POSITIVE ISOTOPICS
(CHART 3.3)

I. There is a need for a new rising tide of excellence.

II. This new excellence will improve the national welfare and the entire capitalist system.

III. The remedy for our educational system is upgrading expectations and standards in education and in our curriculum.

MAJOR NEGATIVE ISOTOPICS

I. There exists a high tide of mediocrity.

II. There is in evidence poor educational performance which puts our system and way of life at risk.

III. There are numerous deficiencies in our present educational system.

These three major positive and negative isotopics of the *A Nation at Risk* text bear further investigation. They can be explained to demonstrate their function as major organizing topics of this particular text. The major set up underlying these binary oppositions is findings and recommendations.

THE NEED FOR A RISING TIDE OF EXCELLENCE

The first and most important principle of *A Nation at Risk* is carried throughout the text in countless references and examples. It is important to point out several of these references to demonstrate the isotopics pervasiveness.

1. In light of the urgent need for improvement, both immediate and long term, the Commission has agreed on a set of recommendations that the American people can begin to act on now, that can be implemented over the next several years, and that promise lasting reform (NCEE, 1983, p. 23).

2. We recommend that the state and local high school graduation requirements be strengthened (NCEE, 1983, p. 24).

3. We recommend that schools, colleges, and universities adopt
   more rigorous and measurable standards, and higher expectations, for academic performance and student conduct, and
   that 4-year colleges and universities raise their requirements
   for admission (NCEE, 1983, p. 20).

4. We recommend more time be devoted to learning the New
   Basics (NCEE, 1983, p. 29).

5. This recommendation consists of seven parts. Each is intended to improve the preparation of teachers (NCEE, 1983,
   p. 30).

These several examples for achieving a rising tide of excellence
demonstrates that this isotopic is a major organizing factor in the *A
Nation at Risk* text. This is set up in contrast to a series of findings on
the abysmal state of contemporary education. Our poor and inadequate system of public schooling is discussed in terms of its jeopard-
izing of the American system. This is the primary and most crucial
binary opposition set up in this text, the current mediocre educational system versus the reformed system of excellence in education.
This organizing isotopic is most evident in a section entitled "Indicators of the Risk". A few of these indicators will demonstrate the
basic opposition.

1. About 13 percent of all 17-year-olds in the United States can
   be considered functionally illiterate. Functional illiteracy
   among minority youth may run as high as 40 percent (NCEE,
   1983, p. 8).

2. The College Board's Scholastic Aptitude Test (SAT) demonstrates a virtually unbroken decline from 1963 to 1980.
   Average verbal scores fell 50 points and average mathemat-

ics scores dropped nearly 40 points (NCEE, 1983, p. 9).

3. There was a steady decline in science achievement scores of U.S. 17 year-olds as measured by national assessments of science in 1969, 1973, and 1977 (NCEE, 1983, p. 9).

4. Average tested achievement of students graduating from college is also lower (NCEE, 1983, p. 9).

These examples demonstrate education as a risky business versus a reformed excellent education. It is also reminiscient of the Paideia texts organizing isotopic of the present evil system versus the salvation of the curriculum proposed by the Commission. In the case of the Commission's recommendations there is a specific curriculum advocated, however. The curriculum of the "New Basics".

THE EXCELLENT NEW CURRICULUM AND OUR IMPROVED NATIONAL WELFARE

The second major isotopic in *A Nation at Risk* concerns the very existence of our society. Our system is at risk but the recommended reforms save our society. This isotopic is commented on frequently.

1. It is their America, and the America of all of us, that is at risk; it is to each of us that this imperative is addressed. It is by our willingness to take up the challenge, and our resolve to see it through, that America's place in the world will be either secured or forfeited. Americans have succeeded before and so we shall again (NCEE, 1983, p. 36).

2. Our present plight did not appear overnight, and the responsibility for our current situation is widespread. Reform of our educational system will take time and unwavering commitment (NCEE, 1983, p. 38).

3. Our goal must be to develop the talents of all to their fullest. Attaining that goal requires that we expect and assist all students to work to the limits of their capabilities. We should expect school to have genuinely high standards rather than

minimum ones; and parents to support and encourage their children to make the most of their talents and abilities (NCEE, p. 37).

These references give one the flavor of the urged for improved curriculum and hence for an improved national welfare.   The opposing isotopics paint a bleak picture of a nation on the precipice.

1.   Our society and its educational institutions seem to have lost sight of the basic purposes of schooling, and of high expectations and disciplined efforts needed to obtain them (NCEE, 1983, p. 6).

2.   Our nation is at risk. Our once unchallenged preeminence in commerce, industry, science, and technological innovation is being overtaken by competitors throughout the world (NCEE, 1983, p. 5).

3.   If an unfriendly foreign power had attempted to impose on America the mediocre educational performance that exists today we might well have viewed it as an act of war (NCEE, 1983, p. 5).

These references are in binary opposition to the recommended excellent curriculum which will save our endangered system.

THE UPGRADED CURRICULUM

The final isotopic has shades of the other two, however, it is distinctive enough to need a separate elaboration. The solution to the problem of a risky curriculum is reminiscent of a much publicized Wendys' commercial. In this particular commercial an elderly lady asks the question of the hamburger's nutritional value. "Where's the beef?" This commercial phrase caught on in America and began to emerge as a rhetorical question concerning the lack of substance in various areas. It appears the Commission is asking the same question of American education. Where is the substance? The answer is that the substance is lacking and it needs, if we pardon the pun, to be beefed up. The Commission's answer comes in the form of the "New Basics" and is opposed to the old deficient system.

(each student should) lay the foundation in the Five New Basics by taking the following curriculum during their 4 years of high school: (a) 4 years of English; (b) 3 years of mathematics; (c) 3 years of science; (d) 3 years of social studies; and (e) one-half year of computer science. For the college-bound 2 years of foreign language in high school are strongly recommended (NCEE, 1983, p. 25).

This recommended curriculum is the core of the Commission's educational reform proposals. This is set up in opposition to the current findings concerning the content of schooling, the curriculum.

Seconday school curricula have been homogenized, diluted, and diffused to the point that they no longer have a central purpose. In effect, we have a cafeteria style curriculum, in which the appetizers and desserts can easily be mistaken for the main courses. Students have migrated from vocational and college prepatory programs to "general track" courses in large numbers. The proportion of students taking a general program of study has increased from 12 percent in 1964 to 42 percent in 1979 (NCEE, 1983, p. 10).

These isotopics have been elaborated upon to show how they are the major organizing principles of *A Nation at Risk: The Imperative for Educational Reform*. These isotopics are interwoven throughout the text. The major isotopics are arranged in binary oppositions. Perhaps a new overarching isotopic can be delineated. It is quite similar to the major isotopic of the Paideia texts. It is the New Basics Curriculum as Salvation versus the Cafeteria Style Curriculum as America's Demise.

GENRE

When we begin the explanation of the generative nature of the genre form and its connection to the text of *A Nation at Risk* we encounter an interesting paradox. The text is defined as an open letter to the American people. A letter connotes a personal message either to a friend or a business or professional associate. However, a letter as a form entails more than just those connotative meanings. The definitions of a letter raise some interesting points for this study. The first definition states that the term letter or epistle is "applied to letters written in ancient times especially to those which rank as literary productions or to those of a public character or addressed to a body of persons" (OED, 1971, 1601). The second definition of interest for this study of genre states that a letter is a "missive communication in writing, addressed to a person or body of persons; an epistle also, in extended use, applied to certain *formal documents* issued by persons in authority" (OED, 1971, 1601). These two definitions set up categories for an analysis of *A Nation at Risk* as a letter. The characteristics that evolve are: (a) the public character of the letter, and (b) the character of letter as a formal document issued by persons in authority.

A Nation at Risk takes the personal aspects of the letter and makes them public. This is not necessarily a negative aspect, however. The letter is addressed to the American people and consequently the pronoun, our, is used extensively. This is to give the letter a quality of being somewhat personal and at the same time a quality of publicness. It is meant to imbue the letter with a feeling of community. There is a continual effort to reinforce the community of believers throughout the document. The emphasis in this example is mine.

> For *our* country to function, *citizens* must be able to reach some *common* understandings on complex issues, often on short notice and on the basis of conflicting or incomplete evidence (NCEE, 1983, p. 7).

> It is *their* America (students), and the America of *all of us*, that is at risk, it is to *each of us* that this imperative is addressed (NCEE, 1983, p. 36).

The attempt to make the reader feel part of a community of concern is an interesting twist to the form of the letter. Since this is a public letter form, the writer(s) attempt to make it as personal as possible.

The aspect of the public document, however, in the second

definition of the letter is for this study the most crucial. The text is for the most part a letter at the salutation point and at the point of closing. The body of the letter or its more documentary nature drifts away from the letter form. It becomes, I suggest, not a letter at all but a rather formal research document. It loosely explains the method of data collection, the findings of the Commission and the recommendations based on those findings. The language in this portion of the Commission's report is characteristic of mainstream research.

> To review and synthesize the data and scholarly literature on the quality of learning and teaching in the nation's schools, colleges and universities, both public and private, with special concern for the educational experience of teenage youth (NCEE, 1983, p. 39).

I hesitate to call this text a research paper disguised as a letter; but it does have traces of that nature. If we are not duped by the apparent genre of the text and begin to investigate it as a public document issued by person or persons in authority, then, the text as genre takes on whole new meanings.

The text as public document recalls the manifesto as a public document. Both of these genres have that generating function of almost requiring the thoughts to be issued in rather edict-like form. Certainly if not in edict-like form then at least in a prescriptive form. The language of *A Nation at Risk* is somewhat less hammer-like than are the Paideia texts. But they are still prescriptive. The word recommend is used to soften the blows. Nonetheless the hammer is still pounding. A few examples are sufficient to illustrate this point. These examples are taken from various places throughout the text.

1. Grades should be indicators of academic achievement so they can be relied on as evidene of a student's readiness for further study (NCEE, 1983, p. 27).

2. Students in high schools should be assigned far more homework than is now the case (NCEE, 1983, p. 29).

3. School districts and State legislatures should strongly

consider 7-hour school days, as well as a 200 to 220 day
school year (NCEE, 1983, p. 29).

These recommendations have a type of edict-like, prescriptive
nature, which is a necessary component of either traditional research findings or public documents. The Commission attempts to
soften its edicts by using the word should in place of must.

With the text, *A Nation at Risk*, we have a dilemma concerning
genre. The text calls itself a letter. However, it seems that in a
number of ways it is not only a letter but also something else, a public
research report. Although this does fit into a classification scheme
for a letter by definition, there is the more important matter of its
generative nature. It appears after some structural explanation of its
form that the community appeal at the salutation and closing
portions of the text are not carried throughout the document. The
body of this letter which conveys the basic message to be communicated is more prescriptive in nature than communicative. It does
communicate but in an ultimately edict-like way. In essence, then,
we do have a letter by genre classification, but by generative function
we have a formal prescriptive document leaning toward a mani-
festo-like document. This is important because as was pointed out
with the Paideia texts, the form of an edict necessitates edict-like
thoughts and prescriptive statements. It appears here again that the
thoughts of the Commission are in a sense limited to the genre form
that is used in this specific situation. Attempting to give it a letter-
like quality with a type of tacked on salutation and closing do not
[revent the body of the document from acquiring this nature.

The salvation of the Five New Basics is given in an edict-like
manner but is covered up with the title of letter. At the surface, or
naive reading this might seem less hammer-like and more melliflu-
ous or subdued even forgotten, but it is there nonetheless.

STYLE

Style or stylization is a "transaction between complex concrete
situation and the residues of previous unsatisfactory solutions and
an individual project" (Ricoeur, 1973b, p. 128), specifically when
discussing theoretical texts. With *A Nation at Risk* its stylization

emerges as the philosophical basis of the theory underlying the text. As already stated with the Paideia texts, the immersion of the theorist or group of theorists in a philosophical tradition precipitates their thinking and writing within the style of that tradition. What is the philosophic tradition that emerges in the style of *A Nation at Risk?* It is the style of essentialism.

There are several basic tenets of essentialism that emerge in the style of the Commission's text. These tenets or epistemes of essentialism should be clarified, elaborated upon and connected to *A Nation at Risk.* There are three basic tenets of essentialism that are significant for this study. They are: 1. The belief that the primary purpose of education is rigorous intellectual training. "This process, the essentialist maintains, and only this, is worthy to be called the purpose of education" (Wingo, 1974, p. 53). 2. The belief that education should foster and aid the physical and emotional well-being of the student. 3. There is a common core of worthwhile knowledge. (This core is "organized in terms of the traditional intellectual disciplines English, mathematics, history, science, and foreign languages" (Wingo, 1974, p. 55). 4. The belief that the role of education is to preserve, conserve, cherish and transmit our cultural heritage.

This tradition of essentialism like the tradition of perennialism is a long running one.

> Essentialism is the dominant educational tradition in America and it always has been; certainly this is true in practical matters of operating our schools. This means that essentialism is more than a related group of abstract ideas about education; it is a living body of school practices (Wingo, 1974, p. 62).

The style/voice of essentialism is loud and strong in some of the past examples of this tradition, which emphasize the same areas of concern as the text, *A Nation at Risk.* A rather harsh indictment of this nation's schools was written by Arthur E. Bestor and entitled *Educational Wastelands: The Retreat from Learning in Our Public Schools* (1953). Hyman George Rickover, a true essentialist, spoke in the essentialist style in *Education and Freedom* (1959) and *American Education - A National Failure: The Problem of Our Schools and What We Can Learn from England* (1963).

When we investigate and explain the style of the Commission's text of 1983, the voices of Bestor and Rickover are audible and resound throughout. It is evident that the individual project and style of the Commission's text is a project that has been attempted or expressed many times.

The first element of style or of the individual project of the essentialist is the notion that education is or should be a series of exercises in rigorous intellectual training.

Bestor in his text *Educational Wastelands* (1953) emphasized the notion that education was synonymous with intellectual training.

> The nation depends upon its schools and colleges to furnish this intellectual training to its citizenry as a whole. Society has no other institutions upon which it can rely in this matter. If schools and colleges do not emphasize rigorous intellectual training, there will be none (Bestor, 1953, p. 14).

This essentialist voice is heard in Rickover's text also. It is striking how similar these texts are to *A Nation at Risk*. Even the titles carry the same message. Rickover discusses intellectual training frequently. Rickover tolls the bell of danger or risk because of the undervaluation of intellectual training in America in his 1959 text, *Education and Freedom*.

> Basically, it is an indifference to intellectual excellence, to matters of the mind. We still think more highly of an athlete than of a brilliant student. We still do not as a people realize that in modern life, as Whitehead said it so elegantly: "The rule is absolute, the race which does not value trained intelligence is doomed" (Rickover, 1959, p. 186).

In 1963 Rickover issued his indictment *American Education - A National Failure*. In this volume he compared American schools to the English system and found our system to be conspiciously lacking. The text evidences the style of the essentialist. It emphasizes this point of rigorous intellectual training.

> Bright people whose mental powers have been developed through rigorous academic education have it in them to contribute enormously to society. A country that succeeded in providing every child with the requisite talent to pursue an

academic education would not only enhance public well-being but would excel in most areas that affect a nation's position in the world (Rickover, 1963, p. 153).

The 1983 text begins to sound very similar to these 1950s and 1960s texts. The reason seems to be that the style as project is the same. It is interesting to note that this emphasis in an essentialist concern with curriculum theory surfaces during times of general conservatism in the United States at least in this century. These earlier representations of essentialist style arose during a conservative Republican administration under Eisenhower. There was also the threat that the Soviet Union would move ahead of America in the space race. It was a time of crisis for the country and its system. There was then a retrenchement of the essentialist and their style. *A Nation at Risk* surfaces during the Reagan administration and another crisis. This time the crisis is an economic one. There is a fear that other nations will out run our industrial and technological capabilities. Again, the retrenched essentialist voice appears. Education is seen by the essentialist as the panacea for these problems. The reason for these problems is in part the shoddy nature of American education.

The Commission's text does give a voice to this facet of rigorous intellectual training.

> We must demand the best effort and performance from all students, whether they are gifted or less able, affluent or disadvantaged, whether destined for college, the farm, or industry.

> Our recommendations are based on the beliefs that everyone can learn, that everyone is born with an urge to learn which can be nurtured, that a solid high school education is within reach of virtually all, and that life long learning will equip people with the skills required for new careers and for citizenship (NCEE, 1983, p. 24).

It must be remembered that the first of the recommendations of the NCEE is for a strong intellectual core program which confirms the first aspect of the essentialist style. We also see that this mainstream theory is a long running one. Certainly the essentialist style reaches farther back than the 1950s, but it appears that this period (1950s) was a time when essentialist style was emphasized most strongly. I posit this strong emphasis is returning with such texts as *A Nation at Risk*. Perhaps return is an incorrect term. It is more like a resurfacing.

The second tenet of the philosophical style of the essentialist texts is the belief that another function of education is to foster the physical and emotional well-being of children. This surfaces as a concern with life-long learning on the part of individuals in our society. The essentialists believe that if a student acquires this life-long learning attitude that their emotional and physical well-being is certain to follow.

Bestor, in his text, discusses this aspect of essentialist style of life-long learning. He is discussing rigorous intellectual training again, but he is now dealing with its results.

> It should be the ideal of liberal education at every level. It can direct the first steps in instruction, it can guide a man's quest for knowledge to the end of his life. A man whose formal education has strengthened these qualities in him is equipped for life in the present and in the future as no merely vocational training could possibly equip him. His is a disciplined mind. And because his mind is disciplined, he himself is free (Bestor, 1953, p. 24).

This element of essentialist style is also in Rickover's texts. This establishes its basic nature to essentialist style.

> In democratic countries a citizen must learn all this and much more besides. He must prepare himself not merely for competence in his chosen calling but must also learn to become a responsible citizen and a contented human being. He needs to learn how to lead a good life no less than an efficient one (Rickover, 1959, p. 100).

> Most of the problems they will have to cope with as individuals and as citizens of this great democracy will involve the use of their minds. Whitehead wrote half a centruy ago that "in modern complex social organisms, the adventure of life cannot be disjoined from intellectual adventure (Rickover, 1963, p. 307).

The Commission's 1983 text carries on this essentialist style and its connection between life-long learning and well-being. *A Nation at Risk* entitles it the learning society. The emphasis is mine.

Also at the heart of the Learning Society are educational opportunities extending far beyond the traditional institutions of learning, our schools and colleges. They extend into homes and work places, into libraries, art galleries, museums, and science centers; indeed, into every place where the individual can develop and mature in work and life. In our view, formal schooling in youth is the *essential foundation for learning throughout one's life.* But without life-long learning, one's skills will become rapidly dated (NCEE, 1983, p. 14).

The second point emphasizes that the rigorous intellectual training received as part of the essentialist project will equip the student with the skills of life-long learning which will provide for a life of freedom and happiness.

The third aspect of essentialist style is the area of knowledge. There is the standard belief among essentialists that there is a common core of essential knowledge to be known. This core involves the areas included in most present day curriculums. This coincides with the idea of rigorous intellectual training. It is rigorous intellectual training in the core program. This common core concept has as one of its proponents Dr. James B. Conant, one of the best known conservative educational theorists. He insists in *The American High School Today* (1959) that every student in the high school must study the common core of four years of English, three or four years of social studies (to include American history), a senior course in American government, either albegra or general mathematics, and one year of natural science (Wingo, 1974). The essentialist glimmerings of this core can be seen in the Bestor text.

Secondary education, for such a student, is conceived of in all countries (if we except some of the American heresies that I have already discussed) as rigorous training in the fundamentals of the various fields of learning - languages, sciences, mathematics, history and the rest (Bestor, 1953, p. 160).

Rickover, in fact, discusses Conant's core program. Rickover in the 1963 text *American Education - A National Failure* discusses this core.

> Dr. Conant drew up a college prepatory high school course which he felt 15 to 20 percent of our youth were able to follow through. It consisted of 4-year courses each for English, mathematics, and foreign languages, and 3-year courses each for science and the social sciences. The program is a *goal* which only a small percentage of American high schools has as yet attained. The goal is, in my estimation, scholastically more modest than what is already being achieved in England by 16 percent of the children who are, moreover, 2 to 3 years younger than the American high school graduate (Rickover, 1963, p. 304).

This long running style of the essentialist is very evident in *A Nation at Risk*. The Commission's recommendation concerning the "Five New Basics" gravitates to the essentialist core. There should be four years of English, three years of mathematics, science and social studies, one-half year of computer science and two years of foreign language (NCEE, 1983). The Commission gives guidelines for implementing this core. The individual style of the essentialist is heard again in this 1983 text.

The final aspect of style in the individual project of the essentialist is closely tied to the core program. Since there is this basic core of knowledge, the primary function of education becomes the transmission of this knowledge. Education, under this style, can be conceived of as Freire does in *Pedagogy of the Oppressed* as banking. The student is the empty bank and the function of the teacher and education is to fill that empty bank with deposits. In the case of the essentialist curriculum the deposits amount to the components of the core. One other aspect must be deposited and that is our cultural heritage.

> The responsibility for transmission does not end with knowledge and skill. The school must play a large role in transmitting to succeeding generations that body of accepted values that are the core of Western Civilization (Wingo, 1974, p. 54).

This aspect of essentialist style is in many of these texts.   In

Rickover's 1959 text, *Education and Freedom* he states:

Today we must have schools which develop in all children - talented, average, and below average - the highest level of intellectual competence of which they are capable; schools that help young people to understand the complex world of today and how it came to be what it is. This means that our schools must return to the traditional task of formal education in Western civilization - transmission of cultural heritage, and preparation for life through rigorous intellectual training of young minds to think clearly, logically and independently (Rickover, 1959, p. 18).

In *A Nation at Risk* this element of essentialist style is evident.

Our concern, however, goes well beyond matters such as industry and commerce. It also includes the intellectual, moral and spiritual strengths of our people which knit together the very fabric of our society - A high level of shared education is essential to a free, democratic society and to the fostering of a common culture, especially in a country that prides itself on pluralism and individual freedom (NCEE, 1983, p. 7).

The style of the essentialist text *A Nation at Risk* is the style of essentialist philosophy. It has been demonstrated that it is one in a continuing line of essentialist texts which saw a strong emphasis in the 1950s and are returning in the 1980s. The Commission's *A Nation at Risk* is essentialist.

At the end of this explanation phase of the hermeneutical process concerning conservative curriculum theory, we can draw some brief conclusions. These methods of explanation seem to validate a number of the suspicions I had at the point of the initial reading.

It seems because of their structural make up (composition, genre, style) these texts are prescriptive in nature and rather tied to a change not of the system but of the processes within the taken for granted system.

It appears that my initial combining of perennial texts and essentialist texts under the heading of conservative curriculum theory can and has been validated. Although they do have many differences, especially in specific curricular agendas, there is a type of shared acceptance of idealist philosophy. Especially the idealist notion of the absolute. That there is, in fact, a specific core of knowledge that everyone should know. The Paideia texts and the Commission's text may, indeed, differ on what comprises that knowledge, but they do agree on the fundamental concept of a body of required knowledge.

Since there is this shared belief that there is an absolute knowledge, then the prescriptive nature of their texts becomes understandable. If I have knowledge that must be given, then I have to give ways or methods by which it can be given. This also reinforces the conservative trend toward the belief in the banking style of education.

This explanation by structural analysis is essential to validate the guesses of an initial reading. However, it is not the end of the hermeneutic process by any means.

THE WORLD OF THE TEXT: APPROPRIATION

The aim of this hermeneutical journey through the texts of conservative curriculum theory has its main aim not only in the interpretation of curriculum texts through an initial reading and structural analysis, but also a process of appropriation and self-understanding. In fact, Ricoeur believes that appropriation is the ultimate aim of all hermeneutics.

> The existential concept of appropriation is no less enriched by the dialectic between explanation and understanding. Indeed, it must lose nothing of its existential force. To "make one's own" what was previously "foreign" remains the ultimate aim of all hermeneutics. Interpretation in its last stage wants to equalize, to render contemporaneous, to assimilate in the sense of making similar. This goal is achieved insofar as interpretation actualizes the meaning of the text for the present reader (Ricoeur, 1974, pp. 91-92).

This concept of appropriation deserves some further comment. An important question arises from this concept of appropriation. How does knowledge of the self derive from texts? In his brilliant text, *The Hermeneutical Theory of Paul Ricoeur*, Klemm discusses this very question. Klemm states:

Ricoeur initially turned to hermeneutics in recognition that the cogito is a vain and empty starting point for a philosophy asking about the meaning of being human, because there is no content to immediate self-consciousness. Knowledge of the self must be mediated by the objectifications and figures of the self, for the cogito gives no insight into the concrete meaning of existence. To gain access to the meaning of human expression of self understanding, Ricoeur's reflection took the path of hermeneutics conceived as "the appropriation of our effort to exist and of our desire to be, through the works which bear witness to that effort and desire" (Klemm, 1983, p. 142).

The object of appropriation is not, as in romanticist hermeneutics, the subjectivity of another author. It is the world that is "projected by the text" (Reagan and Stewart, 1978, p. 145).

In this sense, appropriation, has nothing to do with any kind of person to person appeal. It is instead close to what Hans Georg Gadamer calls a fusion of horizons (Horizonverschmelzung): the world horizon of the reader is fused with the world horizon of the writer, And the ideality of the text is the mediating link in the process of horizon fusing (Ricoeur, 1974, p. 93).

Appropriation is, then, inextricably tied to the interpretation process and the dialectic of sense and reference. Although the naive reading and the structural explanation are rigorous, they still only deal with the sense of the text and not the reference. When we use the conception of appropriation we begin to explore the reference aspect of the dialectic.

Klemm points out one weakness in Ricoeur's accounts which is an important one to acknowledge before any work on the reference of conservative curriculum theory is begun. Klemm states that the account of appropriation by Ricoeur leaves some points of difference unclear.

...the difference between (1) the directly imagined world of the text as a context of meanings into which the self can project itself in a kind of self-forgetfulness in a first "naive" reading, and (2) the reflexively articulated ontological world, which includes me as the reader and the text world projected for the direct reader.   And Ricoeur also is unclear in distinguishing the referent as an extralinguistic object of experience projected into the text-world from the text-world itself (Klemm, 1983, p. 144).

To clarify this weakness Klemm suggests that there are two levels of appropriation. He calls them the surface and the depth level and uses the term world of the text and ontological world respectively.

My basic concern at this point of the study is with the subject of appropriation and a depth level of understanding (the ontological world). Ricoeur discusses the role of the subject in appropriation in the final pages of *Interpretation Theory: Discourse and the Surplus of Meaning.*

> I say that interpretation is the process by which disclosure of new modes of being - or if you prefer Wittgenstein to Heidegger, of new forms of life - gives to the subject a new capacity for knowing himself. If the reference of the text is the projection of a world, then it is not the reader who primarily projects himself. The reader rather is enlarged in his capacity of self-projection by receiving a new mode of being from the text itself.

> Appropriation, in this way, ceases to appear as a kind of possession, as a way of taking hold of things; instead it implies a moment of dispossession of the egoistic and narcissitic ego (Ricoeur, 1974, p. 94).

Ricoeur would also posit that the subject would "open itself to receive an authentic self from the text" (Ricoeur, 1974, p. 94).

Klemm discusses appropriation in this vein also:

> At the deepest level of appropriation, that is, when it is a case of the fully reflexive "I" grasping/responding in correlation with being as such, then the situation might be described as follows (although this is by no means Ricoeur's terminology): the "I" who reads hermeneutically encounters in what is initially not-I the figure of "new being" in the sense described earlier as the appearence of essential authentic Dasein, and that "I" recognizes its estranged self there in that image insofar as it is the figure on which that mode of being appears. "I" can appropriate that mode of being to the extent that it can bring about my essential being in spite of the condition of existential

split and fault. The enabling power as direct appearence of the self to the self, and the interpretation of this event allows the self to return to the self in conscious self-recognition (Klemm, 1983, p. 15).

The reference of the theoretical texts along with the metaphorical processes of literary texts allows for this type of appropriation.

TEXT WORLDS

By reading and interpreting the texts of conservative curriculum theory the authentic "I" or the "I" that I really am becomes in essence clarified. Through the recognition of the "not-I" of the text world and my reflection on the disparity between the not-I of the text world and the appearence of that to the self I am able to, by the recognition of the "not-I", further distinguish my authentic self. So that Ricoeur's original postulate concerning the interpretation of texts ending in self-understanding is for this writer true.

By the theoretical texts critique of the present system of education and its curriculum they present a possible world for the I to inhabit. The remainder of this study will discuss those possible worlds and their connection with self-understanding. The question is not only how can I be who I really am through these texts, but also how do these texts in relating possible worlds enable the self to confront the self and thereby create a more authentic human being? I agree with Ricoeur that these texts are the mediation by which this increased self-understanding becomes possible.

THE LIVED WORLD OF THE SCHOOLS

When I begin to look at the reference of these read and explained texts and begin to relate them to my lived experience or my experiences in the lived world of the schools, I find that these projected worlds are quite sad. In fact, the title of Lillian Rubin's book *Worlds of Pain* comes echoing back as being an appropriate appellation for these worlds and the worlds they critique.

It appears that what these projected worlds accomplish is the substitution of one painful form of curriculum for another. A form that is devoid of choice, devoid of meaning and lastly devoid of hope.

Thus hope refers to that which gives us patience, tolerance, and belief in the possibilities of our children. Hope is our experience of the child's possibilities. It is our experience of confidence that a child will show us how a life can be lived, no matter how many dissappointments we may have felt. Thus hope gives us pedagogy itself. Or is it pedagogy which grants us hope? As with all great values, their ontological roots seem to merge (van Manen, 1985, p. 42).

Through the mediating nature of these texts and their projected worlds and the consequent fusion of horizons I come to a heightened sense of self.

THE CRITIQUED SYSTEM
At points during the reading of these conservative texts their ostensive reference points to a shabby world of mediocre schools. I have found during the ten years I spent in the lived world of the schools that the schools were and continue to be filled with misery. That being-in-the-schools tends toward a move to the inauthentic. Not only is this movement for the students, but also for the teachers, administrators and all other school personnel as well.

There is a loss of independence, freedom, choice and the type of hope van Manen discusses. All of these are necessary to move one toward authentic being. A lack of these produces depencence on others and consequently a movement toward inauthentic being. Pinar discusses this very point in *Sanity, Madness and the Schools*.

The kind of obedience to authority - that schooling engenders is inherently maddening. It requires loss of self to the control of others, atrophying the possibility of morality as well as autonomy (Pinar, 1976, p. 9).

The focus of the critique of these texts, however, does not center its criticism on this mode of fostering inauthentic being and other directedness. It focuses on the need to replace, revise, and replenish the present curriculum. My lived-world experiences of the schools is consistent with the point that Pinar makes in his text.

Maria, a student in one of my English classes in high school, had this to say about schooling and the present educational system in her journal.

3/14/85

If we are bad, we are given extra homework. No wonder we hate homework. We are forced to take certain classes for an allotted amount of time - whether we like it or not. We are suppressed, put under the guidance of incapable teachers, humiliated in classes for not being quick enough, and threatened with authority. So many people think of lunch as their favorite subject because that is the only place where they are really allowed to express their feelings or talk about what they want to talk about...This is what makes getting out at the end of the day such a goal.

This one eloquent expression of the lived experience of one student in high school suggests that for at least her, school is certainly misery. A world of constraints, inflicted pain and coersion.

For a teacher the world of the schools can be just as wretched, just as painful. My lived experience in the schools was one of pain. As a new inexperienced teacher I had hopes of changing the system that I had experienced in high school. I was trying to be the proverbial white knight fighting the dreaded two-headed dragon of apathy and alienation. But, everyday was another hack at the newly shined armor. My initial reaction to the world of the schools was quite reminiscient of Mr. Bucket and Mr. Snagsby's journey into the undisclosed parts of London in Dicken's *Bleak House*. In the book the two characters are walking through this part of London.

Mr. Snagsby passes along the middle of a villainous street, undrained, unventilated, deep in black mud and corrupt water - though the roads are dry elsewhere - and reeking with such smells and sights that he, who has lived in London all his life, can scarce believe his senses. Branching from this street and its heaps of ruins are other streets and courts so infamous that Mr. Snagsby sickens in body and mind and feels as if he were going every moment deeper down into the infernal gulf (Dickens, 1964, p. 321).

Although outwardly the roads and progress of the schools I experienced were, indeed, very dry and smooth, covertly they were deep in mud and contaminated water. As the industrious young knight, I desperately tried to purify some of corrupt waters of the schools process-product mentality and its devestating and maddening effect on students. I tried to clean up the mud of the school's bureaucracy. For nine years as a teacher I, as well as others, tried desperately to deal with the school's bureaucracy. I fought against the hierarchical nature of decision making, the countless menial and degrading tasks that were mandated, and the cold calculating mechanisms of the schools. The results were sometimes minimumly successful. But more often the results were another blow to the armor and pain for the knight.

I could also see the contaminated waters of the educational system and their effect on students. Students talked to me and wrote of the pain in their journals as Maria did. Reading these journals was beneficial for me because I heard through the rush of corrupt waters the voices of anguish and it filled me with anguish to hear them. The anguish arose in me because of the small difference I could make. The waters rusted and corroded the armor of the knight. After nine years of struggling the knight was scarred, weary and frustrated. He was not "burned out" but ready to take the struggle to a different level.

I was encouraged to find texts that critiqued the present system of pain and eagerly read them to view the horizons of possibility they presented. I was eager to listen to texts outside and against my prejudicial pre-understandings to see if those worlds held hope and the promise of emancipation. As I began reading these texts I found myself nodding in assent to many of their criticisms of the present curriculum and the entire educational system. But as I began to carefully and structurally analyze them through the Ricoeurian hermeneutic, the suspicions of my prejudicial understandings began to arise and at some points were confirmed. By their critique of the present system and their advocacy and plan for reform these texts posit and project a new world that I would like to discuss.

THE SAD POSSIBLE WORLDS OF CONSERVATIVE CURRICU-LUM THEORY

The treatment of the possible worlds opened up by the Paideia texts and *A Nation at Risk* will be dealt with separately.

The discussion of the worlds of conservative curriculum theory can draw some information from Ricoeur's "Listening to the Parables of Jesus" which was discussed at the beginning of this study. Ricoeur states:

> To listen to the Parables of Jesus, it seems to me, is to let one's imagination be opened to the new possibilities disclosed by the extravagance of these short dramas (Reagan and Stewart, 1978, p. 245).

It seems to me that to listen to conservative curriculum theory is to "let one's imagination be opened to new possibilities" (Reagan and Stewart, 1978, p. 245), disclosed by the excesses of these theoretical texts and their projected worlds.

THE WORLD OF PAIDEIA - THE SCHOOLS AS DUNGEONS

The world of Paideia is initially a world that is "not-I". From my prejudicial pre-understandings, I came to this projected world of Paideia with suspicions and some distrust. My reconceptualist views are in conflict in many ways with this "not-I" world.

The projected world of Paideia is a world of little freedom. It lacks the emphasis for the development of a critical consciousness. The world that is projected is not a world of new possibilities, but a world that has been pictured previously by other perennial voices. It is a world that emphasizes one culture, one overall world view and maintains the dominance of Western thought. Although it does emphasize a classical curriculum framework, which in some cases may be beneficial, it does so at the expense of emancipation.

The world that Paideia projects and its differences with the critiqued world of the schools can perhaps be best illustrated by a metaphor. Let us call this metaphor the schools as dungeons metaphor.

Dungeon is defined in many ways, but two are significant for this writing. The first definition is the most well known. It is a "strong close cell; a dark subterranean place of confinement; a deep dark vault" (OED, 1971, p. 817). The other definition is not so well known. It is "applied to a person of profound learning or wisdom" (OED, 1971, p. 817).

These definitions can be applied to the projected Paideia world.

From my lived experience in the schools and from my reading, explanation and reflection on the Paideia texts I see the present world of the schools as dungeons. The school system itself is a dungeon and many of those brought up in it are dungeons according to the definition. They are deep in the wisdom of the dungeon. The schools are places of confinement. They are places of confusion and obscurity, hence they are deep dark vaults. A dungeon does not have to be deep in the ground to be a dungeon. The individual cubicle or cell of this dungeon are the various components of the curriculum. The student moves from one cell to another in this deep dark vault of the school. Occassionally rays of sunlight penetrate the dungeon, but they are usually too little and too infrequent to enlighten the entire dungeon. The students and the teachers are the inmates in this dungeon. It is little wonder, as Maria pointed out at the end of her journal entry, that "getting out" is the students' goal and I suggest the teachers' goal too. It is no surprise that there is mediocrity. In the darkness of the vault and its confining influence, who can gain commitment to any project other than escape.

The Paideia texts critique this world for its undemocraticness, its mediocrity and its curriculum. What does it project as a world to take its place? Upon reflection it seems to me that it is just another dungeon. The present dungeon or the fact that it is a dungeon is never addressed. The Paideia world is still a dungeon.

The Paideia texts suggest that what is needed is a drastic change in the cells of the curriculum. The emphasis is on cleaning, polishing and restoring the individual cubicles. At least in the present dungeon the inmates can at points chose which cells they wish to be confined in. The Paideia world projects cells that would be stronger and more secure. There would no longer be choice, but during the entire time in the dungeon all the cells will be required.

So, I feel that the Paideia world, in essence, replaces one dungeon and its system with only another system for the same dungeon. When I begin to reflect on the substitution theory and analyze my own lived experiences, I find that this projected world is definitely "not-I". It is an inauthentic, other-directed type of world. It is a type of world that would encourage inauthentic being characterized by fallenness and being-towards-others (Heidegger, 1962).

This projected world perpetuates the fostering of inauthenticity by requiring students to be in the know about "Classical" subjects and works, but only for knowing sake.

In my own lived experience I found that the present curriculum of the schools, colleges, and even universities fosters this type of "curiosity" and being-towards-others. My own journey toward this study provides perfect evidence of that fact. What was the knowledge to be in the know about? It was the knowldge that others and the curriculum said was the knowledge to be in the know about. I, like many others, kept searching through the dungeon to find a way out. But, the dungeon, its masters and its course of study only provided for studying the intricacies of the dungeon. It wasn't until I recognized that it was, indeed, a dungeon that I was able to become more self-directed. There were only certain moments, specifically people and books that provided this experience for me. I have mentioned those earlier in this study. At first even they were masters in a sense. Being so immersed in other-directedness, I looked to them for direction. Finally with their guidance I managed to find a voice of my own. The dungeon system I have been describing works against such possibilities.

The Paideia world projected is a new curriculum base to the same world that produces inauthentic being or the "I" that "I really was not" or me. It is a world that would promote being-towards-others. Other-directedness or the publicness of the curriculum would encourage this inauthenticity. The required Paideia curriculum framework encourages students to look toward others for direction as does the present curricular system. It would still consist of a system of external rewards and punishments, of prescriptions and grades. This encourages a noncommitment to the learning that is or is not taking place.

If I imagine myself in this world as both a student and a teacher again I envision worlds of pain. As a student I would be looking to others for rewards and direction. As a teacher I would be required to teach specific subjects in specific ways. The dungeon of Paideia would work its misery in these ways.

THE WORLD OF OUR NATION AT RISK - A STRONGER DUNGEON

The same metaphor is helpful in understanding the projected world of the NCEE's work. This text also critiques the present dungeon because it is dealing in mediocrity. Their solution is a stronger more efficient dungeon.

The world of the Commission's text is not a new dungeon. It is concerned with the specific cells within the dungeon/school. The projected world in this case is not a world substitution or replacement but a world of reinforcement and extension.

In the dungeon world of the Commission's text, the student and the teacher are still encouraged to be "they" directed through the dimly lit corridors of the school world. The emphasis is on the individual cells. It appears that certain cells in the dungeon are essential. The students must occupy those cells for certain amounts of time during the four years of dungeon dwelling. The Commission critiques the present dungeon because the students do not spend enough of their four years in those certain cells and projects a world where the students would spend even more time in those certain cells. Students now spend one to two years in the science cell. In the projected world of the Commission's text they would spend three. The dungeon still exists in this world. It's just the amount of time and the content of the cells that is different.

The other change in the Commission's projected world would be tougher standards concerning homework and examinations. This would mean, I imagine, that the students would be taking home larger or greater amounts of dungeon related activities into their homes. So, the dungeon would become an even larger part of their lives.

Another part of this "new" dungeon interior would be higher standards. That would necessitate, I imagine, stricter dungeon masters and even more other-directedness on the part of the students. These higher standards would encourage more external rewards and less internal motivation and direction. It also would place stricter requirements for being allowed into other dungeons of higher learning. The students again would be learning for the sake of a test to enter another other-directed dungeon.

In essence, however, the projected world of *A Nation at Risk* projects even a smaller difference than the world of Paideia. The world that the Commission's text projects is simply the present dungeon made more unbearable by heaping more of the same on to an already devestating system. I have discussed previously how the present system and the lived-experiences in that system produce misery, to concur with Pinar, a type of madness. So that the ultimate goal of the students and teachers in that system is the "getting out" at the end of the day. By projecting a world that simply heaps more of the same curricula onto the system, is to project more misery and pain.

I could hardly abide the present system. This projected world is simply a world where I could not be the "I" that I am now. But, by recognizing that "not-I" in the projected world of the Commission's text I come to a better self-understanding.

I begin to understand that the misery I went through in my lived -experience in the schools was not only because the dungeon was a secure one and I recognized that, but also because that system pulls students and teachers (and we all are in this system) away from authenticity toward the "they" self.

It became obvious to me at this juncture that the trouble I encountered finding a voice to express curriculum thought and my own ideas was due for the most part from spending so much of my time in dungeons. It becomes clear to me that the reason I became so other-directed to the voices of Madeleine Grumet, William Pinar and Philip Wexler was that I was and still am up to a point other-directed.

My uncomfortableness with these mentors, who advocated working in my own voice, was that I was brought up in dungeons that advocated using other voices for expression. It was emphasized countless times not to use the pronouns I or my in your work. The Commission's projected world wants this type of directedness to continue.

This discussion begins to demonstrate and bring to an understanding the self. I begin to have an enhanced understanding of the "I" that I really am. This becomes clear only through the disclosed worlds of the texts where the "not-I" is demonstrated.

Before I understood that I was somewhat other-directed, but now I begin to understand the why and the how of this other-directedness. It must be emphasized that Ricoeur's supposition was correct. It was only through the mediation of objects of consciousness (texts) that this was possible.

As I reflect, then, on the worlds of the conservative curriculum texts, I concur with Ricoeur. By doing the hermeneutic process with the conservative curriculum texts the chief aim of an increased self-understanding has been accomplished. In this study of conservative curriculum texts I have reached a moment of more enlightened self-understanding by listening to these texts. By recognizing the "not-I" in these texts I have come to a closer and more distinct understanding of the "I".

It has made me reflect on my lived-experiences in the school both as as student and as a teacher. I have come to the the realization that for me authentic being is extremely difficult if not impossible to achieve in the present system of schooling or in the projected world of these texts.

The existential/phenomenological discussion has presented the self to the self and I recongize more fully and deeply the "I" that I really am. Thereby I come to an enhanced self-understanding as a result of reading, explaining and understanding these theoretical curriculum texts.

One point must be emphasized. This "method" demonstrates not an end all panecea for every person. But it does suggest that outright rejection of texts and ideas simply because they are in conflict with our prejudicial pre-understandings or our pre-hermeneutical understandings may just be ill-advised and a bit foolish. Texts even from conflictual perspectives are worth, at least for the sake of self-understanding, listenting to.

Ricoeur in "Metaphor and the Main Problem of Hermeneutics" discusses this concept and states:

> the reader is consequently enlarged in his capacity of self-projection by receiving a new mode of being from the text (Reagan and Stewart, 1978, p. 220).

We become by this interpretive process more of a Being-for-oneself and not a Being-for-the-they.

4
Listening to Reconceptualist and Reproductionist Curriculum Theory

LISTENING TO RECONCEPTUALIST AND
REPRODUCTIONIST THEORY

To listen carefully to the voice in reconceptualist and reproductionist curriculum theory is the course that this study runs. It asks the same questions of reconceptualist and reproductionist curriculum theory that were asked of contemporary conservative curriculum theory. Do the texts of this theory set us in motion? Are we renewed by either reconceptualist or reproduction theory? By treating the reconceptualist and reproductionists' curriculum theory as a "text among other texts" (Ricoeur in Reagan and Stewart, 1978, p. 213), is one way of answering these questions.

Two texts will be read in this study. They are *Sanity, Madness and the School* (1976) by William F. Pinar and "Curriculum Forms and the Logic of Technical Control: Building the Possessive Individual" (1982) by Michael Apple. These two texts do not by any means exhaust the various avenues of reconceptualist or reproductionist research or theory, but they are two important texts by the recognized innovators in the respective areas.

The first stage in the process of understanding this theory is to give these texts an initial reading. The first step in that process is to attempt a delineation of those pre-understandings or prejudicial understandings I bring to these texts.

These readings present an interesting type of prejudicial understanding problem. With conservative curriculum theory, my disciplinary background in reconceptualism provoked an attitude of suspicion which I attempted to balance with an open mind and a willingness to listen to what was being said. In the case of these particular texts I face, surprisingly, a very similar problem. I embark upon this hermeneutic journey not with a suspicion that nothing will be put into motion or that we will not be renewed, but that this theory contains without question all these positive qualities. So, in the case of this initial reading, I already possess the willingness to listen which I had to obtain in reading contemporary conservative curriculum theory. But, in the case of this theory I have to attempt to invoke an attitude of suspicion. This is made even more difficult because of my close association with William Pinar the author of one of the texts. This suspicion does not become an iconoclastic blasting of these theories, but an earnest attempt to listen and understand exactly what is being said. In the case of the conservative curriculum theory the danger of not pursuing an in depth hermeneutic reading of the texts was that the reader would simply dismiss the texts as worthless or useless without so much as an initial reading. In the case of the reconceptualist and reproductionist curriculum theory texts the danger is that readers will not go beyond the initial reading and the nod of assent to raise suspicions about the work with which, on the surface, we agree. The attitude of not going beyond the initial reading of what a reader agrees with is quite reminiscent of Wemmick's nodding "aged parent" in *Great Expectations*. The "aged parent" nodded away in response to everything that was said.

A very old man in a flannel coat: clean, cheerful, comfortable, and well cared for, but *intensely deaf* (Dickens, 1965, p. 230).

The point is that a non-hermeneutic reading can allow either total rejection or total acceptance without careful understanding. As a reader of curriculum theory, regardless of its philosophical orientation or apparent lack of one, I do not want to be nodding or shaking my head while being at the same time intensely deaf. What does seem desirable is to apply this hermeneutic-phenomenological reading to the texts of curriculum theory that are read and therefore, explained and understood. It becomes imperative, then, that those same texts function as a type of mediation by which we can achieve a more enhanced self-understanding.

Consequently, in this particular study the hermeneutic-phenomenological reading of reconceptualist and reproductionist texts will be pursued. As with the conservative curriculum theory the works of Paul Ricoeur will be emphasized and used as the basis for the hermeneutic journey undertaken.

AN INITIAL READING

When we begin to read *Sanity, Madness and the School* (1976) by William Pinar, we are at once struck by the difference in attitude of this text, and the attitude evidenced in conservative curriculum theory texts. The attitude is not at all prescriptive, but much more descriptive. A description has two important definitions in this case. The first is "the action of setting forth in words by mentioning recognizable features or characteristic marks" (OED, 1971, p. 697). The second definition is "tracing out or passing over a certain course or distance" (OED, 1971, p. 697). These two definitions bear an important resemblance to the stated purpose of this text.

> Thus, we will examine the lebenswelt (to use Heidegger's term), the world of the lived experience of person's-in-school, including various modalities of experience, such as thought, images, feelings, reveries, and so on (Pinar, 1976, p. 1).

In the reconceptualist text, then, we do not encounter a series of prescriptions or an attitude of prescription from the very start of the text. At this point of an initial reading it appears that this is in keeping with the essence of reconceptualist theory. Pinar, the recognized innovator of this form of curriculum theory, is keeping within the boundaries that he sets out interestingly enough in a much later work.

> It is not that reconceptualists do not speak to this constituency (schoolpeople) of the curriculum field. But there is a conscious abandonment of the technician's mentality. There are no prescriptions or traditional rationales...What is necessary is a fundamental reconceptualization of what curriculum is, how it functions, and how it might function in emancipatory ways. It is this commitment to a comprehensive critique and theory development that distinguishes the reconceptualist phenomenon (Giroux, Penna and Pinar, 1981, p. 94).

So, it is in essence this distance from a close proximity with a type of traditionalist-prescriptive nature that makes at least this text inherently descriptive.

Whereas conservative curriculum theory has focused on the present system and rearranging within that system, this text immediately as a function of its descriptive nature critiques the system which it describes. In a section entitled "Afterword" Pinar reaffirms this non-prescriptive nature of his concepts and theory.

It is not a model to imitate or emulate, but a sketch to be filled in idiosyncratically (Pinar, 1976, p. 91).

The very nature of being opposed to the "banking" concept of education suggests that Pinar rejects the present prescriptive nature of education in the traditionalist sense. But, I am getting ahead of myself. This particular theory can be seen not as a prescriptive extrinsic force for change, but as a moment of critique which causes certainly reflection and eventually praxis.

The next important aspect that Pinar discusses is Paulo Freire's concept of banking education. Pinar highlights the characteristics of banking education. It is relevant to this study to discuss three of these concepts in relation to Pinar's study and its inherent differences with contemporary conservative curriculum theory. Three of the points that Freire lays out are: 1) the teacher teaches and the students are taught; 2) the teacher knows everything and the students know nothing; and 3) the teacher chooses and enforces his choice, and the students comply (Friere, 1970, p. 59), (Pinar, 1976, pp. 2-3). It strikes me as I read these points that these three characteristics apply to American education as it exists in the schools that I have had personal experiences in and generally as well, as Pinar correctly states. We can see these characteristics in classrooms when teachers mistake authoritarianism for authority. This distinction is raised by Rachel Sharp in her text, *Knowledge, Ideology and the Politics of Schooling: Towards a Marxist Analysis of Education:*

A distinction needs to be made between authoritativeness and authoritarianism. It seems feasible to open up the relationships between teachers and taught, without simultaneously abrogating the authority of the knowledge which the teacher possesses, and the responsibility that flows from that knowledge to pupils who lack it (Sharp, 1980, p. 165).

This is a precise distinction that is missed in many classrooms today. Students will raise questions. Why are we studying this? These types of questions are met with replies which re-establish the banking model. The teacher's reply in a situation such as this might well be that the students are studying a certain topic because that teacher wills it to be so. It is interesting to begin to understand not only the process of schooling in terms of the banking concept, but also to view the dissemination of curriculum theory under the same terms. It appears at this point that a major difference, from the point of inception, of Pinar's type of theorectical work is that it is not using a banking concept of the uses of curriculum theory. This strikes me as a major difference between conservative curriculum theory and reconceptual theory. Conservative curriculum theory suggests a modified banking concept of theory use and reconceptualist theory does not. The modified banking concept of theory appears to be: 1) the theorist (practically oriented) pontificates, the practitioner is instructed; 2) the theorist knows everything and the practitioner knows nothing; 3) the theorist chooses and the state, the local school district and the federal government enforce the choice and the practitioners comply. At an intitial reading it appears that Pinar, at the beginning of his text, paints a fairly black and white picture of American education. As I read the text I am caught up in this picture and I do agree that American education is in an abysmal state, yet I wonder about those teachers and students who for lack of better expression fall through the cracks, those students and teachers who do not accept the model of banking education. I believe there are moments of freedom within that system. Pinar and his ability to critique that system is evidence that these moments do exist. Perhaps a valid question could be raised on how to capitalize on those moments of freedom. Although Pinar does paint, at this point, a fairly black and white picture, he does not give lists of requirements for new curricula like Adler and the National Commission on Excellence in Education do.

The next important stage in Pinar's study, *Sanity, Madness and the School* in the section entitled "Analysis" that I have been discussing is the delineation of the "twelve effects of schooling" (Pinar, 1976, p. 3). I would like to list them and then comment on those effects.

THE TWELVE EFFECTS OF SCHOOLING

1. Hypertrophy or Atrophy of Fantasy Life

2. Division or Loss of Self to Others via Modeling

3. Dependence and Arrested Development of Autonomy

4. Criticism by Others and the Loss of Self-Love

5. Thwarting of Affiliative Needs

6. Estrangement from Self and Its Effects upon the Process of Individuation

7. Self-direction Becomes Other-direction

8. Loss of Self and Internalization of Externalized "Self"

9. Internalization of the Oppressor; Development of a False Self-System

10. Alienation from Personal Reality Due to Impersonality of Schooling Groups

11. Desiccation via Disconfirmation

12. Atrophy of Capacity to Perceive Aesthetically and Sensuously (Pinar, 1976, pp. 3-28)

My comments on these twelve will not specifically deal with all twelve separately for as Pinar correctly states:

> In actuality, these effects cannot be clearly distinguishable. They overflow, if you will, into each other, and manifest themselves in the idiosyncratic manner of each individual. For purposes of elucidation and generalization, such analysis is useful (Pinar, 1976, p. 3).

My initial reading and responding to these effects will by necessity be a blending of some of these effects. Pinar wishes, it appears, to uncover or analyze the nature of schooling and how it fosters madness, dehumanization or one-dimensionality. He then will suggest an "ambience which is schooling for sanity" (Pinar, 1976, p. 3).

The first area to ponder is the atrophy of fantasy life and how the school fosters this movement. Pinar posits that the school has "two distortive effects upon the fantasy life" (Pinar, 1976, p. 3). Those two effects are: 1) If a student is forced by the basic nature of school to be "absent" through daydreams and other means, then "one becomes 'absent' most of the day, day after day" (Pinar, 1976, p. 5). In a sense, according to Pinar, one is not living in the "real world". "In fact, one may be designated, at some point, as psychotic" (Pinar, 1976, p. 5); 2) If the student is present only through psychic violence, then accordingly one becomes "impoverished and one-dimensional" (Pinar, 1976, p. 5). I would concur with this supposition. I think we see more and more of the "one-dimensional" student in the classroom everyday. Many educators and educational theorists have witnessed this type of student and call them by different names. We even discuss their emptiness under different terminology. The conservative theorists call this emptiness and one-dimensionalness by the appellation, laziness and choosing the "general track" (NCEE, 1983, p. 18). Michael Apple in *Education and Power* discusses these "one-dimensional" students. He does not use the same language, but discusses the actions of these students. The most frightening aspect of this is that the students who effectively initiate psychic violence are usually those students in the academic tracks. They are the brighter students. Apple discusses their actions.

> In the daily routine of the school, one met the minimal demands of the institution - and tried to keep these demands as minimal as possible - and at the same time one's group structured its own agenda as well (Apple, 1982, p. 105).

Although Pinar's work and Apple's work have very distinctive differences, which will be discussed later in this study, they are speaking about the same type of phenomena. This first effect of schooling, the atrophy of fantasy life, that Pinar discusses confirms my initial feeling that there would be many points of agreement with his text.

This second characteristic effect of schooling is an important one to discuss. It is "the division or loss of self to others via modeling" (Pinar, 1976, p. 5). Pinar explains the effects of modeling, regardless of the model, upon the individual in a significant passage.

> To get someone to desire to be like someone else, teachers must teach children to be dissatistifed with themselves. Dissatisfaction with oneself is almost always the introjected non-acceptance by a significant other...Such introjection is necessarily violent; internalization of external condemnation necessarily represents a violation of self. Such introjection means "existent" along side the self is a non-acceptance of that self; the merging becomes a self turned against itself, a divided self, or, in the extreme cases, a self lost to others (Pinar, 1976, p. 6).

The results of this process of losing one's self is carried over into many of the other effects of schooling. My initial reaction to this concept is one of agreement. I again agree with Pinar's assertion that this effect of modeling that is encouraged in most schools and implicitly in many curriculums fosters this effect. We see many students in schools today not writing or working to please themselves, but to follow a model. They write to produce a product which follows the model of a perfect product. Teachers are even encouraged and proded to correct papers based on models provided by external agencies. But, there are still those teachers and students who manage, despite the circumstances, to overcome these factors. The problem as Pinar astutely points out is that in the majority of cases the system of banking education makes these moments of sanity extremely difficult to achieve. If schooling does produce people who are only playing at being something they are not, then our educational system needs more reform than either *The Paideia Proposal* or *A Nation at Risk: The Imperative for Educational Reform* propose.

The next significant effect of schooling is the "thwarting of affiliative needs" (Pinar, 1976, p. 12). Our need to affiliate and share a sense of community with our peers is effectively thwarted in schools.

So that in schools we build a spirit of competition rather than a spirit of cooperation.

> Even the most superficial observation of life-in-school reveals that affiliative needs not merely go unmet, they are activley thwarted, in several ways.

Pinar elaborates on the various ways in which the students come to view one another with suspicion and mistrust in their competition for the "love" of the teacher. I would again concur with him on this view of the school. How many times have we seen or participated in the almost ritualistic competition within the schools. There is competition for grades, scholarships, and various other "prizes" associated with academic competition. There are few rewards which emphasize community work or any type of work associated with a group effort. The results of this competition spirit are in most cases devastating. Students become angry in these situations. Where does the student vent his anger?

> Since the child cannot re-act to the violence of the teacher, i.e., vertical violence he "displaces" his anger and aggression and expresses it horizontally...In the context of the school, this phenomenon is manifested in the disagreement, arguments, and fights among children (Pinar, 1976, p. 15).

It appears, at this initial reading stage of the hermeneutical process, that, according to Pinar, school is not only responsible for destroying our concept of self but at the same time destroying our ability to work effectively with our peers. This focus of Pinar is distinctly different from that of the conservative theory. His focus is not on how the schools can produce more efficient workers, students, or soldiers for the corporate system, but on how schools might foster the growth of the self-directed individual. This difference in focus is an important distinction which will be discussed in the explanation section of the study.

The schools' tendency to foster other-directness is another important effect Pinar discusses. The child, after years of coping with doing assignments and various other tasks he does not necessarily agree with, begins to look less and less to intrinsic motivation and more and more to extrinsic motivation. The child becomes other directed. This effect blends in with the effects of modeling. Again the students are doing things to please others. They complete homework assignments to please the teacher and their parents, not themselves. A recent concrete example of this doing things for extrinsic rewards is a Pizza Hut contest. Students in this activity were rewarded for reading a certain number of books by getting a free pizza. The important question that Pinar implicitly asks was not asked of this contest. Why were the students reading books? I would suggest, as Pinar does, that it was for the extrinsic reward. Perhaps, this type of contest is not harmful when it stands alone, but when it is reinforced by countless other instances it can have devastating effects.

> The process is particularly prevalent in chronological adults, especially in those who have been schooled for many years. Such people often marry for financial or social reasons rather than for love, obtain Ph.D.'s for status rather than to inquire and to learn, and they often have children to vicariously live their emptied-out lives over rather than to propagate the species (Pinar, 1976, p. 19).

I agree that this devastating comment about the schooling acquired in this country is accurate. This concept of empty lives is a frightening one. If we as human beings are constantly searching outside ourselves and looking to others for meaning, then those meanings provided could assume any categories. Tyrants, in any form, desire empty people who are extrinsically motivated.

In the next section entitled "Loss of Self and Internalization of Externalized Self" Pinar elaborates on the very concept of empty people. In this case the self becomes objectified. It becomes, as Pinar states, a role. To emphasize what has already been said about schooling Pinar elaborates in a fine passage where he quotes from Camus' *The Rebel*.

> Thus, schooling produces hollow men, obedient automata programmed to compute the correct computations, strangers to themselves and to others, but madmen to the few who escaped, half-crazed, to search for what has been robbed them. The radical test for one of the latter lies in his decision to be

stronger than his condition and if his condition is unjust, has only one way to overcome it, which is to be just himself (Pinar, 1976, p. 20).

This section reiterates the frightening effects of schooling discussed in the preceeding section. Pinar, in this text, is questioning the basic system of education in the United States. This is something that the conservative texts never did. This questioning of the basic system is a chief characteristic of the Pinar text and one that is, in Ricoeur's terms, worth more than an initial reading.

The "development of a false self-system" (Pinar, 1976, p. 20) is the ninth consequence of schooling. A false self-system is the other result if the externalized "self" is not internalized. This concept was initially developed by R. D. Laing in *The Divided Self*.

> The child will develop a false self-system, a facade, a mask to prevent friction with the instructor and/or to protect (or so he might think) the real self. Both of these possibilities are dehumanizing and hence, to some extent, maddening (Pinar, 1976, p. 20).

This consequence also produces an empty human being. The child may think that they are merely playing the game in school. But, the continuation of this playing the game day after day produces dire results.

> For as several writers have pointed out, rather than protecting the self, the false self-system isolates it from genuine and intense contact with others, rendering the self crippled, violated, withered. It may die, leaving a walking-talking automation who works, sexes, sleeps, but who never lives. Or, if the self fights for life, the conflict, if manifested in socially unacceptable behavior, may earn the person the designation of 'schizophrenic' (Pinar, 1976, pp. 21-22).

Pinar concludes at the end of this section that schooling leaves little choice but dehumanization in one form or another. This is an important recognition that the conservative curriculum theory misses. They very seldom, if ever, question the concrete results of their theories. Pinar at this point in his text presents a convincing argument concerning the cost in human terms of our present educational system. It is not tied to the causes that initiated the conservative theory. What precipitated their concern with the education of our children was not a concern for the process of becoming human as in the case of Pinar's work, but with the status of the United States as a world leader in commerce and military strength. This difference alone makes this reading and responding to Pinar's work important. Pinar is concerned with what it means to be human and how schools destroy that development. This is an area that the conservative theory I have read does not deal with in any way. It will have to be seen in this initial reading whether Pinar suggests some alternatives to this basic dehumanizing system.

Pinar discusses, in effect, ten determental effects of the "impersonality of schooling groups" (Pinar, 1976, p. 22). He states that the large groups that children learn in, groups of more than twelve to fifteen, can contribute to the overall dehumanizing effects of school. These larger groups preclude the possibilities of sharing and realizing "personal realities" (Pinar, 1976, p. 22). There is little time for working in solitude, a necessary requirement for the development of the self.

> In fact he (Kierkegaard) viewed the ability to be with oneself the supreme test of the individual, for those who cannot tolerate solitude are reduced to mere 'social animals'...The sheer impossibility of seclusion, of quiet in the school forces us to ignore ourselves and eventually empty ourselves out (Pinar, 1976, p. 23).

Pinar suggests that even the make up of class size and other grouping factors in schools foster not self development but dehumanization. I found in my own teaching experience that moments of solitude for either the teacher or the student were very difficult if not impossible to achieve. If, indeed, solitude is a requirement for the development of the self, then schools are not to any large extent providing it. In fact, the most current research in the conservative mileu, effective teacher practices, suggests that the most effective instruction takes place in large groups (Berliner, 1979). This brings about the call for more large group instruction. The emphasis in this case is on cognitive learning. This may be more efficient. But, where is the concern for the development of the individual? This again emphasizes the difference between Pinar's text and the conservative theories.

The remaining sections of Pinar's "Analysis" continue to discuss the consequences for the self of schooling. Most of the areas pertinent to this study have already been discussed. One section entitled "Atrophy to Perceive Aesthetically and Sensuously" does contain one more additional effect worth noting. The subjects covered in schools from science to something as aesthetic as a poetry class are discussed in narrowly cognitive ways. "Works of art come to have little or no impact upon the perceiver, unless it be a narrowly cognitive one" (Pinar, 1976, p. 27). The ability to trust our feelings about a work are eroded. If our responses to objects, no matter what the type, can't be critique, counted, charted or graphed they are considered worthless. It appears that, according to Pinar's text, we are taught to mistrust our feelings. One only has to remember their first college literature course to remember what the reaction was to a paper filled with emotive comments about the works personal meanings. Pinar discusses this consequence.

> Inspection renders the object lifeless, analysis murders, and the intellectual's gaze turns to stone. Ours is an age petrified by cognition, moribund by scholarship (Pinar, 1976, p. 27).

Pinar concludes this section of his text with an insightful final comment. We must remember that he is critiquing the system of public schooling.

> The cumulative effect of the schooling experience is devastating. We graduate, credentialed but crazed, erudite but fragmented shells of human possibility (Pinar, 1976, p. 28).

In the next section of the text Pinar tackles the question of the type of curriculum needed in the schools. It is to that section we now turn.

The next section of *Sanity, Madness and the School* is entitled "Critique and Rationale". In this section Pinar lays out the basis for his alternative to the existing system of schooling. At the heart of his concept is a humanities program, but he is very careful to distinguish it from what exists in the schools as a humanities program. He also separates it from the type of programs that Adler or The National Commission on Excellence in Education would suggest. Rather than a humanities curriculum Pinar entitles his concept as a "humanities ambience" (Pinar, 1976, p. 29). It is the basic intent of this ambience that makes it distinct. The movement away from a prescriptive type of theory is evident.

> Retaining the sense of the word ambience in our context, refers to areas of study traditionally regarded as the Humanities, e.g., literature, philosophy, the fine arts. "They" enchance the central design or theme, i.e., the individual person's journey toward sanity, but they are clearly secondary. It is beyond the scope of this investigation to specify the methodology by which these traditional areas of study would be taught. Let it suffice to reiterate the obvious; "they" are not to be "deposited". "They" are precisely areas of study, useful only to the extent to which the individual person finds them helpful or in some way pertinent to his journey. It is the journey, i.e., the process of individuation, of psycho-social and moral development, that must be our central concern (Pinar, 1976, p. 29).

In this passage the difference between prescriptive theory and descriptive theory can be seen. Pinar is not issuing the seven or eight magical steps to change the schools for the better, as the conservative theory has a tendency to do. It appears he is merely suggesting that the ambience he is proposing is a theory to consider. It is an important characteristic of this reconceptualist theory. I find this lack of prescribing refreshing.

Another important facet of Pinar's theory is mentioned in the first few pages of this section. It is another demarcation that widens the gulf between this reconceptualist theory and conservative theory. As mentioned previously, the conservative curriculum theory emphasized congitive development. *A Nation at Risk* bemoaned the lack of substanative course work in schools. They were concerned with the cognitive development of the student almost to the exclusion of other facets. *The Paideia Proposal* wanted to implement a required curriculum based on cognitive development of the students because the cognitive development of the students was in such a precarious state. Pinar mentions the cognitive craze of the sixties and discusses it. I think for the most part that cognitive emphasis has returned in the conservative theory of the eighties.

The complusively cognitive emphasis of curriculum specialists during the nineteen-sixties accentuated much of what was already wrong with American society. In a culture whose classical dilemma has been and is the hypertrophy of the intellect at the expense of feeling and sensuality, this emphasis on the cognitive represents the continued cultivation of the maddened schizoid, frighteningly prototypical (Pinar, 1976, p. 30).

A number of things are contained in these statements. The point of emphasis not on the cognitive but on the individual's development is implicit in this statement. This shift of emphasis is again a key characteristic in this reconceptualist text. But, another important point is emphasized, which is an integral part of this theory it seems to me. We see evidenced in Pinar's work a connection between society and the school. He is not treating schooling as a box divorced from the rest of society. But, he implicitly treats schooling as an integral part of society. This is a major tenet, I think, of this reconceptualist theory. It has ramifications. If we treat the school as a separate entity divorced from the society, then the reform of schooling becomes the simple process of giving prescriptive solutions to limited problems contained only within the school. This is the inherent nature of conservative curriculum theory. Pinar's theory opens up a whole new area. If schooling is only a reinforcing part of the maddening process, albeit an important one, then what is needed is not only the reform of schooling, but the reformation of society as well. Perhaps, schooling is the place to start this change. This crucial characteristic of reconceptualist theory is one that I can agree with.

Another important difference is in Pinar's basic theory of knowledge. In his theory is the concept that knowledge is produced by our separate journey toward humanization or individuation. Therefore, the concept of knowledge being a black box that we eventually grasp larger and larger pieces of is not behind his theories. I think his basic view of knowledge leads to his condemnation of the overemphasis on cognitive development and on the price of being human. After initially reading this theory, we shutter to think of what is perpetuated in the name of education in our schools. It seems in our endeavor to improve education through the emphasis on cognitive development in the eighties, we have, to a great extent, forgotten the individual. This is the major difference in emphasis in Pinar's text.

> The individual must not only be the 'point of departure,' but the 'point of termination' as well. Against him or her must every dimension of the program be evaluated. Any "program" committed to sanity and humanization is condemned to fail unless the individual person is the "point" around which the curriculum is integrated (Pinar, 1976, p. 3).

Pinar is calling for a type of change that is not called for in the conservative theory. It is not only calling for the rearrangement of curriculum within a specific system, but also it is advocating changing the system. This clearly distinguishes this theory from the rest.

There is also a call for a change in the basic relationship between students and teachers. It is in sharp contrast to the banking concept of the teacher/student relationship. This concept of the teacher knowing everything and the students knowing nothing is quite obvious in the conservative theory. Pinar calls for a different type of relationship which accentuates the private realm. It centers on this text's concern for the development of the inner life and the process of individuation.

> Not until educators relinquish such roles, come out from behind their "professional" masks, and try to meet their students somewhere in the space that inevitably separates them, not until then can we envision the possibility of genuine communication and of mutual influence: of education (Pinar, 1976, p. 33).

Pinar appears to advocate that this "humanities ambience" he is discussing might be one way to move toward this genuine education. This theory, at the point of initial reading, seems to contain the qualities of a text that initiates renewal and motion (Ricoeur in Reagan and Stewart, 1978).

Pinar then begins a review of the literature of English educators to "establish a sense of the historicity of this essay within the 'literature' and to lay some preliminary theoretical groundwork for our curricular view" (Pinar, 1976, p. 33). He discusses: *Literature as Exploration* by Louise Rosenblatt, *Sense and Sensitivity* by J. W. Patrick Creber,

The Disappearing Dais by Frank Whitehead, *The Exploring Word* by David Holbrook, and *The Universe of Discourse* by James Moffet. The concern in this study is not with his review of each text, but with some of the conclusions he draws as a result of his study of other texts.

> We have seen how these writers have laid important and necessary groundwork for humanizing English classes. We have also seen, excluding Mr. Holbrook, their inability to resolve the contradiction of allegiance to two 'poles': respect for the discipline and respect for the person (Pinar, 1976, p. 45).

Pinar makes an important distinction later on that same page. He states that we should not be too critical of these attempts because their goal is unattainable in the present context of the classroom. Here we see, again, that the emphasis is not, like in the literature he surveyed, to rearrange the curriculum within the present context or structure, but the point is the system needs to be changed. Apparently most attempts at educational reform are dealing only with symptoms of the problems not the causes. In Pinar's terminology we in many of our proposed curricular changes are only dealing with the symptoms of madness not the causes. This is one of the chief characteristics that distinguished Pinar's text and at this initial point is renewing.

Pinar's comments on the use of books is interesting when it is compared to the use Adler and the Paideia Group would advocate. The Paideia Group would suggest that reading and discussing "great books" is an end in and of itself. Pinar comments on this suggestion when discussing Rosenblatt's text.

> However, to suppose that social sensitivity, self-awareness, etc., can be achieved merely or even primarily by reading and discussing one's readings is to ignore the dynamics of psycho-social-moral development, the theory of which must be the basis for any program, English or Humanities, which aspires to achieve such objectives (Pinar, 1976, p. 35).

Again, Pinar's basic concern for the development of the individual is heard. Pinar next lays out his rationale for a humanities ambience.

Pinar suggests that there are three elements that comprise an adequate conceptualization of this type of education. They are: 1) an adequate image of man "that reflects the reality and, most importantly, the possibility that is human being (Pinar, 1976, p. 45); 2) a workable model of psycho-social development; and 3) an adequately explained "activity we believe permits, in fact, fosters psycho-social development, i.e., growth toward the image of man we seek to become, i.e., sane men" (Pinar, 1976, p. 46). It is important to read these elements at this point.

Pinar discusses the image of man in this section. He consequently discusses the development of that type of individual and activities that foster that development. The image is based to a large extent on the writings of existential psychology. Such writers as: Carl Rogers, Abraham Maslow, and R. D. Laing are included in this section. The image of man that results is certainly different from the image of man that is implicit in the conservative curriculum theory texts. It seems that man, as presented in the conservative texts, is an empty vessel needing to be filled or a tabla raza that needs to be inscribed. The image of man presented in Pinar's *Sanity, Madness and the School* presupposes the existence of a self. The objective of the humanities ambience then is to develop that self. In the words of Carl Rogers to facilitate the process of becoming is the goal. In the words of Maslow it is to facilitate the process of "self-actualization". Pinar expresses the image and the goal in a succinct way.

> To become a person might well be the objective of our Humanities "program". Instead of the de-humanized, automatized, maddened men school now "produces," we aspire to establish the "favorable psychological climate" Rogers mentions so that our students might become persons, become themselves, become sane (Pinar, 1976, p. 56).

Pinar then discusses the conceptual frameworks that could be used to examine this process of becoming. He charts two. One framework is taken from the text *Radical Man: The Process of Psychosocial Development* by Hampden Turner. The other suggested framework is The Kohlberg Moral Judgment Scale. Pinar's contention is that a curriculum that fosters the process of individuation will enable students to achieve the highest levels of development on these scales.

> Such 'courage to be,' to stand without crutches, is obviously difficult. However, it is possible. It is our responsibility as curricular theorists and as educators to design an ambience in which possibility becomes actuality (Pinar, 1976, p. 59).

We can view in the schools that the self does die a little everyday. It appears to be inherent to the system. Having or theorizing in a text that the primary purpose of schooling should be the development of the individual is suggesting that the system that presently exists as education is in error. But, from my experiences in the schools and the resulting other directedness that I have had to battle since those experiences, I have to concur with Pinar that the system is the problem. The conservative theory never questions the taken for granted in the curriculum. They view the students as simply lacking the necessary componets of knowledge that the schools are supposed to provide. The issue is not a question of more adequately filling the vessel, but working with the vessel itself. The suspicion I had at the beginning of this study, that I would be nodding to a great deal of this work, seems to be confirming itself. But, this is the intitial reading stage. The entire hermeneutic reading must be accomplished before any definitive conclusions can be made.

The final section of the text is entitled "Synthesis". It is in this section that the components of the humanities ambience are discussed. There are two components to the ambience. There is the nuclear component and the cortical component.

> The nuclear component refers to the center of the ambience, the curricular nucleus of human growth and development, while the cortical component refers to peripherial elements. They are, however, interdependent and mutually supportive; together they constitute a total humanizing ambience in which persons can develop their intellectual, moral and psycho-social potentialities (Pinar, 1976, p. 60).

Pinar's delineation of the nuclear component develops a radical departure from the everyday schools to which most teachers and students are accustomed. Pinar spends approximately twenty pages explicating this aspect of his theory. At this point of an initial reading I will discuss what I find to be the most significant passages.

One important aspect of self development, according to Pinar, is self disclosure. Therefore, any program that provides for self development must also provide for self disclosure. The ambience that Pinar wishes to develop is based on that primary assumption. The schools as they are set up today do not, as the text stated earlier, facilitate the desire for self disclosure. Pinar suggests the alternative. There needs to be, according to Pinar's text, the development of a free flow of conversation that encourages "dialogical encounter" (Pinar, 1976, p. 64). This can only be accomplished if the ambience that is developed is characterized by tenderness, gentleness and sensitivity. The curriculum of the present schools is certainly not characterized, Pinar has suggested, in this way. It is necessary to conceptualize a program that would be characterized in this way. Pinar develops the alternative.

> The activity currently available to us and which offers the possibility of encounter, of intense and authentic meetings among persons, is the Training Group, the T-Group, or what Rogers terms the basic encounter group. It is the experience we can design that is most likely to develop the segments of the development cycle, despite individual differences. It unites 'theory and activity, intelligence and affect and strengthens simultaneously various segments of the cycle, according to the imbalance in each individual' (Hampden Turner in Pinar, 1976, p. 64).

This group would, of course, be a small group most likely between nine and twelve members. It seems to have a great potential for self development for the process of individuation. This group type education relies on the dialogical model of education not on the banking concept. The teacher no longer is the banker making deposits but part of the group. The artificiality is removed from the process. The teacher becomes the group leader.

Pinar discusses the use of "psychedelic" drugs in the cause of fostering the development of the individual. Pinar states:

> It is Roszak, who argues, oversimply, that the so called psyche-

delic revolution is reducible to this syllogism: change the prevailing consciousness and one changes the world; the use of dope ex opere operato changes the prevailing consciousness; therefore, the universal use of dope changes the world. As we have seen, there is tentative yet impressive evidence that the syllogism is maybe true, although one appends to such a judgement that the data we have derived from the thoughtful and careful use of these drugs. This writer would tend to be skeptical that the indiscriminate use of any drug insures a healthy change in consciousness (Pinar, 1976, p. 75).

I would certainly agree with Pinar concerning the indiscriminate use of drugs and the change that develops in consciousness. But, I also would posit that this form of encounter education would not be facilitated in any way by the use of drugs. The type of education that this theory suggests, I believe, would eventually eliminate the need for the use of drugs on the part of many individuals. There use in any way in the educational process is not necessary.

In this process of learning, the notion of interdependence takes a different meaning. Learning viewed as a transactional process means active interactions among peers rather than among superiors and subordinates. Such a view implies mutual aid in coping with difficulties that cannot be solved by the teacher-banker. The leader, if present, is himself a member of the process. He also must be willing to disclose himself authentically and intensly to others. In Friere's terms he must be the teacher-student, not the teacher-banker (Pinar, 1976, p. 79).

This type of education is a type not seen in our schools and for that part not even on our college campuses. It is a type of education that should be attempted. We see also a different type of presentation in this text. Pinar is not suggesting or positing a panacea for the educational community. His method is not prescriptive. These are not the magical seven or eight steps to a more perfect educational system. His theories are simply suggestions. For those of us who have suffered through the trendy solutions and panaceas of prescriptive curriculum theory, Pinar's presentation is a renewing breath of fresh air.

The results of this type of encounter education are many. The most important point to emphasize is that instead of automatons this type of education may produce self-directed individuals who just might change the world.

Thus, we as curricular theorists can establish conditions which, in all likelihood, will result in various categories of behaviors - self-directing behaviors, sensitivity to internal and external realities, abilities to adapt flexibly - that are manifestations of authentic, humane, sane persons (Pinar, 1976, p. 80).

This type of encounter education holds, it seems at this point of initial reading, much potential for improving the nature of education as we know it. While conservative theory perpetuates the system, this theory changes it. Pinar eloquently states the polarity. "This writer submits that, once again, the choice we face daily is between sanity and madness, and the choice is being made against us" (Pinar, 1976, p. 86).

It is extremely significant that Pinar devotes only one page to the cortical component of his theory. This is the component that becomes the area of prescription for most curriculum theory. This is the portion where we are instructed in how to improve the nature of our course offerings, the content of our courses and other practical concerns. Pinar's lack of specifics is significant. For the text to suggest the content of this type of encounter education would be ludicrous. It will be a result or an outgrowth of the individual groups.

Hence the realms mentioned here are illustory and prototypical; their role in the life of the student and their status in the total ambience is contingent upon the particular institutional setting and the needs and desires of the participants (Pinar, 1976, p. 87).

This comment makes any traditionalist uncomfortable. What do I do? This is the question that is not answered by this theory. It is proof to a certain extent that what Pinar has said about education is true. We as educators are still other directed. We continually look to others for direction. The point of Pinar's theory is that what one does is idiosyncratically devised in this type of education. Perhaps our uncomfortableness with this lack of specifics is proof that more of this encounter education is needed.

CURRICULAR FORM AND THE LOGIC OF TECHNICAL CONTROL: BUILDING THE POSSESSIVE INDIVIDUAL

The next text to be read is written by Michael Apple. The text is entitled "Curriculum Form and the Logic of Technical Control: Building the Possessive Individual" (1982). This text has appeared in several places. It has been included in Apple's text entitled *Education and Power* (1983), but it stands by itself as a text to be analyzed. In this study, I will be reading the text which is included in a book entitled *Cultural and Economic Reproduction in Education: Essays on Class, Ideology and the State* (1982). Apple is recognized as one of the chief developers of reproduction theory in the United States so it is important in this hermeneutic process to analyze one of his texts.

When we begin reading this text, we are once struck with the differences not only between this text and the conservative curriculum theory, but also with the difference between reproductionist theory and reconceptualist theory. It is difficult to categorize its uniqueness. Perhaps, it can again be best characterized as an attitude. Our common sense notions of the reality of the schools are not directly appealed to as in the conservative curriculum theory texts. Nor are we guided through a questioning of our perceptions of education as in Pinar's *Sanity, Madness and the School*. It appears at the outset of this reading that the attitude of the text is one of confrontation, even anger. Confrontation is evident from the very first sentence of the text. In the first section entitled "Corporated Ideologies: Reaching the Teacher" (Apple, 1982, p. 247), there is the first sentence.

> It does not require an exceptional amount of insight to see the current attempts by the State and industry to bring schools more closely into line with 'economic needs' (Apple, 1982, p. 247).

All of the connotations of the concept of confrontation are exemplified in this opening statement. Qualities such as: challenging, clashing, conflicting, defying, disputing, fighting, battling and repelling are in this very first passage. Neither is the work prescriptive nor is it descriptive, but it is confrontational. This is no doubt connected to the inherently political nature of this work. This text as a function of its confrontational nature takes on and does battle with the present system of education in the United States. Therefore, unlike the conservative curriculum theory it sees its task not as prescribing practical suggestions to be implemented within the present system, but the task is to challenge that present system and to expose its inherently unjust nature.

The first aspect that Apple establishes is the fact of the close tie between the economic needs of a nation and the resultant programs in schools. In this particular text Apple seems to be concerned with the close tie between corporate needs and curriculum forms. Apple, in this particular passage, quotes from James O'Connor's *The Fiscal Crisis of the State* (1973).

> I am not implying that the level of practice in schools is fundamentally controlled in some mechanistic way by private enterprise. As an aspect of the State, the school mediates and transforms an array of economic, political and cultural pressures from competing classes and class segments. Yet we tend to forget that this does not mean that the logics, discourses, or modes of control of capital will not have an increasing impact on everyday life in our educational institutions, especially in times of what has been called 'the fiscal crisis of the state'. This impact, clearly visible in the United States (although I would hazard a guess it will become more prevelent in Europe and Latin America as well), is especially evident in curriculum, in essence in some very important aspects of the actual stuff that students and teachers interact with (Apple, 1982, p. 249).

It is obvious that the confrontational nature of this text is evident in this passage. But, another important point to observe is this text's tying of the school to the larger social context of society. Apple, in this text, is pointing out the inherently political nature of schooling. This is a fact that conservative theory either leaves unaddressed or discussed in matter of fact terminology. This disclosing of the political nature of education and all intellectual activity is a chief characteristic of this and other reproductionist texts. Pinar alludes to this in an article entitled "The Reconceptualization of Curriculum

Studies" (1981). Pinar labels Apple as a reconceptualist, but it seems the term reproductionist may be more appropriate.

> Apple and Marxists and neo-Marxists go further and accept a teleological view of historical movement, allying themselves with the lower classes, whose final emergence from oppression is seen to be inevitable. A number of reconceptualists, while not Marxists, nonetheless accept some variation of this teleological historical view. And many of these, at least from a distance, would seem to be 'leftists' of some sort. Nearly all accept that a political dimension is inherent in any intellectual activity (Giroux, Penna and Pinar, 1981, p. 93).

Consequently, the confrontational nature of this text begins to make sense when focused through the lens of its political make up. This political and conflictual analysis of curriculum is certainly different from the type of taken for granted nature of the prescriptive conservative curriculum theory.

Apple is focusing on a different aspect of curriculum from most curriculum theory. It is somewhat reminiscient of Pinar's basic focus.

> In this essay, I shall be particularly interested in curricular form, not curricular content. That is, my focus will not be on what is actually taught, but on the manner in which it is organized. As a number of Marxist cultural analysts have argued, the working of idealogy can be seen most impressively at the level of form as well as what the form has in it (Apple 1978; Jameson 1971; Williams 1977). As I shall argue here, this the key to uncovering the role of ideology 'in' education (Apple, 1982, p. 250).

The texts Apple refers to are: "Ideology and Form in Curriculum Evaluation" by Apple in Willis' *Qualitative Evaluation* (1978), *Marxism and Form* by Fredric Jameson (1971), and *Marxism and Literature* by Raymond Williams (1977). Apple, therefore, is discussing the ideological as well as economic influences and impacts on schools. This seems to be a type of curriculum theory that needs to be done. Most teachers and students in the schools where I have had experiences do not question, to any great extent, the inherently political nature of their work. Even those who are prescribing more efficient programs are not questioning the inherently political nature of those prescriptions.

Apple situates the development in the curricular form in schools within the trends that affect various phases of social life. The one major area he is concerned with is forms of control. He infers that the various forms of control usually associated with industry are moving into schools.

the development of new forms of control, the process of deskilling, the separation of conception from execution, are not limited to factories and offices. These tendencies intrude more and more into institutions like schools (Apple, 1982, p. 250).

Apple then discusses the three basic forms of control. They are: a) simple control; b) technical control; and c) bureaucratic control (Apple, 1982). Simple control is the most obvious and overt form of control. It occurs when we are told what to do and the consequences of not doing it. Technical control is a bit more complicated. "They are controls embedded in the physical structure of your job" (Apple, 1982, p. 251). The concept of bureaucratic control is discussed by Apple.

(It) signifies a social structure where control is less visible since the principles of control are embodied within the hierarchical social relations of the workplace (Apple, 1982, p. 251).

The primary rationale for discussing these forms of control is to demonstrate how these forms are intruding into schools. Technical control, the controls that appear to be just part of the job, are the most pertinent for this study of curricular form. The basic consequence of this technical control, according to Apple, is deskilling. This process of deskilling is the crucial concept in Apple's text. This is the point at which Apple draws the connections between industry and education. Those connections are not very often uncovered by educational theorists and I think that Apple's linking the two areas is an important and insightful point in the text. He, earlier in the text, discusses the Ryerson Plan, where teachers, in the summer, spend time in the corporate world and bring those expeiences back to the students. However, Apple appears to be less concerned with these overt manifestations of the connections between corporations and schools and more interested in the subtle and covert connections.

This is especially evident in the discussion of deskilling. The key to understanding the concept of deskilling is to remember that in this process conception is divorced from execution.

> When jobs are deskilled, the knowledge that once accompanied it, knowledge that was controlled and used by workers in carrying out their day to day lives on their jobs, goes somewhere. Management attempts (with varying degrees of success) to accumulate and control this assemblage of skills and knowledge. It attempts, in other words, to separate conception from execution. The control of knowledge enables management to plan; the worker should ideally merely carry these plans out to the specifications, and at the pace, set by people away from the actual point of production (Apple, 1982, p. 252).

Apple's thesis is that this form of control is making inroads into our nation's schools. In other words, teachers are becoming deskilled. They are beginning to merely execute and not conceive the programs they are utilizing. Schooling, of course, is different in many respects from industrial line work, and according to Apple, it has been "relatively recently" (Apple, 1982, p. 253) that this type of control has entered into the schools.

Apple feels that there are examples of this type of control gaining access to the schools. The best examples of this type of technical control are in the "rapid growth in the use of prepackaged sets of curricular materials" (Apple, 1982, p. 253). These materials contain everything a teacher is normally required to conceptualize. They cover every step from the writing of behavioral objectives through tests on the designated material. Apple is correct. There are a plethora of these materials available. I have, in a paper entitled "Freedom from Control: Toward an Abolition of Teacher Texts and Minimum Competency Tests in English Education" (Reynolds, 1988), discussed the use of these types of materials in the specific subject field of English. They contain essentially the same characteristics Apple alludes to in his explication of science materials. He discusses primarily elementary materials, whereas my discussion centered on secondary materials. The characteristics are the same.

The material specifies all of the goals. It includes everything a teacher 'needs' to teach, has the pedogogical steps a teacher must take to reach these goals already built in, and has the evaluation mechanisms built into it as well. But that is not all. Not only does it prespecify nearly all a teacher should know, say and do, but it often lays out the appropriate student responses to these elements as well (Apple, 1982, p. 254).

This is, indeed, true. In fact, as Apple demonstrates in his science text and I found to be the case in an English series entitled *Scholastic Literature Units 5100*, there is a specific script for the teacher to read. Apple's primary focus, is again, not only the specific textual analysis, but also the results of using this type of curricular form.

I think I would concur with Apple that these types of materials are in widespread use across the curriculum and across the nation. I do believe it is a frightening and dangerous trend. However, not every teacher uses these materials unquestioningly. This question of blind acceptance and use of these materials is a major facet that Apple must deal with in this text.

The result, Apple posits, of deskilling is the necessity of reskilling (Apple, 1982). His application of this concept of reskilling to curricular form is a significant point. When teachers lose their craft through deskilling, it is replaced. They are reskilled in terms of management techniques. This explains many of the courses, in-service workshops and literature that currently abounds in education and curriculum theory.

The growth of behavior modification techniques and classroom management strategies and their incorporation within both curricular material and teachers' repetoiries signifies these kinds of alterations. That is as teachers lose control of the curricular and pedagogic skills to large publishing houses, these skills are replaced by techniques for better controlling students (Apple, 1982, p. 256).

This is a point of agreement between my lived experience and Apple's text. We can observe countless examples of these types of strategies and techniques evident in today's educational system. The entire trend labelled as "effective teacher practices" is a prime example of this type of reskilling. In their research summarized in an issue of *The Peabody Journal of Education* entitled *Good Schools: What Research Says About Improving Achievement* (1984), edited by Willis Hawley and Susan Rosenholtz with Henry Goodstein and Ted Hasselbring, this literature defines teaching as a science or set of skills that can be learned. These skills center on classroom management, time usage and teacher expectations. This is certainly a case where conceptual responsibility for curricular form is being replaced by classroom management strategies. Its most prevelant form is found in Madeline Hunter's courses in effective teaching. It appears, therefore, that to a certain extent this reskilling has begun. In fact, in many school districts in Upstate, New York, courses that instruct teachers in these new skills are required of new teachers and in some cases all teachers in a school district (this is especially true in Wayne county). I agree with Apple that this reskilling process is taking place. It appears at this point of initial reading that Apple's critique concerning the business ideology entering the day to day practice in schools is somewhat accurate. Teachers are becoming "proletarianized" (Apple, 1982, p. 256). It is interesting to interject at this point that, even though Apple disclaims any conspiratorial theories, that this type of feeling prevades the text. Perhaps, it is a result of the overall attitude of confrontation that was discussed previously.

In Pinar's text, *Sanity, Madness and the School*, we noted that one consequence of the schools maddening nature was the "thwarting of affiliative needs" (Pinar, 1976, pp. 12-16). Students begin to mistrust each other and there is a loss of community. In Apple's text we read that one of the results of the technical control through prepackaged materials is a loss of community among teachers. It is similar to factories and the workforce.

> With the increasing employment of prepackaged curricular systems as the basic curricular form, virtually no interaction between teachers is required. If nearly everything is rationalized and specified before execution, then contact among teachers about actual curricular matters is minimized (Apple, 1982, p. 257).

It is quite interesting to see exactly why this fact of the lack of communication between teachers concerns Apple. At this point of reading Apple's text with its conflictual nature, it seems Apple finds it important that there is another consequence of the phenomenon of deskilling and reskilling. The additional aspect is the possibility that it might generate opposition to this enforced curricular form. In the industrial field, for example, increased control lead to the opposition from unions and quite possibly to the rise of unions. As far as the educational field is concerned, Apple states:

> Even given the ideology of professionalism (an ideology that might make it difficult for collective struggles to evolve) which tends to dominate certain sectors of the teaching force, other state employees, who thought of themselves as professionals, have gained a greater collective sense in response to similar modes of control (Apple, 1982, p. 257).

Again, we recognize the sense of struggle in this passage. The point Apple is making is that together teachers can fight this on set of technical control. I would agree that this might be one effective way to challenge the forms of control evident in education today. Perhaps, a united effort on the part of teachers might break the hold of the behavioralist techniques and effective teacher techniques that are reskilling them. However, the point should be raised that this will be all but an impossible task unless the individual teacher questions these techniqes. If they are trained in a type of banking education where these behavioral techniques are emphasized, then the task is a monumental one.

Apple next tackles the question of the acceptance of control in a section entitled "Accepting Technical Control". Apple's text confronts and struggles with the question of just how these materials end up in our schools. His analysis of the problem is quite candid.

> It occurs in large part because schools are a rather lucrative market. These sets of materials are published by firms who aggressively market where there is a need, or where they can create needs. It is simply good business practice in terms of profit margins to market material of this type, especially since the original purchase of the 'system' or set of modules means

increasing purchases over the years (Apple, 1982, p. 258).

This is only a partial explanation of the reasons for the adoption of this prepackaged material, however. Apple discusses five basic reasons in addition to the economic one for the growth of these materials especially in the 1950s and 1960s. They can be summarized as: 1. the views of educationists that teachers were "unsophisticated in major curriculum areas" (Apple, 1982, p. 259) led to teacher proof materials; 2. the cold war led to the need for the efficient and guaranteed production of more scientists and technicians, hence the need for prepackaged materials; 3. the National Defense Act gave "cash credits to local school districts for the purchase of new curricula created by the private sector (Apple, 1982, p. 259); 4. The rise in credibility of behavioral and learning psychology coincided with the principles of the materials and therefore, increased their legitimacy; and 5. the trend of the federal government to let the private sector produce these products (Apple, 1982). These trends are returning at the present time with the emphasis on minimum competencies, back to basics, and new teacher proof materials (Reynolds, 1988).

One of the major facets of these materials, according to Apple, is that they facilitate more tightly controlled teaching through accountability. It answers the call from parents, government, industry, and local administrators for accountability.

The fact that the form taken by these curricular systems is tightly controlled and more easily made 'accountable', that it is usually individualized, that it focuses on skills in a time of perceived crisis in the teaching of 'basic skills,' etc., nearly guarantees its acceptability to a wide array of classes and interest groups (Apple, 1982, p. 260).

Apple has made the case in his text that the teachers in American schools are being deskilled through the use of a specific curricular form, namely prepackaged units. I agree that this seems to be happening and that it is a dangerous and frightening trend. The theory of the conservatives does not question this aspect of the curriculum at all. In fact, it seems at this point that the materials Apple is discussing would fit perfectly well within the framework of either the Paideia program or the curriculum advocated by the National Commission on Excellence in Education.

There is another point that Apple deals with that at this point of the initial reading strikes this reader as being quite significant. Apple discusses the results of the use of this material on the students.

> But what kind of subjectivity, what kind of ideology, what kind of individual may be produced here? The characteristics embodied in the modes of technical control built into the curricular form itself are ideally suited to reproduce the possessive individual, a vision of oneself that lies at the ideological heart of corporate economies (Apple, 1982, p. 261).

It is interesting to note that while this seems to this reader the most important aspect of the entire text Apple spends a relatively short amount of the text to discuss it. The type of individual we are producing and that our society recognizes is not a true autonomous being.

> Important aspects of our cultural apparatus represent a world in which the society recognizes each member as an individual; but that recognition is dependent almost entirely upon technical skills (Apple, 1982, p. 262).

In these prepackaged materials the students as well as the teachers actions and thoughts are controlled. The teachers are told what to do and say and the students are required how, by pre-specified instructions, to respond. Learning becomes, according to Apple, mastery of sets of instructions, competencies and skills. The important point it seems at this reading is the view of knowledge that these materials presume. It is the view, as Apple sees it, that knowledge is a commodity and can be accumulated just as one accumulates possessions. This view of knowledge also seems to prevade the conservative curriculum theory which I have previously discussed. This view of knowledge as a commodity produces an individual, who desires to accumulate as much of this commodity as possible. Knowledge as a result of these materials is equated with technical skills. A student desires to acquire more and more of these skills.

> The particular kind of individualism we are witnessing here is an interesting shift from an ideology of individual autonomy,

where a person is his or her own boss and controls his or her destiny, to a careerist individualism. Here the individualism is geared towards organizational mobility and advancement by following technical rules (Apple, 1982, p. 263).

The prime motivation for this type of individual is to acquire knowledge as technical skills to facilitate upward mobility. I think we do see these types of students in schools today. Students that are more interested in grades and what is on the test than they are in learning is evidence of this phenomenon. Even the much discussed 'yuppies' are evidence of this trend. Their primary concern is accumulation of wealth and career advancement to obtain that wealth. These 'yuppies' are for the most part highly educated and it seems to me educated to be possessive individuals. One of their marks of accomplishment and consequently fulfillment is owning (possessing) a BMW automobile. They are a perfect example of Apple's new possessive individual and proof that we are producing them in school.

The final section of Apple's text is entitled "Resistances". His primary point in this section is to acknowledge that the picture he has painted of American education is a bleak one. But, more importantly that not all teachers nor all students are unquestion-ingly part of this deskilling-reskilling phenomenon. Apple suggests that there are resistances. Some teachers may subvert the material in interesting ways.

It was employed only three days a week instead of five days which were specified. As the teacher put it, 'Listen, if we worked hard we'd finish this stuff in two or three months and besides it's sometimes confusing and boring. So I try to go beyond it as often as possible, as long as I do not teach what is in the material to be covered by the series next year' (Apple, 1982, pp. 264-265).

It appears that this is a bit of a short coming of this text. At this point of the initial reading I would like to see much more of the discussion of resistances. However, Apple does call for more research in this vein, especially in the area of content analysis. He calls, interestingly enough, for analysis based on structuralist and post-structuralist thought. I would, of course, agree that this type of analysis should be done. He calls for readings of in use curriculum that might be similar to the very one I am using and applying to his work. I think this certainly would be an interesting avenue for research.

Apple concludes his text in much the same attitude as he opened his text. It is the conflictual attitude of confrontation that closes the text. He discusses those resistors who seem to slip through the cracks and emerge from this prescribed system not as possessive individuals. Apple posits that there are ways to resist the system. He does not advocate overt resistance because the times are against it. However, he does advocate trying to find methods to resist the system in the cracks the system leaves open. He believes that those cracks exist and so do I. He then closes his text with a benediction calling for resistance. This returns the reader to the confrontation mind set. It is this character that gives this work its uniqueness. It distinguishes this text from the conservative theory that only advocates the rearrangement of curriculum within the system. This theory is calling for contesting that system.

> Our task is to find them (openings for resistance). We need somehow to give life to resistances, the struggles. What I have done here is to point to the terrain within the school (the transformation of work, the deskilling and reskilling, the technical control, and so on) over which these struggles will be fought. The resistances may be informal, not fully organized or even conscious; yet this does not mean that they will have no impact...Our own work should help in this contestation.

EXPLANATION: THE STRUCTURAL ANALYSIS OF RECONCEPTUALIST AND REPRODUCTIONIST CURRICULUM DISCOURSE

The next aspect in this hermeneutic arch is the explanation through structural analysis of the texts of reconceptualist and reproductionist texts. This explanation phase or structural analysis of texts has three facets. Ricoeur explicates these three phases in "The Hermeneutic Function of Distanciation" (1973). These three aspects include: (a) the text as composition; (b) the text as genre; and (c) the text as style. In this specific study of reconceptualist and reproductionist curriculum theory texts the two texts, *Sanity, Madness and the School* (1976) by William Pinar and "Curricular Form and the Logic of Technical Control: Building the Possessive Individual" (1982) by Michael Apple will be structurally analyzed with these concepts forming the basis.

This structural analysis is an important bridge between the initial reading and the in depth understanding of these texts, which leads to an enhanced self-understanding. I have discussed in detail in the previous chapter the specifics of each of the three aspects of a structural reading (refer to the section entitled "Explanation: The Structural Analysis of Conservative Curriculum Discourse").

RECONCEPTUALIST AND REPRODUCTIONIST CURRICULUM THEORY — AN EXPLANATION

William Pinar's text *Sanity, Madness and the School* is the first text to be explained. This text will be explained using the three facets Ricoeur delineates. The first area of explanation will be the area of composition.

SANITY, MADNESS AND THE SCHOOL — COMPOSITION

The first step in the process of explicating the Pinar text is to examine the major isotopics that emerge as crucial to the very make up of the text. It is interesting that in the case of this reconceptualist text the major isotopics fall into a pattern of binary opposition. Even though the content of this text is very different from that of the conservative texts, the isotopics follow a somewhat similar pattern. Both of these distinctly different theoretical texts are organized by this concept of binary opposition. In the Pinar text we have a hierarchy of preferred concepts laid out in contrast to the devasting consequences of the present dehumanizing system. The Pinar text presents the possibility of an encounter education as opposed to the madness of the present 'banking' educational system and its catastrophic effects. The major isotopics are listed in chart 4.1. These are presented in a hierarchical order which is developmental.

SANITY, MADNESS AND THE SCHOOL
CHART 4.1

MAJOR NEGATIVE ISOTOPICS

I.   Banking education exists and produces negative psycho-
     logical and phenomenological consequences.

II. The major purpose of education is control and oppression
     of the individual human spirit. There exits education that
     leads to madness.

MAJOR POSITIVE ISOTOPICS

I.   There is the possibility of an encounter (dialogical) educa-
     tion within a humanities ambience.

II. The major purpose of education is emancipation or libera-
     tion of human beings. There can exist education for sanity.

The three major isotopics in *Sanity, Madness and the School* allow
the writer and therefore, the reader to organize the content of this
text around the three intertwined major isotopics. Again, we do not
have a fictional text, consequently the particular definition used of
isotopics as organizing factors appears relevant. The first major task
is to explicate these isotopics separately to see their organizing
principles concretely. It is interesting to note in the case of this
reconceptualist text it is more relevant than in the conservative texts
to discuss the negative isotopics first and then the positive isotopics.
This is the result of the critique emphasis of this particular reconceptual text.

BANKING EDUCATION AND ITS EFFECTS

There first and it seems most important principle of the Pinar text
is explicitly and implicitly mentioned throughout the work. The
major impact of this particular isotopic becomes quite evident if a list
of references to the isotopic from the text is given.

1.   Hence to speak about American schooling is to speak
     about the 'banking' or digestive concept of education, the
     latter term being the one Sartre employed to describe the

process in which information is 'fed' to pupils by teachers in order to 'fill them out' (Freire, 1970, p. 62, ft. 2. Pinar, 1976, p. 2).

2.   Freire elaborates on the concept; noting that teachers are primarily narrators, bestowing knowledge as a gift upon those whom they consider to know nothing. Teachers project onto their students an ignorance which necessarily negates the possibility of education and knowledge as a process of inquiry. The effects are decidedly injurious (Pinar, 1976, p. 2).

3.   Teacher-bankers, however, deposit rather than inquire. Freire lays out in outline fashion, their attitudes and practices (Pinar, 1976, p. 2):

(a) the teacher teaches and the students are taught;

(b) the teacher knows everything and students know nothing;

(c) the teacher thinks and the students are thought about;

(d) the teacher talks and the students listen - meekly;

(e) the teacher disciplines and the students are disciplined;

(f) the teacher chooses and enforces his choice, and the students comply;

(g) the teacher acts and the students have the illusion of acting through the action of the teacher;

(h) the teacher confuses the authority of knowledge with his own professional authority, which he sets in opposition to the freedom of the students;

(i) the teacher is the Subject of the learning process, while the pupils are mere objects (Freire, 1970, p. 59 in Pinar, 1976, pp. 203).

4.   What is the psychological, or more precisely, the phenom-

enological (in David Cooper's sense) impact of such attitudes and practices? The cummulative effect is madness (Pinar, 1976, p. 3).

5. Students, "good" students that is, more than comply with the instructions of the teachers. They come to depend upon them; they come to need them, just as they came to need the instructions of their parents...With domination, concomitant dependence, loss of freedom, the development of autonomy is arrest (Pinar, 1976, pp. 7-8).

6. Even "liberal" teachers who hold "discussions" and employ the so-called inquiry method make children feel inadequate. Regardless of the method, as long as the "banking concept is operative, the teacher pretends knowledge and projects ignorance onto the students (Pinar, 1976, p. 11).

7. If the child comes to rely on the teacher for instruction (broadly defined), he cannot feel close to his peers. The tie is vertical, not horizontal, and because the relationship is a "transferred" one, the child competes for the "love" of the teacher just as he would for the "love" of the parent. As a result, his peers become his competitors, and ultimately, his enemies. As Freire writes, 'the dominated consciousnesses is dual ambiguous, full of fear and mistrust' (Freire, 1970, p. 166 in Pinar, 1976, p. 13).

8. Thus, schooling produces hollow men, obedient automata programmed to compute the correct computations, strangers to themselves and to others, but madmen to the few who escaped, half-crazed, to search for what has been robbed from them. The radical test for one of the latter "lies in his decision to be stronger than his condition and if his condition is unjust, has only one way to overcome it, which is to be just himself" (Camus, 1956, p. 30 in Pinar, 1976, p. 20).

9. The schooling process obviously precludes such experience (aesthetic experience). The focus is study, development of the intellect, and in a culture whose classic dilemma is the hypertrophy of the intellect, such foci preclude the development of an aesthetic and sensuous sen-
   sibility (Pinar, 1976, p. 28).

10. The cummulative effect of the schooling experience is
    devastating. We graduate, credential but crazed, erudite
    but fragmented shells of human possibility (Pinar, 1976, p.
    28).

These several examples from *Sanity, Madness and the School* (1976)
of the banking education concept and its disastrous results, demonstrate the extent to which this major isotopic permeates the text. This
is the primary view of the present educational system that is critiqued in this Pinar text. It is criticizing the basic system or form of
education in the United States. It is not arguing over specifics in the
curriculum because they are only symptomatic of the far greater
problem of the system's constitution and function. This banking
system causes, as elaborated by Pinar, empty shells of humanity.
This annulling education is set up in binary opposition to what Pinar
alludes to as a "humanities ambience" (Pinar, 1976, p. 29). I have
called this, encounter education. A major portion of *Sanity, Madness
and the School* is devoted to setting up, discussing, and commenting
upon the structure and idiosyncratic content of this alternative
system of education. However, several comments should provide a
clear and concise portrait of this opposing isotopic.

1. We can conceptualize the Humanities ambience by differentiating between two types of components: the nuclear and
   cortical. The nuclear component refers to the center of the
   ambience, the curricular nucleus of human growth and
   development, while the cortical component refers to
   peripherial elements. They are, however, interdependent
   and mutually supportive; together they constitute a total
   humanizing ambience in which persons can develop their

intellectual, moral and psych-social potentialities (Pinar, 1976, p. 60).

2.   It is the Humanities ambience we envision that fosters "free exchange of conversation" and encourages "dialogical encounter" that encourages synergeistic, "I-Thou" relationships all contributing to the psycho-social and moral development of the individual, in his search for himself and others in the desert of technocratic, maddened "civilization" (Pinar, 1976, p. 64).

3.   The activity currently available to us and which offers the possibility of encounter, of intense and authentic meetings among persons, is the Training Group, the T-Group, or what Rogers terms the basic encounter group (Pinar, 1976, p. 64).

4.   In this process of learning (transactional process), the notion of interdependence takes a different meaning. Learning viewed as a transactional process means active interactions among peers rather than among superiors and subordinates. Such a view implies mutual aid in coping with difficulties that cannot be solved by the teacher-banker. The leader, if present, is himself a member of the process. He also must be willing to disclose himself authentically and intensely to others. In Freire's terms, he must be the teacher-student, not a teacher-banker (Pinar, 1976, p. 79).

5.   Education, as discussed in this investigation, obviously means something very different. It means that persons must be free to design their own learning environment in collaboration with peers and teacher-students. The important point is that persons find themselves, and then develop their potentialities, which implies freedom from formal or technical dictation (Pinar, 1976, p. 84).

6.   What form would this perspective take programmatically? As we noted earlier, the emphasis would be on the individ-

ual in small group work, in solitude, and in areas of inquiry traditionally associated with the humanities: literature philosophy, dance, and the visual arts, etc. (Pinar, 1976, p. 93).

7. Materials and other artifacts, the usual emphasis in curriculum, are viewed as less consequential than the actors and their operations. Leaders and mentors must manifest experientially, an adequate level of psycho-social development (Pinar, 1976, p. 93).

8. It is not a model to imitate or emulate, but a sketch to be filled in idiosyncratically (Pinar, 1976, p. 93).

9. Humanities curriculum is to provide the conditions that make more likely the possibility of emergence from the current, dehumanized onotological modes (Pinar, 1976, p. 91).

10. While more evolved dialogical techniques would further further expression and hence achievement in these areas, they are not necessarily prerequisites for heightened awareness and integration of self. If the mentor-student relationship and the small group function correctly, the student's attentiveness will turn inward as well as outward, the strength of his encapsulation will be diminished, and the disintigrative elements in her personality will begin to coalesce, with commensurate gains in intellectual, psycho-social and moral development (Pinar, 1976, p. 94).

These ten examples clarify the basic and primary opposition within the Pinar text. This opposition is interesting when it is compared to the basic primary oppositions in the conservative curriculum theory. Again, we have the age old opposition between good and evil. It is taken to a different level, however, in the Pinar text. In this case it is opposing system to system instead of simply changing components within that system. In the particular case of the Pinar text, the first isotopic in binary opposition is the madness of the present banking system versus the emancipatory nature of the "humanities ambience".

DEHUMANIZATION THROUGH EDUCATION

The second major isotopic is inextricably linked to the first major isotopic we have just discussed. It concerns the psycho-social aspects and effects on the individual of the present educational system, centering on the process of dehumanization. The school system in the present milieu fosters, according to Pinar, madness, which he holds to be synonymous with dehumanization. References to the dehumanization process abound in the text and establish it as an important isotopic. Pinar elaborates upon this dehumanizing phenomenon, when he expands upon the twelve effects of the present schooling system.

1. The self turned against itself seeks to be like someone else. The seeking is dangerous; one's identity is constantly in question since it resides outside oneself. One feels ontologically insecure, and such insecurity prevents and arrests man's ontological vocation of becoming more human, more himself. Such insecurity also increases the likelihood of being designated schizophrenic (Pinar, 1976, p. 6).

2. Parents collude with teachers, criticizing their children if their marks fail to meet their standards which, of course, they often fail to meet. Again, at home, the child is made to feel deficient; he cannot possibly get "A" in everything; he must be only "above average" or "average", and since his attitude toward himself is contingent upon the attitudes of others, he necessarily comes to experience himself as "average" or perhaps even "below average"; he comes to share the view he is "not living up to his potential". One's sense of worth, one's love for oneself, contingent as it has become upon performance and resulting attitudes of others, is bound to be diminished (Pinar, 1976, p. 12).

3. The school-ordained drive for excellence and achievement is

often the drive for poignant unhappiness, the loss of self-love (Pinar, 1976, p. 90).

4. Estranged from the source of biography, of lived experience, one floats on the surface, vulnerable to social waves and storms, likely to be blown off course without the rudder that is unconsciousness of Self (Pinar, 1976, p. 90).

5. The process of dehumanization, of becoming not oneself, can be experienced as a loss of attentiveness, a loss of energy, psychic as well as physical. One may increase one's intake of food or alcohol or knowledge, but this draining or hemorrahaging, often only peripherally conscious, continues. Psychically, the lack is filled by introjection of some image, some mask, typically the reflection of those in politically, and under some certain, usually rare circumstances, psychically superior positions. Regardless of the nature of the image to be internalized, the process itself can only result in the development of a false system (Pinar, 1976, pp. 90-91).

These few examples from the text demonstrate the pervasiveness of the second major isotopic of the dehumanizing educational system. The opposing isotopic would have to be in this case the emancipatory potential of the "humanities ambience" developed by Pinar. This new type of education is alluded to frequently in the text. The major concern in this isotopic is the result of that type of education. I will cite here a few to demonstrate the isotopics' emphasis.

1. Such "courage to be", to stand without crutches, is obviously very difficult. However, it is possible. It is our responsibility as curricular theorists and as educators to design an ambience in which possibility becomes actuality (Pinar, 1976, p. 59).

2. We do not assume that "good standards" are external to people, derived from curriculum guides or whatever, and to

which students must aspire; rather this program assumes that man is an end in himself and that standards are within persons and are discoverable through processes of personal expression (Pinar, 1976, p. 88).

3. The objective is threefold: first, the student is to become more aware of what was before preconscious, his Lebenswelt, to be more able to see this level of experiencing without or at least aware of preconceptions acquired through conditioning. Secondly, the student is to learn to articulate the dynamics of his or her biographic situation, and to be able to converse with his mentor freely about those dynamics. Thirdly, the student learns to make his behavior more congruent with his discovered intentions and motives; namely he is not only to integrate intellectually and emotionally the complex elements that are operative in his life, but behaviorally as well (Pinar, 1976, p. 93).

This education for madness versus the education for sanity is a major isotopic in *Sanity, Madness and the School*. The important point to remember here again is there is actually the emphasis on changing systems as well as curricula in this opposition. It is not a false choice as the choices in conservative curriculum theory oppositions are, but a true choice. Pinar submits "the choice we face daily is between sanity and madness, and the choice is being made against us" (Pinar, 1976, p. 86).

These enumerated isotopics clearly explain that there exist basic binary oppositions in the Pinar text. It is also obvious that these isotopics are intricatly intertwined into one another. The overriding opposition might be Education toward Madness versus Education toward Sanity.

GENRE

The generative function of genres that Ricoeur suggests in his text, "The Hermeneutic Function of Distanciation", becomes quite interesting when we explain *Sanity, Madness and the School*. Perhaps Pinar's isotopics and their language are in many respects generated by the genre he uses to express them.

Pinar, unlike the conservative theorists, does not classify his work in the title. Although, as was demonstrated with the conservative texts, an advertised genre does not necessarily provide the reader with an accurate representation of the advertised genre.

Pinar's text can be classified as an essay or thesis. There are several characteristics of this genre. The classification can be subdivided into formal and informal essay. What is quite unique about Pinar's essay is that he combines both of these types into one. I would like to first give the general characteristics of the genre known as essay, then discuss the blendings Pinar uses. A formal thesis or essay has basically three major characteristics. They are: 1. There is a seriousness of intention; 2. There is a logical organization; and 3. There is a proposition set forth and defended. The word essay is from the French meaning attempt. As the term suggests it is a modest and/or incomplete but worthwhile treatment of a subject. Bacon in his work with the essay defined the essay as a brief philosophical discourse. I believe Pinar's text contains all of these qualities. There is another facet to his work, however. The classic definitions of essays reach us through the two masters of the essay form, Montaigne and Bacon. Montaigne's concept of the essay is now considered to be the classic definition of the informal essay. The informal essay possessed three qualities. The three qualities are: intimateness, informality, and gracefulness. The formal essay, the Bacon essay, has two basic characteristics. One characteristic is that it is quite dogmatic and the other characteristic is that it contains formal exposition.

If we take a close look at Pinar's use of the genre there is a unique blending of all these characteristics, a blending of the formal and the informal. The salient points of these qualities of this definition for structural analysis of Pinar's text can be clearly delineated. The first point is the reference to the essay as a formal thesis and its three characteristics. The second point is the characteristic of an attempt. The final and perhaps most interesting point is the blending of the informal and formal properties of the genre. *Sanity, Madness and the School* fits all the properties of this classificatory scheme. But this explanation is also an opportunity to examine the generative function of this genre classification. It does seem ultimately important because most curriculum theory is written within this genre.

The first step in the explanation of essay as a genre is to analyze its classifying function. We must begin then with the essay as a formal thesis. Before using specific statements from the text, a general discussion of the characteristics is in order. It is difficult to divide this text into the formal and informal aspects because they are inextricably linked. However, to grasp the generative and classificatory nature it is important to proceed in this manner.

The first characteristic of a formal thesis is its seriousness of intent. The author is trying to establish that the subject he is dealing with requires serious attention. There is little question that there is serious intent on the part of Pinar in his text. This is evidenced by one of the major isotopics. The entire text is set up in binary opposition. It is discussing the psychic well-being of humanity. The opposition speaks to the seriousness of intention. The opposition is education toward madness or education toward sanity. It is important to point out that this seriousness of intention is provided in the same manner in which the conservative texts present their prescriptive theories. There is the use of comparison and contrast based on the nature of the binary oppositions. Not only is this seriousness of intention part of a classification schemata, but it also generates a certain type of language and language usage. It is also necessary if we have this seriousness of intention to present material in a logical sequence or order. In the case of *Sanity, Madness and the School* the logical order is based on sound and logical research. There are three basic sections: Analysis, Critique, and Rationale and Synthesis. This organization contributes the basic seriousness of purpose. The setting forth and defense of a proposition is a logical consequence of this type of logical organization. The proposition is set up in the analysis portion and then carried throughout the text where it is defended.

If we consider the serious intention as an aspect of this text as an essay, the Pinar text certainly possesses this characteristic. The text is discussing, as has been stated, the psychic well being of the human being. Pinar's proposition is that schools are driving people toward madness. It is interesting to analyze the word serious. There are many meanings attributed to this term. Thoughtful and subdued in appearance or manner is one definition that can be considered. Another definition that is appropriate is having important or dangerous consequences. The final definition that might be considered is that serious means requiring much thought or work. With each paragraph of the Pinar text we are reminded of the seriousness of the situation and it is stated in a serious manner. These statements and paragraphs are not dogmatic edict-like statements as in many of the conservative texts. The language is still forceful, however, far from being staccato-like; the language is adagio. It is in an easy graceful manner. Rather than being edicts rammed home in a forceful march-like tempo, Pinar's text slowly, gracefully and seriously presents its descriptive statements.

1. From serious study of schools (both urban and sub-urban) and from considerable exploratory reading, this writer is able to identify and explicate twelve effects of schooling (Pinar, 1976, p. 3).

2. Thus, we will examine the lebenswelt (to use Heidegger's term), the world of lived experience of person's-in-school, including various modalities of experience, such as thoughts, images, feelings, reveries, and so on. We will focus the inquiry on the impact of teachers on students, the impact of the oppressors on the oppressed. Only by such a focus can the effects of the process of schooling be known (Pinar, 1976, p. 1).

3. This writer submits that, once again, the choice we face daily is between sanity and madness, and the choice is being made against us (Pinar, 1976, p. 86).

4. We are faced with the choice of increasing control or freedom, of deepened humanity or depersonalization between a world frighteningly similar already to Orwell's nightmare or the possibility of human world: it is the difference between sanity and madness (Pinar, 1976, p. 81).

These serious and convincing statements run throughout the Pinar text. In an essay readers, when they are decoding, expect to find these serious types of statements. The writer encoding under the genre of the essay tends to make these kinds of statements. Pinar does make these kinds of serious statements, despite his adagio manner. The genre in this case as a generative process does not only generate the form, but also the type and nature of the statements made in that form. It is possible, therefore, to state that the genre may be responsible for generating certain types of thoughts.

The second aspect of the essay is that there is a logical organization. In *Sanity, Madness and the School*, the organization is fairly straight forward and based on the basic organizing principles of a propositional essay. We have already seen how this text is organized in the initial reading section. The following chart (4.2) of organization reinforces the point.

SANITY, MADNESS AND THE SCHOOL - STRUCTURE
CHART 4.2

I.   INTRODUCTION

II. ANALYSIS

III. CRITIQUE AND RATIONALE

IV. SYNTHESIS

    A. NUCLEAR COMPONENT

    B. CORTICAL COMPONENT

V.   AFTERWORD

The organization is so logical that it is possible to outline the plan. Therefore, Pinar's text demonstrates an additional characteristic of the essay.

A third characteristic of a formal essay is that there is a propositon set forth and defended. This characteristic is certainly evident in the Pinar text. The initial proposition is stated in the introduction. It is then defined, delineated and defended throughout the remainder of the text.

We shall explore this charge that the process of socialization is roughly equivalent to going mad and specifically we shall look at the special contribution of schooling to psychic deterioration. Afterward we shall suggest the outlines of a rationale for a sort of schooling that will arrest the deterioration and, in fact, promote growth in its intellectual, moral and psycho-social dimensions (Pinar, 1976, p. ii).

The proposition, therefore, is set forth. The proposition is defended throughout the text and in the last section entitled "Afterword" it is reinforced.

The question of the age, at the broadest conceptual level, is who is man? What is the possibility that is being human? In this writer's lifetime, one notes the process of disintegration which commences at birth and which is roughly equivalent to the process of socialization or acculturation. A more natural and correct relation of self to self, of self to others, becomes distorted into role, mask, intrapersonal and interpersonal estrangement (Pinar, 1976, p. 88).

The Pinar text, therefore, fulfills the third characteristc of the essay genre.

The Pinar text does fulfill the basic genre features that are characteristic of the essay. Yet, the informal adagio gracefulness is present in all these aspects. This specific aspect will be dealt with in the discussion of style.

It must be remembered that Ricoeur, in discussing the aspects of genre, is positing the two functions of genre. One function is the classificatory scheme that has been discussed. The second facet of the genre is its generative function. Stated simply, the thought and messages produced within a certain genre code are shaped by that code. The ideas expressed within the code are in essence limited by that code. In the case of the essay, I believe there is somewhat more flexibility than within, say, the manifesto. If we look at the form we see that the ideas expressed must: 1. be presented with a seriousness of intention; 2. be presented within a logical framework; and 3. be presented and defended within a propositional format. At once the writer is limited to these forms of composing. The writer becomes proficient in the code. He must achieve a basic competency.

In the particular case of the Pinar text, however, we do observe a type of flexibility. Even though there is the limitation of the genre of formal essay, which necessitates producing certain information in certain ways, the author can facilitate a blending. However, even with this blending the writer still must master the competence thereby producing an adequate essay. There is not in this form as much of a prescriptive nature as in the manifesto form of *The Paideia Proposal: An Educational Manifesto*, it allows more flexibility.

As readers decoding the genre, again, we are working within the code of the essay. We treat the material accordingly. I believe we look for a seriousness of purpose, a logical organization and a proposition set forth and defended. We are pleasantly surprised if the effort is as readable as the Pinar text.

As a result of studying *Sanity, Madness and the School* as a formal essay, the isotopic of Education toward Sanity has been given by the genre a very thoughtful and logical nature. The verification of the pre-hermeneutical reading is becoming established. The descriptive nature is present.

STYLE

When we begin to consider the aspect of style as a part of the explanation process with *Sanity, Madness and the School*, we face a somewhat different problem than we did with the conservative curriculum theory texts. It is the problem of language. The use of language in style is ultimately important. Ricoeur in "The Hermeneutic Function of Distanciation" discusses the use of language. The emphasis is mine.

> Because style is a work which individualizes, that is, which produces something individual, it retroactively points to its author. Thus the word "author" belongs to the stylistic. "Author" says more than "speaker". *The author is the artisan of a work of language*...Man individualizes himself by producing

individual works (Ricoeur, 1973, p. 139).

There is a difference between this reconceptualist text and the texts of conservative theory. The difference is in the use of language. It is the difference between the use of everyday language and the use of philosophic language.   In the conservative curriculum theory texts the opaqueness of the everyday language and its accessibility denies or at the very least hides the ideological basis of the texts. The appeal of the everyday language claims that there is a simple and basic application for the theories. The ideological bases of these texts had to be uncovered.   Therefore, when we analyzed style in these texts, the philosophical bases were uncovered.   The texts, by common sense appeal, covered up the ideological foundation upon which they were built.   It was, therefore, most important to uncover that very foundation upon which they were built.

Pinar's text, on the other hand, does not use the opaque everyday language.   His ideological or philosophical basis is made clear.   In fact, he discusses this problem of a hidden philosophical basis in the opening paragraph of his text.   The emphasis is mine.

> Much has been written about the deleterious effects schools have on children. However, the cogency of much that has been written is weakened because *the criticism has usually a firm, identifiable theoretical base. By providing such a base, both the clarity and cogency of criticism will be strengthened.* As well, the outlines of reformation will be sharpened. One obvious and compelling base is the science of persons: psychology, or to employ a term of more use to our inquiry, the science of persons in relation to persons: social phenomenology (Pinar, 1976, p. 1).

We understand from the outset of the text that Pinar's orientation or philosophical style is phenomenological and existential. It is quite interesting to note that while using this existential-phenomenological philosophic basis, Pinar advocates each individual educator filling out his own cortical component idiosycratically. He practices in his work the philosophy.   It is next to impossible to aline Pinar with the same method of stylistic analysis we used with the conservative theorists because Pinar's work is idiosyncratic.   It is a perfect example of the individual author working with a language.   The analysis of style must then become an analysis of how this particular author/text uses language. I return to the point I made earlier concerning the insertion of the adagio gracefulness into the formal essay genre. This, I believe, is the essence of the style of this text. The task becomes an analysis and explanation of this adagio gracefulness.   There are two additional componets of style, which are inextricably interwoven within the adagio gracefulness. These need to be analyzed in the Pinar text also.   They are the existential-phenomenological terminology and the personal tone of the text.

It is important to explicate the term, adagio. It has basically one definition which is "a direction in musical time in which a piece is to be sung or played: slowly, leisurely and gracefully" (OED, 1971, p. 25). It is the characteristic uniqueness of this Pinar text. It can be compared to the difference between a staccato march tempo, which interestingly enough further ties the style of the conservative curriculum theory texts to the militarism of a "Stars and Stripes Forever" march and an adagio concerto by Bach i.e., "Concerto No. 2 for Violin and Orchestra in E major, S. 1042". The style is in contrast to the fast pace "getting and spending" society. The conservative texts written in the "getting and spending" style reinforce the tempo of society and cover up the ideology. In contrast we have a text with a style such as Pinar's.   Its contrast to the technical rationale of mainstream style and pace is one of its chief characteristics. For a moment when we first read in the style of Pinar, there is a shock. The language is quite different from what we are accustomed to in educational/curriculum theory and in a Brechtian sense we are "alienated". Whether or not this is a conscious effort by the author is not in question. The text as a work presents this alienation.

The idea of alienation towards an enlightenment is not a new concept. It dates back to the Romantic poets. It is also a concept that Bertolt Brecht used in his ideas of theater. Brecht expanded the concept and placed emphasis on its social implications. It is relatively difficult to condense this concept, but it is important to have a basic understanding of it to appreciate its application for an adagio style.

When we are accustomed to anything, in this particular case a type of curriculum theory text (conservative, prescriptive), then it is easy for us to assume that it has always been so. We begin to accept the inevitability of what we are used to. It becomes natural. But, when something different, new or unique is offered to us, we begin to recognize that what we are used to is not natural or inevitable. We may choose to accept or reject it. Now, when that something familiar is made strange to us, we recognize that the natural could be otherwise. For Brecht this concept dealt with political and economic systems, but, I think that this concept applies to the adagio style of *Sanity, Madness and the School*. This shock or alienation of the natural is reinforced by the three major components of the style. Those components are: 1. the adagio gracefulness; 2. the existential-phenomenological terminology; and 3. the personal idiosyncratic voice.

The adagio pace immediately jars us by its contrast to the pace of everyday existence. Perhaps the best way to illustrate the pace is to contrast it with the everyday pace. In chart 4.3 I have put two passages from the Pinar text and two passages from the *Paideia Proposal*. I think that his makes the graceful pace rather clear. The emphasis is mine.

SANITY, MADNESS AND THE SCHOOL
CHART 4.3

1...the central pedagogical question becomes: *how and under what conditions can one come to himself, however incipiently?* It is within this ontological context that educational strategies must be conceptualized and evaluated (Pinar, 1976, p. 89).

2...the leader, if present, is himself a member of the process (learning). He must also be willing to *disclose himself authentically and intensely to others* (Pinar, 1976, p. 79).

THE PAIDEIA PROPOSAL:
AN EDUCATIONAL MANIFESTO

1...To achieve the desired quality of a democratic education, a one track system of schooling for twelve years *must aim directly at three main objectives and make every effort to achieve them to a satisfactory degree* (Adler, 1982, p. 16).

2...To learn how to do any of these things (skills) well, one must not only engage in doing them, but *one must be guided in doing them by someone more expert in doing them oneself* (Adler, 1982, p. 52).

These examples only lean toward an explanation of the characteristic style of the Pinar text. It is a holistic style that a subdividing explanation can come to grips with, but not entirely analyze.

Another characteristic of this style is the terminology used by the text. It reinforces the adagio pace and the alienation previously discussed. The text does not possess the everyday language characteristic of conservative texts. It is the language of existentialism and phenomenology. The language does not cover up the ideological basis of the text, but on the contrary it opens it up. The language reinforces the positive aspects of alienation and at the same time reveals and discusses the philosophical basis or style of the text. Specific examples from the text demonstrate this concept. The text is full of examples. Almost every paragraph is written with the existential-phenomenological terminology. However, a few examples are sufficient to denomstrate this emphasis. This terminology is a necessary constituative element of the adagio pace. The terminology reinforces the pace and the pace reinforces the terminology. It is impossible and irrelevant to attempt to ascertain which one proceeds the other. I have emphasized the terminology.

1. *One's biography,* the public and personal manifestations of one's psyche, and one's calling, which is to say the work one is to do in the public world, becomes more congruent with established social biographical modes, less idiosyncratic and organic, less a matter of itself and more a matter of *collusion with current ontological styles.* Estranged from the *source of biography, of lived experience,* one floats on the surface vulnerable to social waves and storms, likely to be blown off course without the rudder that is *consciousness of self* (Pinar, 1976, p. 90).

2. "They" (subjects in the humanities ambience) are precisely areas of study, useful only to the extent to which the individual person finds them helpful or in some way *pertinent to his journey. It is this journey, i.e., the process of individuation, of psycho-social and moral development, that must be our central concern* (Pinar, 1976, p. 29).

This existential-phenomenological language is a characteristic of the Pinar text, *Sanity, Madness and the School*. We observed the terms and disclosure of the philosophic basis. There is a problem in using this type of sophisticated language, however. Some readers may reject the text because of the difficulty or unfamiliarity of the language. I will discuss this aspect later in the study.

The final aspect of the style of the Pinar text that needs to be explicated is its personalness. Unlike the conservative theory produced by committee or group with their prescriptions for success. Pinar's text is idiosyncratic or personal. It is not a group who impersonally issues edicts or recommendations, but an individual making some important suggestions. It is reinforced by the frequent use of the pronoun I, other personal pronouns and some specific nouns. A method of idiosyncratic writing, we are all interestingly enough forced away from in education. It is part of the shock that the style of this text renders.

The personal style is reinforced numerous times throughout the text. The personal style, too, contributes to the overall adagio style. Some examples help to illustrate this aspect of style. I have emphasized the personal voice.

1. This *writer-educator* answers these questions with a tentative "yes", and in the following chapter he will describe a rationale for a humanities "program" that may indeed be schooling for sanity. It seems, at this historical juncture, nothing less will do (Pinar, 1976, p. 28).

2. True intellectuality and intelligence, it has been said, overly simple to be sure, is the ability to think what you feel and feel

what you think. This *writer contends* such connection is the beginning of genuine intelligence (Pinar, 1976, p. 70).

3. This *writer submits* once again, the choice we face daily is between sanity and madness, and the choice is *being made against us* (Pinar, 1976, p. 86).

The style of this Pinar text is defined as the adagio, existential-phenomenological and personal style. It has been demonstrated that this is one of the more important aspects of the Pinar text. It is the style that produces critical thought about education. The style of this text takes us out of the tempo of everyday life, slows us down, allows us to reflect on what seems natural, and returns us to everyday existence. But, we return in many cases with a changed outlook on the educational process.

"CURRICULAR FORM AND THE LOGIC OF TECHNICAL CONTROL: BUILDING THE POSSESSIVE INDIVIDUAL
    The explanation of Michael Apple's text begins with the explanation and delineation of the major isotopics evident in this reproductionist text.

COMPOSITION
    The structural analysis of "Curricular Form and the Logic of Technical Control: Building the Possessive Individual" reveals two major isotopics. They are set up in binary opposition between control and freedom. In this case, as in the Pinar text, it is important because of the aspect of critique to put the negative isotopics first.

CHART 4.4

MAJOR NEGATIVE ISOTOPICS

I. There is a deskilled, reskilled possessive individual that comprises the teaching force that is technically controlled.

II. There exists a prepackaged educational curriculum.

MAJOR POSITIVE ISOTOPICS

I. There is a need for resistant pedagogy.

II. There is a need for a critical analysis and use of prepackaged curriculum materials.

These are the major negative and positive isotopics of the Apple text. Each pair of isotopics requires further explanation to demonstrate its organizing function. The major opposition is set up, in essence, between what is and what ought to be.

THE CONTROLLED, DESKILLED, RESKILLED AND POSSESSIVE TEACHING FORCE

The first and most important principle of critique in Apple's text is carried throughout the text and is responsible for the remaining isotopic. It is, therefore, pervasive and crucial to the set up of the Apple text. The references to this isotopic are frequent. Several examples will demonstrate this fact.

1. As we shall see, the development of new forms of control, the process of deskilling, the separation of conception from execution, are not limited to factories and offices. These tendencies intrude more and more into institutions like schools (Apple, 1982, p. 250).

2. Deskilling is part of a long process in which labor is divided and then redivided to increase productivity, to reduce "inefficiency", and to control both the cost and the impact of labor (Apple, 1982, p. 251).

3.   When jobs are deskilled, the knowledge that once accompa-
      nied it, knowledge that was controlled and used by the
      workers in carrying out their day to day lives on their jobs,
      goes somewhere. Management attempts (with varying
      degrees of success) to accumulate and control this assem-
      blage of skills and knowledge (Apple, 1982, p. 252).

4.   Notice as well the process of deskilling at work here. Skills
      that teachers used to need, that were deemed essential to the
      craft of working with children - such as curriculum delibera-
      tion and planning, designing teaching and curricular strate-
      gies for specific groups and individuals based on intimate
      knowledge of these people are no longer necessary (Apple,
      1982, p. 255).

5.   While deskilling the deskilling involves the loss of craft the
      ongoing atrophication of educational skills, the reskilling
      involves the substitution of the skills and ideological visions
      of management (Apple, 1982, p. 256).

6.   As teachers lose control of the curricular and pedagogic skills
      to large publishing houses, these skills are replaced by
      techniques for better controlling students (Apple, 1982, p.
      256).

7.   The particular kind of individualism we are witnessing here
      is an interesting shift from an ideology of individual auton-
      omy, where a person is his or her own boss and controls his
      or her destiny, to a careerist individualism. Here the indi-
      vidualism is geared towards organizational mobility and
      advancement by following technical rules (Apple, 1982, p.
      263).

8.   Increasing rationalization and a more sophisticated level of
      control tend to encourage people to manifest an interesting
      array of traits: a rules orientation, that is, an awareness of
      rules and procedures and a habit of following them; greater

> dependability - that is, performing a job and a relatively consistent level,...and the "internalization of the enterprise's goals and values" (Apple, 1982, pp. 263-264).

These statements do reveal that this isotopic is a major organizing factor in the Apple text. This isotopic is set up in binary opposition to a different type of pedagogy, a resistant pedagogy. Therefore, the major binary opposition in the text is set forth. The current deskilled and reskilled teacher, who is technically controlled, is set up in contrast to teachers that exist, and hopefully will exist, and who utilize various forms of resistance to this type of deskilling-reskilling phenomenon. This resistant teacher is also one that is under the deskilling-reskilling process. Apple provides us with some examples of this type.

RESISTANT PEDAGOGY

The opposing isotopic of resistance is mentioned throughout the second section of the text.

1. The fact that individual teachers like most other workers may develop patterns of resistance to these patterns of technical control or the informal cultural level alters these messages (powerful, social) (Apple, 1982, p. 269).

2. The contradictory ideologies of individualism and cooperativeness that are naturally generated out of the crowded conditions or many classrooms (you can't be an isolated individual all the time when there are twenty to thirty other prople around with whom the teacher must cope) also provide countervailing possibilities (Apple, 1982, p. 269).

3 ....just as blue- and white-collar workers have constantly found ways to retain their humanity and continually struggle to integrate conception and execution in their work (if only to relieve boredom) so too will teacher and students find ways, in the cracks so to speak, to do the same things (Apple, 1982, p. 269).

In the case of this opposition, it is the forces of technical control against the teacher who struggles to find an integration between conception and execution.

PREPACKAGED EDUCATION

The second major isotopic in "Curricular Form and the Logic of Technical Control: Building the Possessive Individual" concerns the effect of the form of educational materials used in our educational system. The prepackaged form leads, as Apple sees it, to the present educational dilemma. This isotopic is commented on frequently.

1. ...rapid growth in the use of prepackaged sets of curriculum materials. It is nearly impossible now to walk into an American classroom, for instance, without seeing boxes upon boxes of science, social studies, mathematics and reading materials ("systems" as they are sometimes called") (Apple, 1982, p. 253).

2. The material specifies all the goals. It includes everything a teacher "needs" to teach, has the pedagogical steps a teacher must take to reach these goals already built in, and has the evaluation mechanism built into it as well (Apple, 1982, p. 254).

3. The goals, the process, the outcome, and the evaluative criteria for assuring them are defined as precisely as possible by people external to the situation. In the competency measure at the end of the module, this extends to the specification of even the exact words the teacher has to say (Apple, 1982, p. 255).

This major isotopic is set up in opposition to the critical use of these prepackaged materials. The critical use of these materials is an integral part, as has been demonstrated, of a resistant pedagogy.

THE CRITICAL USE OF CURRICULUM MATERIALS

The opposing isotopic posits the possibility of making moments of opposition to the existent flood of prepackaged materials. There are many references to this concept. Again, we observe the similarities between this desired resistance and total resistant pedagogy.

1. On the other hand resistances will be there. This same teacher who disagreed with the curriculum but used it also was partially subverting it in interesting ways. It was employed only three days a week instead of five (Apple, 1982, pp. 264-265).

2. Students and teachers may also find ways of creatively using these sytems in ways undreamed of by state bureaucrats or corporate publishing. (I must admit, however, that my repeated observations in classrooms over the last years make me less than totally optimistic that this will always or even very often be the case (Apple, 1982, p. 265).

3. It is easy to forget something: that this is not a good time, ideologically or economically, for teachers who engage in overt resistances. Given a difficult ideological climate and given the employment situation among teachers today - with thousands having either been laid off or living under the threat of it - the loss of control can progress in a relatively unthreatened manner (Apple, 1982, p. 269).

These examples demonstrate teaching as deskilled, reskilled labor versus the risky business of resistant pedagogy. It leads us to view the prepackaged materials as the cause and the possible solution to this educational/curriculum dilemma. Again we see the critiqued system set up in opposition to the desired actions.

The isotopics that have been elaborated demonstrate their basic and major organizing functions and character. The isotopics are interwoven throughout the text, "Curricular Form and the Logic of Technical Control: Building the Possessive Individual". A new overarching isotopic might emerge from this analysis. This new isotopic might be The Struggle Against A Controlling System.

GENRE

When we begin to analyze the genre of "Curricular Form and the Logic of Technical Control: Building the Possessive Individual", we are as with *Sanity, Madness and the School* dealing with the formal essay, that is, the academic essay. In the case of the Apple text we are dealing with the genre both as a classificatory scheme and as generative of certain thought processes. Again, we are not told by any means the specific genre as in the conservative curriculum theory texts.

Apple's text can be classified as a formal essay or thesis. What is unique about Apple's text is that he stays within the basic parameters of the formal essay (It is a dwelling within the Bacon style of essay). There is more of a dogmatic tendency in the Apple text than in the Pinar text. It appears that rather than the intimateness, informality and gracefulness that we found in the Pinar text, the Apple text has relied more on the formal and less on the informal aspects of the genre. This is reinforced by his use of the language of struggle, which I will discuss later in this study.

To reiterate, the characteristics of the formal essay are a necessary step in this explanation of genre. They consist of: 1. a seriousness of purpose; 2. a logically organized format; and 3. the setting forth of a proposition. The first step in the explanation of this essay as a genre is to analyze Apple's text within this classificatory scheme.

The first characteristic of a formal essay-thesis is its seriousness of intention. There is a little question that Apple is posing a serious binary opposition or major isotopic. The overriding opposition speaks to a certain level of seriousness. The text is discussing the day to day work lives of teachers. The opposition is between the technically controlled and the resistant pedagogue although there is a possibility that they could be one and the same. In Apple's text the definition of serious as having dangerous or important consequences is certainly applicable. The statements and paragraphs all through the Apple text are made: not in a prescriptive, staccato style like in the conservative curriculum theory texts; not in a descriptive, adagio style like in the Pinar text; but in a conflictual style, in the langauge of struggle. The seriousness concerns the dangers of both the control and the resistance. Apple, in a conflictual and somewhat forceful style, presents his serious intention in the language of struggle.

1. I want to argue that ideologies are not only global sets of interests, things imposed on one group by another. They are embodied by our common sense meanings and practices (Williams, 1977). Thus, if you want to understand ideology at work in schools, look as much at the concreta of day to day curricular and pedagogic life as you would at the statements made by spokespersons of the State or industry (Apple, 1982, p. 242).

2. Yet, we tend to forget that this does not mean that the logics, discourses, or modes of control of capital will not have an increasing impact on everyday life in our educational institutions (Apple, 1982, p. 249).

3. We need somehow to give life to the resistances, the struggles. What I have done here is to point out the terrain within the school (the transformation of work, the deskilling and re-skilling, the technical control and so on) over which these struggles will be fought (Apple, 1982, pp.2 269-270).

These statements made by Apple are continuously made in the text. Again, as readers we are decoding within the genre and we expect to find statements of this serious nature. The writer, who is encoding within the genre, is most apt to make serious types of statements. The genre, once again, as a generative process generates the type and nature of the statements made. Apple makes these types of statements even though they are in the language of struggle. Genres appear to be generating certain types of expression and to a certain degree thoughts.

The second characteristic of the essay genre is that it contains a logical organization. In "Curricular Form and the Logic of Technical Control: Building the Possessive Individual" there is a very logical organization. It is based on the propositional nature of the formal essay. In the initial reading the organization was discussed. The following chart (4.5) demonstrates the organizational aspects of the Apple text and its relationship to this qualification of the genre.

CURRICULAR FORM AND THE LOGIC
OF TECHNICAL CONTROL: BUILDING
THE POSSESSIVE INDIVIDUAL" — STRUCTURE
CHART 4.5

I. Corporate Ideologies:Reaching the Teacher

   A. Deskilling and Reskilling

   B. Controlling Curricular Form

   C. Accepting Technical Control

   D. The Possessive Individual

II. Resistances

The organization is so logical that it is possible to outline the overall plan. The Apple text fulfills the second characteristic of the genre of formal essay.

The third characteristic of the essay genre is the traditional propostional nature. This characteristic is in evidence in the Apple text. The initial proposition is stated on the third page of the text. It is then explicated, extended and defended. There is the characteristic thesis statement and its defense. Apple even refers to the genre by name.

In this essay, I shall be particularly interested in curricular form, not curricular content. That is my focus will not be on what is actually taught, but on the manner in which it is organized. As a number of Marxist cultural analysts have argued, the working of ideology can be seen most impressively at the level of form as well as what form has in it (Apple, 1978; Jameson 1971; Williams, 1977). As I shall argue here, this is a key to uncovering the role of ideology "in" education (Apple, 1982, pp. 249-250).

The proposition is set forth in the Apple text. It is set forth in an agrumentative manner characteristic of the propositional nature of the genre. In the last section of the text entitled "Resistances" the proposition is clarified.

Yet I am not arguing for a crude kind of functionalist perspective, where everything is measured by, or is aimed toward, its ability to reproduce an existing static society. The creation of the kind of ideological hegemony "caused" by the increasing introduction of technical control is not "naturally" pre-ordained. It is something that is won or lost particular conflicts or struggles (Johnson, 1979, p. 70) (Apple, 1982, p. 264).

Apple's text contains the third characteristic of the essay genre. There is a unique aspect to Apple's treatment of the essay genre. It is the insertion of the style of struggle. That is the aspect that we turn to next.

STYLE

When we explain the aspect of style in connection with "Curricular Form and the Logic of Technical Control: Building the Possessive Individual", we are again faced with the language problematic. Apple's use of language is ultimately important when we discuss style and his text. We do not face the language of the everyday. In the conservative texts the apparently unencumbered language hid some underlying philosophical biases. In the text of a reproductionist like Apple the underlying philosophy is made quite clear.

Apple, therefore, does not use everyday langauge or as Ricoeur discusses it, ordinary language.

By ordinary language I mean that use of natural languages (English, French, German and so on) whose aim is communication and whose means are a tatic of polysemy reduction. By communication I mean the attempt to convey information from speaker to hearer concerning concrete situations of everyday life which are differently experienced by the individual members of the speech community. A certain amount of univocity is reached by specific means requiring a minimal technicity in the use of works which I call the reduction of polysemy (Reagan and Stewart, 1978, p. 127).

Ricoeur discusses speaking and hearing and I am suggesting that similar consequences occur in writing and reading. In the conservative texts what is actually, then, this ordinary language makes this minimal technicity of words, and makes the texts readily understandable. However, it may be used to cover up the philosophical bias of those texts.

The philosophical orientation of the Apple text is made quite clear from the start of the text. The emphasis is mine.

As a number of Marxist cultural analysts have agreed, the working of ideology can be seen most impressively at the level of form as well as what the form has in it (Apple 1978: Jameson 1971; Williams 1977). As I shall argue here, this is a key to uncovering the role of ideology "in" education (Apple, 1982, p. 250).

We understand the orientation of Apple in this and other texts. The philosophical style of the text is Marxist. The analysis of style must become, therefore, a determination of the stylistic of this particular reproductionist. It is the insertion of the language of struggle into the essay genre that I have explicated previously. The explanation of the style must become the explanation and analysis of the language of struggle.

First, it is interesting to look at the term struggle and its various meanings. The term struggle has several interesting meanings that are relevant to the discussion of Apple's text. They are: 1. "to offer obstinate resistance; 2. to make violent efforts to escape from restraint; 3. to make great efforts in spite of difficulties; and 4. to contest persistently" (OED), 1971, p. 3104). All of these definitions fit the language style of the Apple text. I referred to it earlier as the conflictual voice. It is a style of confrontation.

The style of this Apple text, the style of struggle, is like that of the Pinar text in one respect. It possesses that shock quality. Its style is in contrast to the everydayness of the conservative theory texts. In fact, it is their very perceptions and prescriptions that are contested. As we said with the Pinar text, the alienation of the natural is produced. It is also produced in the Apple text. However, it is accomplished in a very different way. It is produced not by an adagio gracefulness, but by the language of struggle. The language of struggle and the alienation it produces are achieved by the three major components of the style of struggle. Those components are:

1. the conflictual tone; 2. the Marxist, neo-Marxist terminology; and 3. the appeal for participation.

The conflictual tone of Apple's text is in contrast to the opaque common language of the conservative texts. It is the voice that urges resistance and contestation both of which are an integral portion of the definition of struggle. Specific references from the text will illustrate this conflictual tone. The emphasis is mine.

1. Yet these internal conditions need not preclude teachers from also making these commodified cultural from their own, to generate their own *creative responses to dominant ideologies,* in a manner similar to what the counter-cultural groups studied by Marxist ethnographers have done to commodified culture. These groups transformed and reinterpreted the products they bought and use so that they become tools for the creation of alternative pockets of resistance (Apple, 1982, p. 265).

2. On the other hand, *resistance will be there.* This same teacher who disagreed with the curriculum but used it, also *was partially subverting it in interesting ways* (Apple, 1982, p. 264).

3. One would expect *resistances to ideological practices* I have discussed in this essay on the part of students as well as teachers, *resistances that may be specific by race, gender and class* (Apple, 1982, p. 267).

4. The formation of ideologies - even those of the kind of individualism I have examined in this essay - is not a simple act of imposition. It is produced by concrete actors and embodied in lived experiences that may *resist, alter or mediate these social messages* (Johnson 1978) (Apple, 1982, p. 267).

Another characteristic of the langauge of struggle is the terminology used by the author of the text. This terminology reinforces both the language of struggle and the alienation of the natural. Thus, the Apple text does not use everyday terminology as the conservative curriculum theory texts do, but it uses the language of Marxist analysis. This terminology, rather than covering up the philosophical bases of the text, reveals that basis. The terminology is pervasive in the text. The examples below are illustrative of this fact. The terminology is, of course, an integral part of the style/language of struggle. I have highlighted the terms.

1.   For as I shall argue here, some of the *ideological* and *material* influences of our kind of *social formation* on teachers and students are not most importantly found at the levels of these documents or plans (Apple, 1982, p. 247).

2.   As I shall argue here, this is the key to *uncovering the role of ideology "in" education* (Apple, 1982, p. 250).

3.   In order to understand part of what is occurring in the school and *the ideological and economic pressures* being placed upon it, we need to situate it within certain long term trends in the capital accumulation process (Apple, 1982, p. 250).

4.   For just as the everyday discourse and patterns of interaction in the family and in say, the media are increasingly being subtly *transformed by the logic and contradictions of dominant ideologies* (Gitlin 1979), so to is the school, a site where these *subtle ideological transformations occur* (Apple, 1982, p. 253).

5.   All of these conditions do not mean that schools are immune or autnomous from *the logic of capital*. The logic will be mediated (in part due to the school as a *state apparatus*); it will enter where it can in partial; distorted or coded ways (Apple, 1982, p. 255).

The final aspect of the style of the Apple text that requires explanation is its call for action both collective and individual. This is certainly consistent with both the conflictual tone and Marxist terminology. It is also consistent with the several definitions of struggle and their emphasis on persistent contestation. In fact, they are all rather inseparable. It is not the Paideia Group issuing edicts for educators to follow, but the theorist calling for collective or individual resistance to the imposed curriculum. It is a call, in

Marxist terminology, for praxis.

Regardless of whether collective or individual resistances are possible, the text uses plural pronous and nouns to advocate this resistance. The sense is of a group. Even though resistances may be on the individual level, there is a sense that there may be many individuals. The call for resistance is in evidence in many places in the text. A few examples can serve as an illustration.

1. Take teachers for example. While technical controls could possibly lead to unionization within the school most resistances will be, by necessity, on an individual not a collective level (Apple, 1982, p. 267).

2. ...hegemony is always contested. Our own work should help in this contestation (Apple, 1982, p. 269).

3. So too will teachers and students find ways, in the cracks so to speak, to do the same things (resistances) (Apple, 1982, p. 269).

The style of this Apple text is defined as the language of struggle. It has been demonstrated that it is a crucial aspect of this text. It is a style that facilitates critical thought about our educational system. It is a style that shocks us and causes us to return to our educational system with our views in many cases altered.

TEXT WORLD

When we begin to discuss the possible worlds of the text in connection with reconceptualist and reproductionist texts, the recognition of the "not-I" and its consequent illumination of the existent-I becomes, for this writer, much more difficult. In the case of the conservative theory texts it was through the recognition of the "not-I" of the possible text worlds, and my reflection on the disparity between the "not-I" of the text world and the appearance of that to the self, that I was able to further distinguish the existent-I. In the case of the reconceptualist and reproductionist texts, there is some recognition of the "not-I". This recognition, however, is much more difficult to reach. This is the result of several factors specific to each text. I will explain these factors later in the study.

The reconceptualist and reproductionist texts critique the present educational system. In fact it is their major point of emphasis. They also, as a result of this critique, project a possible world for a potential-I to inhabit. The remainder of this study on reconceptualist and reproductionist texts, like the analysis of the conservative texts, will concentrate on the discussion of those possible worlds. More importantly, however, the study will focus on the fusion of horizons between the possible worlds of the texts and the sense of the world of the potential-I.

The problem with the reconceptualist and reproductionist texts is the process of finding the world of the potential-I in moments of fusion with the worlds of the texts. This is a different process from the understanding of self with the conservative texts. This process involves more reflexsive participation to get to the "I". How does one fuse with the other (in this case the text world) and at the same time, in essence, refuse the other? It becomes, to a certain extent, a process of relocating, after the fusion, the specificity of one's own voice that is evident in the Pinar and Apple texts. It is the problem with which I started this journey. This finding of the potential-I leads to some forms(s) of agency that is discovered through and in the potential-I. In other words it becomes a gaining of a sense of self, who can act in the world with his own voice. This is the major focus of the entire study. With these curriculum theory texts this agency is not in the theoretical space, but action must have a specificity and that specificity of action (agency) with one's own voice is what this "new" hermeneutic leads one to. In the conservative texts, with their prescriptive nature, we had a world that was "not-I". It allowed for a clearer picture of the existent-I. The possible world of the conservative texts was a world where the potential-I found no dwelling place. The worlds of the conservative texts were much easier to discuss because fusion with these texts was not a problem.

There is an interesting paradox to this comparison of the conservative theory texts and the reconceptualist and reproductionist texts. The paradox involves the very different worlds of these texts and their presentation and organization. It has been demonstrated that, although these texts, their worlds and their language are unlike in nature, the very organization of presentation is quite similar.

Organization is centered upon binary oppositions. The major iso-topics of all the texts are set up in binary oppositions. In all cases a set of positive isotopics is posed in opposition to a set of negative isotopics. How do such diverse worlds and consequences come from such similar reasoning? Is part of the difficulty with the texts of Pinar and Apple their use of this type of reasoning? Would a different mode of presentation or form facilitate this discovery of the potential-I and the consequent result of agency. Is this the space to which this hermeneutic points? These are important questions that need a suggested resolution. They will be discussed in this section of the study.

The discussion of the text worlds in this particular investigation becomes a discussion of all of these problems and possibilities. The text worlds of the Pinar and Apple texts each present a unique set of problems. Therefore, it is necessary to deal with each of them separately.

SANITY, MADNESS AND THE SCHOOL

When I reflect upon this Pinar text and attempt to distinguish the "not-I" of this text world, I encounter a number of problems. The primary problematic is the difficulty in recognizing and delineating the "not-I" aspects of the Pinar text. There are several reasons for this difficulty. I would like to elaborate on them.

The first reason for the difficulty in delineating aspects of the "not-I" in the Pinar text centers on the mentor-student relationship between myself and William Pinar. It is very difficult for a student, no matter how open or nonthreatening this relationship is, to question or oppose concepts that his mentor has established. In my particular case there has been the desire to play it safe and simply parrot or reproduce the work of my mentor. In order to do this I would have to agree with everything that he proposed. This type of work (the simple reproduction of Pinar's work) is not in one's own voice. Therefore, it produces little individual agency. If one begins to reflect on the work of their mentor and through that reflection begins to see the "not-I" within it, then one initiates work that speaks with its own voice. This does not preclude, however, common projects with the mentor because one has established a clearer sense of his own intentions and, therefore, can identify those common projects. It is, nonetheless, a difficult problem to overcome. But, it must be overcome. Nietzsche stated in Thus Spoke *Zarathustra: A Book for Everyone and No One* that "one repays a teacher badly if one remains only a pupil" (Nietzsche, 1961, p. 103). This hermeneutic method has helped this writer to carefully read and explain his mentor's work and, thereby, find moments of "not-I" within the text world.

The second problem which causes difficulties in determining the "not-I" is the style of adagio gracefulness in the Pinar text. The style of adagio with its penetration of the informal into the formal diminishes and blurs the distance between the reader and the self. It also blurs the ground of the relationship to Pinar's argument. This blurring results from many factors which are important to discuss. Perhaps the best way to express the difficulties that the adagio style poses is to say that is is difficult to find a potential-I when one is dancing in adagio. The reader is swept up in the style and pace of the text. Its personal and direct address allows the reader to lose himself. The reader is situated by the voice of the writer. The dancing metaphor is apt because the relationship with the text becomes quite similar to the relationship of two dancers. When we are dancing, we can lose ourselves to the music. Sometimes we are even surprised when the music ends. The method of direct address in the Pinar text is an invitation to dance with the text. In the particular case of *Sanity, Madness and the School* the ideas or the writer's argument becomes blurred in the informal presentation so that the fusion with the text is so strong it is very difficult to refuse the invitation. The text is so flexible with its lack of prescription that the "not-I" becomes, at the point of initial reading and even at the point of the explanation, very difficult to see. We are, therefore, faced with a paradox. The most open text and reading experience leads, at the surface level, to the least sense of the reader's own voice and agency. However, this hermeneutic reading process with its reflective moment allows the reader to, after the dance as it were, assess the fusion and to analyze lack of the "not-I". It allows the reader to refuse in fusion and expand in the dispossession. Ricoeur's discussion of the role of the subject in appropriation bears reiteration within our discussion of fusion. The emphasis is mine.

> I say that interpretation is the process by which disclosure of new modes of being - or if you prefer Wittengenstein to Heidegger, of new forms of life - gives to the subject a new capacity of knowing himself. If the reference of the text is the projection of a world, then it is not the reader who primarily projects himself. The reader rather is enlarged in his capacity of self-projection by receiving a new mode of being from the text itself. Appropriation, in this way, *ceases to appear as a kind of possession, as a way of taking hold of things; instead it implies a moment of dispossession of the egoistic and narcissitic ego* (Ricoeur, 1974, p. 94).

This type of appropriation (dispossessive) is the type of appropriation that causes the difficulties I have been discussing. A text, in this case the reconceptualist and reproductionist texts, enlarge our capacity of self-projection. This is what I have been calling the potential-I. This study then concentrates on these texts and their ability to project new avenues for the potential-I. Without the reflective moment in this hermeneutic process, the moment of the "dispossession of the egoistic and narcissitic ego" (Ricoeur, 1974, p. 94), this projection of possible avenues would remain unnoticed. The process would then degenerate into a quest for appropriation as possession alone. The question is clarified. How does the reader avoid this possessive type of search with texts where there are several moments of fusion? The answer revolves around the hermeneutic reading that has been pursued in this study. It is one way that attempts to deal with such a problem.

This hermeneutic reading also permits the recognition that the binary opposition set up in the Pinar and Apple texts are similar to the binary set up in the conservative texts. This awareness would lead to a sense of agency that would permit the reader to write his own theoretical texts using a different method of organization. Since the conservative, reconceptualist and reproductionist texts project very different worlds, then the organizational presentation of these worlds should be different. They are not. This can be reflected upon within two perspectives. The first perspective would indicate that the organization is generative of thought and, therefore, it is little wonder these reconceptualists and reproductionist texts present problems. Their message is ultimately different than the conservative texts, yet it is presented in the same organizational way. A second perspective, one which I think is closer to being correct, would indicate that the organization is the same. However, that is the point for creativity within these texts. It is the point of the insertion of the style of adagio gracefulness or the language of struggle. It appears, upon reflection, that both texts use the standard organizational technique but manage to subvert it in important ways. Whereas the conservative texts use the binary oppositions to criticize the present system on the one pole, they set up their prescriptions for success on the opposite pole. This makes finding the "not-I" relatively easy. Reconceptualist and reproductionist texts proceed quite differently within the same matrix. Both texts organize their critiques as one of the bi-polar opposites. The other pole is not a set of prescriptions. It is the point of entry for suggestions, in the case of the Pinar text, and for the overall method of direct address and adagio style. It is the point, in the case of the Apple text, for the language of struggle and its suggestions. This manipulation of binary oppositions compounds the difficulty of the process of the identification of the "not-I". The binary set up of these texts then is an additional problem for the Pinar and Apple texts. The recognition of similarities between the Pinar text and the text of the conservatives enables one to question that organizational method and possibly use another method to write his own texts. It might also lead the reader to develop his own method/voice to insert within this oppositional organization. It would not be the same as the adagio gracefulness or the language of struggle. However, it would attempt to manipulate this organizational form toward one's own project. This reflection, on the similarity among the organizational strategies of the representative curriculum theory texts, has led to a sense of agency for this writer. A sense of specificity for the potential-I and its agency.

The problems that cause difficulties in finding the "not-I" have been discussed. They are not insurmountable difficulties. But they must be addressed in order to begin to reflect on the "not-I" that is in the Pinar text. This reflection upon the difficulty in finding the "not-I" has also aided in the understanding of the Pinar text. It is now possible, after recognizing the fact that there is the potential to lose one's voice in the text, to find these "not-I" characteristics.

The "not-I" characteristics in the world of the Pinar text allow for refusal within the larger context of fusion. There are bascially two major "not-I" characteristics in the projected world of *Sanity, Madness and the School*. The properties of these "not-I" characteristics are very different from the "not-I" characteristics of the conservative texts. In the Pinar text there are no prescriptions. The reader must reflect upon the fusion closely to uncover and recover these "not-I" properties. After that process, I find two points of "not-I"ness in the Pinar text which blend into each other. It allows the reader the ability to avoid becoming another Pinar and reflect on the potential-I.

The first point of the "not-I" is the extremity or the degree to which Pinar states his case. Although it is very easy for the reader to get swept up in this extremity, it is a point of the "not-I". I can begin to refuse within an overall fusion. Pinar's critique of the present educational system states that the end result of schooling is "devastating". "We graduate, credentialed but crazed, erudite but fragmented shells of human possibility" (Pinar, 1976, p. 28). Pinar also states that students and teachers are "not themselves: quite literally, they are out of their minds; they are mad (Pinar, 1976, p. 7). In this text the term madness is equated with de-humanization and one-dimensionality. The definition of madness is based on humanistic psychology particularly that of R. D. Laing. Therefore, Pinar must oppose this definition with a definition of sanity composed from the same basic source. This demonstrates an interesting point. There appears to be levels of "not-I"ness. This extreme point, proposing that education is toward madness, leads or propels a reflection concerning the level of "not-I" in the projected world.

The "not-I" in the extreme position is that I do not consider de-humanization and madness, synonymous. Madness connotes closure, a condition that only professional consultation can assist in any real way. Mad is defined as "implying violent excitement or extravagant delusions; maniacal, frenzied' (OED, 1971, p. 1688). The process of schooling does lead to de-humanization. But, whether these de-humanized students and teachers are mad is certainly a point that is debatable. A point of "not-I"ness. I have certainly witnessed the twelve effects of schooling, that Pinar elaborates on, in students and in myself. Is this madness? For the sake of reflection, let us accept the connection between de-humanization and madness. What possible or projected world does this lead to?

The projected world of the Pinar text is a world that emphasizes becoming more authentic, self-actualized with a heightened consciousness. Its suggested plan is the development of these possibilities through the use of a "humanities ambience". The projected world advocates developing, through work in solitude and work with others, the movement toward authenticity or the process of becoming. Much of this potential world is based upon the concepts of Abraham Maslow in *Toward a Psychology of Being* and *Challenges of Humanistic Psychology*. It also receives support in the works of Carl Rogers specifically: *On Becoming a Person* and *Carl Rogers on Encounter Groups*. The concept of self-actualization expressed by Maslow and the concept of becoming or actualizing expressed by Rogers are the "not-I" portion of the projected world. This process of self-actualization is not the hermeneutical process of self-understanding. As we have demonstrated our self-understanding, in hermeneutic theory, is mediated by cultural objects such as texts. It is through the understanding (initial reading, explanation and reflection) upon those objects that our self-understanding is enlarged and then is a fusion between the horizons of possibility in the text and the horizon of the potential-I. Ricoeur discusses this in *Interpretation Theory: Discourse and the Surplus of Meaning*.

> Only interpretation that complies with the injunction of the texts, that follows the "arrow" of the sense and that tries to think accordingly, initiates a new self-understanding. In this self-understanding, I would oppose the self, which proceeds from the understanding of the text, to the ego, which claims to proceed it. It is the text, with its universal power of world disclosure, which gives a self to the ego (Ricoeur, 1974, pp. 94-95).

This is very different from the self-actualization process of Maslow as described by Pinar in *Sanity, Madness and the School*.

All of these he (Maslow) suggests, are steps toward the actualization of self; the person will come to learn what is constitutionally right for him. He will come to know who he is. One cannot choose wisely for life unless he dares listen to himself, his own self (Pinar, 1976, p. 55).

Pinar also defines Roger's views of the self-actualization process. It is quite similar to the process Maslow discusses.

Carl Rogers presents a view which is in basic agreement with Maslow's. Rogers argues that intrinsic to man is a tendency to actualize himself. Within a human being is the urge to expand, extend, develop, mature; within him is the tendency to express and actualize all the capacities of his organism (Pinar, 1976, p. 55).

The basic "not-I" of this humanistic psychological view is that, it proposes a type of "possession or a way of taking hold of things" (Ricoeur, 1974, p. 94). The hermeneutic process proposes a dispossession of the ego. This difference between possession and dispossession is an important "not-I" portion of the projected text world. To summarize the basic "not-I" of the Pinar text are the extreme stands on schools producing madness and humanistic psychology's view of the self and self-understanding.

Despite these crucial "not-I" qualities, which enable me to better understand the voice in which I am speaking, the Pinar text's vision or projected world is large enough so that I can find a source for individual agency. At the same time I can find some sense of a collective voice that I can join. In other words, the projected world of the Pinar text is a world where the potential-I can find moments for dwelling. Yet the road to that projected world for me is not the exact same road as the one which Pinar travels. Pinar's road and my road are moving toward a similar potential world, but the roads to that world are not the same. They may, indeed, intersect at points and have some commonality. Hopefully that stems from the broadness of the vision of each road. My potential-I, therefore, is put into motion through the reflection upon the Pinar text. The sense of agency is arrived at also. By the realization of my intention(s) or having gained, through the process of dispossession, a sense of my own intentions, I have a sense of self who can act independently and jointly in the world with a voice that is my own. Ironically, near the end of this study, when the desire is for closure the process has lead to a point that may be only a beginning. Now I also have, after doing this hermeneutic process, a specificity for action. This is an essential element because no one acts in general. Consequently, in the dispossession process of differentiating myself from the Pinar text, one finds a sense of the potential-I and a sense of agency. Admittedly this was difficult to achieve and I was even reluctant to go about this process.

The specificity of agency/action is to work independently and collectively with those of broad vision like Pinar to, in fact, make education and our society not a dungeon or a reformed or revised dungeon, but a process of liberation. This reading of Pinar's text has exhibited then a fusion/refusal of possible worlds and roads to those worlds of the text and the sense of the world of the potential-I. In so doing it has enabled a sense of agency.

"CURRICULAR FORM AND THE LOGIC OF TECHNICAL CONTROL: BUILDING THE POSSESSIVE INDIVIDUAL"

With Apple's text the "not-I" is much easier to elucidate. Apple's text also projects a potential world. The possible world of freedom and justice. An educational world where teachers choose freely what they teach, and an educational world where the teacher's conception and execution are closely integrated, is the projected world of the Apple text. As in the Pinar text the possible world is one where the potential-I finds comfortable dwelling spots. It is a world that the potential-I with its sense of agency could work toward. Just as the reader can get caught dancing in adagio, he can get swept up in any text that has a strong sense of agency and that moves toward possible worlds that the potential-I could inhabit. Without a reflective moment it is easy to get caught up in a form that, upon further reflection, we realize is "not-I". There is in the Apple text a somewhat more radical sense of contrast than was evident in the Pinar text.

To return to the road metaphor, Apple is, I think, traveling toward a similar destination to Pinar and this writer. The "not-I" becomes then the road Apple chooses to travel along. Just as Pinar's road in *Sanity, Madness and the School* was upon reflection a different road than mine, so too is Apple's road.

This sense of the "not-I" comes from the sense of struggle and confrontation in the potential world of the Apple text. This sense of struggle which was discussed in the explanation of Apple's text rests the potential-I at the moment of critique and resistance. The projected world is one of confrontation and conflict toward a goal of liberation. Although the world of liberation is a worthy world-goal, this is a path where the potential-I finds little place to comfortably travel. It is ironic that in a text that most directly calls for specific action, the sense of individual agency is somewhat limited. My potential agency is not Apple's sense of agency. Upon reflection it seems that in the ways Apple calls for resistances, he is being somewhat prescriptive. This may explain the ease with which I can find the "not-I".

> The real question is not whether such resistances exist...Our task is to find them. We need somehow to give life to the resistances, the struggles...hegemony is always contested. Our own work should help in this contestation (Apple, 1982, pp. 269-270).

The world of resistances and struggle would be somewhat lacking if those who are participating in the contestation are not clear in their own sense of agency. If those who are doing the contesting are resisting in Apple's voice and not their own voice, then the struggle amounts to a parroting of Apple's strong sense of agency and various impressions of it.

Apple calls for this individual agency which we have seen is, perhaps, ultimately important and in my case allows me momentarily to be caught up in his text. At the same time there is an ommission in his road. There is a question left unanswered. How does the individual teacher obtain a sense of agency from which to carry on the struggle? In certain cases it may be possible by just reading texts like Apple's that allow the reader to get carried away with his plan for struggle. But, that somewhat uninformed action is "not-I". Quite seriously, I am convinced it is not the ideal world or path that Apple envisions. This establishes, once again, the necessity for a hermeneutic reading. The reader must venture beyond the initial reading at which point he can become pulled in by a strong undertow of style and voice. He, with this hermeneutic, can pursue an explanation and a reflection upon the texts he initially reads. A moment of comprehension and understanding may be achieved.

The "not-I" of this form of the Apple text clarifies the sense of the potential-I. In the Pinar text the clarification came after a dispossession in fusion with the text. With the Apple text the dispossession was not as difficult to determine. The style of confrontation was not as successful in luring me in as was the adagio style. The "not-I" was readily apparent. But, we have a different phenomenon with the Apple text. In the conservative theory texts with their prescriptive nature, it was easy to find the "not-I" also. I do not equate the Apple text with the conservative theory texts.

I referred to the point that the sense of one's agency is limited in the Apple text. It is limited, but it still exists and certainly to a greater extent than in the conservative texts. Apple's vision is wide enough for me to find a sense of my own agency. I can listen to Apple's text and realize that what it is saying about schools and teachers is true to my lived experiences. We must, indeed, attempt to change the schools from the dungeons that they are. Yet, after reflecting upon the Apple text, I have come to realize an important point as I did with the Pinar text. Unless we carefully read, explain and reflect on these texts and situations and through that process come to a sense of our own voice, to a sense of agency, then our writings, efforts and attempts to free the inmates from the impositions of the dungeon might well stay in the theoretical space and not move toward action.

In a small way this study has shown me a road upon which to continue my journey. It is not Pinar's road. It is not Apple's road. It is my own road. The agency will be to try to provide readers with a way to find their own voices and senses of agency in a world that is against such labors. The risk of such agency is evident. But, I believe the work is worth the risk.

Afterword

This is the completion of one phase of my journey. I feel much like the character St. John at the closing pages of the Voyage Out.

> He was terribly tired, and the light and warmth, the movements of the hands, and the soft communicative voices soothed him; they gave him a strange sense of quiet and relief. As he sat there, motionless, the feeling of relief became a feeling of profound happiness (Woolf, 1925, p. 325).

As I conclude this study of curriculum theory and the hermeneutical reading process, a few comments are necessary. I would like to discuss three aspects I feel to be important. First, I will review the contents of the study. Second, I will discuss the possibilities for further applications of this hermeneutic reading. Finally, I will make some closing comments.

This study was the application of Paul Ricoeur's hermeneutical phenomenology to the texts of curriculum theory. The first chapter of the study dealt with the journey of readings that brought me to the work of Paul Ricoeur. The second chapter discussed the life, philosophy and hermeneutic theory of Paul Ricoeur. The third chapter was the application of this hermeneutic reading to the texts of conservative curriculum theory texts. The texts included: *The Paideia Proposal: An Educational Manifesto, Paideia Problems and Possibilities* and *A Nation at Risk: The Imperative for Educational Reform*. It was comprised of: an initial reading; a structural analysis of the composition, genre, and style of each text; and the existential discussion of possible worlds of the text and their facilitation of self understanding.

The fourth chapter was an application of this same hermeneutic reading to the texts of reconceptualist and reproductionist curriculum theory. The texts included were: *Sanity, Madness and the School* and "Curricular Form and the Logic of Technical Control: Building the Possessive Individual". The same hermeneutic reading was applied to these texts.

The ultimate aim of this hermeneutic process was increased self-understanding. Ricoeur mentions this in his essay, "Metaphor and the Main Problem of Hermeneutics".

Allow me to conclude in a way which would be consistent with a theory of interpretation which lays the stress on "opening up a world". Our conclusion should also "open up" some new vistas. On what? Maybe on the old problem of imagination, which I cautiously put aside. We are prepared to inquire into the power of imagination, no longer as a faculty of deriving "images" from a sensory experiences, but as the capacity to let new worlds build our self-understanding...(Reagan and Steward, 1978, p. 148).

This aim was achieved in the chapters where the hermeneutic reading was applied. The ultimate goal of the process was achieved. The process has reached the point that Ricoeur discusses earlier in the same essay.

I would say that interpretation is the process by which the disclosure of new modes of being - or, if you prefer Wittgenstein to Heidegger, new "forms of life" - gives to the subject a new capacity of knowing himself. If there is somewhere a project and a projection, it is the reference of the work which is a projection of a world; the reader is consequently enlarged in his capacity of self-projection by receiving a new mode of being from the text itself (Reagan and Stewart, 1978, p. 145).

The journey toward an improved self-understanding was successful for this writer. Since that is the case, then there are some interesting possibilities to discuss. Possibilities for further use of the hermeneutic reading developed in this study.

APPLICATIONS FOR THE HERMENEUTIC READING

There exists possibilities for the future use of this hermeneutic reading by this writer and possibly other writers as well. There are at least two areas where this type of study might, indeed, be somewhat useful.

The first area is quite obviously further hermeneutic readings of other texts in the fields of curriculum theory. There are many areas in curriculum theory and educational theory that this particular study has not touched on at all. Hermeneutic readings of conceptual-empiricist theory could be very enlightening. Some of the most

recent areas of curriculum theory could be read within this hermeneutic. Areas such as: feminist curriculum theory, structuralist
curriculum theory, post-structuralist curriculum theory or other
areas with the rubric of reconceptualist, reproductionist or critical
curriculum theory could be read within a hermeneutic viewpoint.
The works of Aoki, Apple, Daignault, Eisner, Giroux, Grumet, Pinar,
Macdonald and others could be hermeneutically read. The ultimate
aim being the existential dwelling within the posited worlds of the
texts toward an improved sense of the "I".

Another area of readings could be in the area of the actual
materials that are presented to classroom practitioners in in-service
workshops or district training seminars. A concrete example might
be the hermeneutic reading of Madeline Hunter's "effective teaching steps" materials that are being widely distributed and used in
school districts across the nation. This is one area I hope to pursue
myself in the near future.

The list of texts that this reading can be applied to seems somewhat endless. It might be wise, for all of us as human beings
attempting to understand ourselves and the world around us, to
approach all the texts we read in this manner. It is a rigorous process
and requires much time and commitment, but the results just may be
worth the effort.

However, I do not think this hermeneutical reading must be
applied to texts (books or articles) alone. There are possibilities to
treat other types of educational phenomenon as texts. Classroom
teachers or observers might take a class period or several periods as
a text and apply this hermeneutic reading to the class as text. It might
be possible, therefore, for ethnographers to apply this hermeneutic
to the transcripts and observations the collect. Not only would this
facilitate the understanding of the observed events, but work toward a greater self-understanding as well.

This study has also discussed the importance of language and its
various uses. Ricoeur, in "Creativity in Language", divides language into basically three types. They are: common language,
scientific langauge and poetic language (metaphor). The study of
metaphor and metaphoric langauge and its application to curriculum theory texts poses some further interesting paths of investiga-

tion. The metaphoric language by its very nature is quite facilitative of the referential nature of texts. Perhaps, the use of metaphoric language in curriculum theory texts would indeed facilitate the positing of alternative/possible worlds. Since these "stories" would be more readily understandable, it might also widen the audience for theoretical work. It is not within the parameters of this study to discuss curriculum theory written as poetry, fable or parable, however, it is an interesting direction that this type of study could precipitate. Metaphor was used in this study to enhance understanding. The use of metaphoric language in theoretical texts provides another interesting path for this type of research to take. Again, this is an area that needs further work.

The specifics of all these possibilities would of necessity have to be worked out idiosyncratically. The possibilities are there. It is up to individuals to apply them. The results might well be very interesting and very revealing. They would certainly, in this writer's opinion, be worthwhile. I am convinced there are also other possibilities. I hope that this study will bring more of those to light. It is a new area where much can be done. The question is whether we think self-understanding is worth the effort. I believe it is.

Again, these are only possibilities and directions where this study could eventually lead. These are also possibilities for paths along my own journey. For me they are ultimately important and so I will no doubt travel down some of those "roads not taken". I leave this part of my journey and move on with the same words with which I began. I look forward to the possible paths that lie ahead.

The voyage had begun, and had begun happily with a soft blue sky, and a calm sea. The sense of untapped resources, things to say as yet unsaid, made the hour significant...(Woolf, 1925, p. 24).

Bibliography

Adler, M.J. (1983). *Paideia problems and possibilities*. New York: Macmillan Publishing.

Adler, M. J. (1982). The paideia proposal. New York: Macmillan Publishing.

Anyon, J. (1979). Ideology and Unites States history textbooks. *Harvard Educational Review, 49* (3): 361-386.

Apple, M. W. (Ed.) (1981). *Cultural and economic reproduction in education*. London: Routledge and Kegan Paul Ltd.

Apple, M. W. (1982). *Education and power*. London: Routledge and Kegan Paul Ltd.

Apple, M. W. (1979). *Ideology and curriculum*. London: Routledge and Kegan Paul Ltd.

Aronowitz, S. (1981). Politics and higher education in the 1980's. In H. A. Giroux, A. N. Penna & W. F. Pinar (Eds.), *Curriculum and instruction: Alternatives in education* (pp. 455-465). Berkeley: McCutchan Publishing Corporation.

Atkinson, M. (1972). A precise phenomenology for the general scholar. *Journal of General Education, 23*, 261-297.

Austin, J. L. (1962). *How to do things with words*. Oxford: Claredon Press.

Barthes, R. (1972). *Mythologies*. New York: Hill and Wang.

Barthes, R. (1975). *The pleasure of the text*. New York: Hill and Wang.

Barthes, R. (1977). *Roland Barthes*. New York: Hill and Wang.

Benveniste, E. (1971). *Problems in general linguistics*. Mary Elizabeth Meek, Trans.) Coral Gables: The University of Miami Press.

Berstein, R. J. (1976). *The restructuring of social and political theory*. New York: Harcourt Brace Jovanovich.

Bestor, A. (1953). *Educational wastelands: The retreat from learning in our public schools*. Urbana: University of Illinois Press).

Bleicher, J. (1980). *Contemporary hermeneutics: Hermeneutics as method, philosophy, and critique*. Boston: Routledge and Kegan Paul Ltd.

Bourgeois, P. (1973). *Extension of Ricoeur's hermeneutic*. The Hague: Martinus Nijhoff.

Bowles, S., & Ginitis, H. (1976). *Schooling in capitalist America: Educational reform and the contradictions of economic life*. New York: Basic Books.

Brown, N. O. (1970). *Life against death: The psychoanalytic meaning of history*. London: Sphere Books Ltd.

Brown, R. (1973). *Knowledge, education, and cultural change: Papers in the sociology of education*. London: Tavistock Publications Ltd.

Cawelti, J. (1976). *Adventure, mystery, and romance: Formula stories as art and popular culture*. Chicago: University of Chicago Press.

Culler, J. (1982). *On deconstruction: Theory and criticism after structuralism*. Ithaca: Cornell University Press.

Culler, J. (1981). *The pursuit of signs: Semiotics, literature, deconstruction*. Ithaca: Cornell University Press.

Culler, J. (1981). *Structuralist poetics: Structuralism, linguistics, and the study of literature*. Ithaca: Cornell University Press.

Daignault, J. (1983, October). *Analogy in education: An archeology without subsoil*. Paper presented at the fifth conference of *The Journal of Curriculum Theorizing*, Dayton, Ohio.

Daignault, J. (1984, October). *Curriculum beyond words, with words*. Paper presented at the sixth conference of *The Journal of Curriculum Theorizing*, Dayton, Ohio.

Daignault, J., & Gauthier, C. (1982). The indecent curriculum machine. *The Journal of Curriculum Theorizing, 4* (2), 177-197.

Daignault, J. (1982, October). *To make someone know as we make someone laugh: A perverse analysis of promise and desire in curriculum*. Paper presented at the fourth conference of *The Journal of Curriculum Theorizing*, Airlie, Virginia.

Derrida, J. (1982). *Margins of philosophy*. (Alan Bass, Trans.). Chicago: University of Chicago Press.

Derrida, J. (1976). *Of grammatology*. (Gayatri Chakravorty Spivak, Trans.). Baltimore: The Johns Hopkins University Press.

Derrida, J. (1978). *Writing and difference*. (Alan Bass, Trans.). Chicago: University of Chicago Press.

Descombes, V. (1980). *Modern french philosophy*. (L. Scott-Fox & J. M. Harding, Trans.). New York: Cambridge University Press.

Dickens, C. (1977). *Bleak house*. New York: W. W. Norton and Company.

Dickens, C. (1965). *Great expectations*. New York: Penguin Books.

Eagleton, T. (1976). *Criticism and ideology*. London: Verso Editions.

Eagleton, T. (1983). *Literary theory: An introduction*. Minneapolis: University of Minnesota Press.

Eagleton, T. (1976). *Marxism and literary criticism*. Los Angeles: University of California Press.

Earle, W. (1972). *The autobiographical consciousness: A philosophical inquiry into existence*. Chicago: Quadrangle Books.

Eco, U. (1983). *The name of the rose*. New York: Harcourt Brace Jovanovich.

Eco, U. (1984). *Semiotics and the philosophy of language*. Bloomington: Indiana University Press.

Fitzgerald, F. (1980). *America revised: History schoolbooks in the 20th century*. New York: Vantage Books.

Foucault, M. (1970). *The order of things: An archaeology of the human sciences*. New York: Vantage Books.

Foucault, M. (1972). *The archeology of knowledge and the discourse on language*. New York: Tavistock Publication Limited.

Foucault, M. (1973). *The birth of the clinic: An archaeology of the medical perception*. New York: Random House.

Foucault, M. (1973). *Madness and civilization: A history of insanity in the age of reason*. New York: Randon House.

Foucault, M. (1978). *Discipline and punish: the birth of the prison*. New York: Random House.

Foucault, M. (1978). *The history of sexuality*. (Vol. 1). New York: Random House.

Frankfort Institute for Social Research. (Eds.). (1973). *Aspects of sociology*. Boston: Beacon Press.

Frege, G. (1952). On sense and reference. *Philosophical Writings of Gottlob Frege* (Max Black & Peter Geach, Trans.). Oxford: Blackwell.

Freire, P. (1981). *Pedagogy of the oppressed* (B. Ramos, Trans.). New York: Continuum. (Original work published 1968)

Freud, S. (1960). *The ego and the id* (J. Riviera, Trans.). New York: W. W. Norton and Company. (Original work published 1923)

Freud, S. (1965). *The interpretation of dreams* (J. Strachey, Trans.). New York: Avon Books.

Frye, N. (1973). *Anatomy of criticism: Four essays*. Princeton University Press.

Gadamer, H. G. (1975) *Truth and method*. New York: Crossroad Publishing.

Geertz, C. (1973). *The interpretation of cultures.* New York: Basic Books.

Gerhart, M. (1979). *The question of belief in literary criticism: An introduction the the hermeneutical theory of Paul Ricoeur.* Stuttgart: Akademischer Verlag Hans-Dieter Heinz.

Giddens, A. (1979). *Central problems in social theory: Action, structure, and contradiction in social analysis.* Berkeley: University of California Press.

Giroux, H. A., Penna, A. N., & Pinar, W. F. (Eds.). *Curriculum and instruction: Alternatives in education.* Berkeley: McCutchan Publishing Corporation.

Giroux, H. A. & Purpel, D. (Eds.). (1983). *The hidden curriculum and moral education: Deception or discovery.* Berkeley: McCutchan Publishing Corporation.

Giroux, H. A. (1981). *Ideology, culture, and the process of schooling.* Philadelphia: Temple University Press.

Giroux, H. A. (1983). *Theory, and resistance in education: A pedagogy for the opposition.* New York: J. F. Bergin.

Greene, M. (1978). *Landscapes of learning.* New York: Teacher's College Press.

Gress, J. R. & Purpel, D. (Eds.). (1978). *Curriculum: an introduction to the field.* Berkeley: McCutchan Publishing Corporation.

Grotowski, J. (1968). *Towards a poor theater.* New York: Simon and Schuester.

Grumet, M. (1983). The line is drawn. *Educational Leadership, 40(4),* 28-38.

Grumet, M. (1983). Response to Stet and Wanowski. *The Journal of Curriculum Theorizing, 5(2)* 124-128.

Hall, C. (1979). *A primer of Freudian psychology.* New York: New American Library.

Heidegger, M. (1962). *Being and time* (J. Macquarrie & E. Robinsin, Trans.). New York: Harper and Row Publishers.

Hoy, D. C. (1978). *The critical circle: Literature, history, and philosophical hermeneutics.* Berkeley: University of California Press.

Hutchins, R. M. (1953). *The conflict in education in a democratic society.* New York: Harper and Brother.

Hutchins, R. M. (1936). *The higher learning in America.* New Haven: Yale University Press.

Ihde, D. (1971). *Hermeneutic phenomenology: The philosophy of Paul Ricoeur*. Evanston: Northwestern University Press.

Jacoby, R. (1975). *Social Amnesia: A critique of contemporary psychology from Alder to Laing*. Boston: Beacon Press.

Jameson, F. (1971). *Marxism and form: 20th century dialectical theories of literature*. Princeton: Princeton University Press.

Jameson, F. (1981). *The political unconscious: Narrative as a socially symbolic act*. Ithaca: Cornell University Press.

Jameson, F. (1972). *The prison house of language: A critical account of structuralism and Russian formalism*. Princeton: Princeton University Press.

Jaspers, K. (1965). *Nietzsche: An introduction to the understanding of his philosophical activity* (C. F. Wallraff & F. J. Schmitz, Trans.). Tucson: University of Arizona Press. (Orginial work published 1935).

Karabel, J. & Halsey, A. H. (Eds.). (1977). *Power and ideology in education*. New York: Oxford University Press.

Kaufmann, W. (1974). *Nietzsche: Philosopher, psychologist, antichrist* (4th Ed.). Princeton: Princeton University Press.

Klemm, D. E. (1983). *The hermeneutical theory of Paul Ricoeur: A constructive analysis*. Lewisburg: Bucknell University Press.

Krell, D. F. (1977). *Martin Heidegger: Basic writings*. New York: Harper and Row Publishers.

Kurzweil, E. (1980). *The age of structuralism: Levi-Strauss to Foucault*. New York: Columbia University Press.

Lapointe, F. H. (1972). A bibliography of Paul Ricoeur. *Philosophy Today, 16*, 28-33.

Marcuse, H. (1976). *The aesthetic dimension: Toward a critque of Marxist aesthetics* (H. Marcuse & E. Sherover, Trans.). Boston: Beacon Press.

Maslow, A. (1968). *Toward a psychology of being* (2nd ed.). New York: Van Nostrand Reinhold Company.

National Commission on Excellence in Education. (1983). *A nation at risk: The imperative for educational reform*. Washington, DC: U.S. Government Printing Office.

Nichols, B. (1981). *Ideology and the image: Social represensation in the cinema and other media*. Bloomington: Indiana University Press.

Nietzsche, F. (1966). *Beyond good and evil: Prelude to a philosophy of the future* (W. Kaufman, Trans.). New York: Random House.

Nietzsche, F. (1968). *The birth of tragedy and the case of Wagner* (W. Kaufman, Trans.). New York: Random House.

Nietzsche, F. (1958). *The portable Nietzsche* (W. Kaufman, Trans.). New York: Viking.

Nietzsche, F. (1961). *Thus spoke Zarathustra: A book for everyone and no one* (R. J. Hollingdale, Trans.). New York: Penguin Books.

Norris, C. (1983). *Deconstruction theory and practice*. New York: Methuen and Company.

Ohmann, R. (1976). *English in America: A radical view of the profession.* New York: New Oxford Press.

The Padeia Proposal: A Symposium. (1983). *Harvard Educational Review, 53(4).*

Palmer, R. E. (1969). *Hermeneutics: Interpretation theory in Schleier-macher, Dilthey, Heidegger, and Gadamer.* Evanston: Northwestern University Press.

Persell, C. H. (1977). *Education and inequality: The roots and results of stratification in America's schools.* New York: The Free Press.

Petrie, H. C. (1981). *The Dilemna of Enquiry and Learning.* Chicago: The University of Chicago Press.

Pettit, P. (Ed.). (1977). *The concept of structuralism: A critical analysis.* Berkeley: University of California Press.

Pinar, W. (Ed.). (1974). *Curriculum theorizing: The reconceptualists.* Berkeley: McCutchan Publishing Corporation.

Pinar, W. (Ed.). (1974). *Heightened consciousness, cultural revolution, and curriculum theory.* Berkeley: McCutchan Publishing Corporation.

Pinar, W. (1976). *Sanity, madness, and the school.* Meerut, India: Sadhna Prakashan.

Pinar, W. & Grumet, M. R. (1976). *Toward a poor curriculum.* Dubugue: Kendall/Hunt Publishing Company.

Rassmussen, D. M. (1971). *Mythic-symbolic language and philosophical anthropology: A constructive interpretation of the thought of Paul Ricoeur.* The Hague: Martinus Hijhoff.

Reagan, C. E. & Steward, D. (Eds.). (1978). *The philosophy of Paul Ricoeur: An anthology of his work.* Boston: Beacon Press.

Reagan, C. E. (Ed.). (1978). *Studies in the philosophy of Paul Ricoeur*. Athens: Ohio University Press.

Reynolds, W. (1981). *English teaching and ideology*. Unpublished paper.

Reynolds, W. (1988). Freedom from control: Toward an abolition of teacher materials and minimum test in English education. *The Journal of Curriculum Theorizing 7:4*, pp. 65-86.

Reynolds, W. (1983). *The prose and the passion: What does it mean for a man to read?*. Unpublished paper.

Reynolds, W. (1984). *Reading curriculum theory: A deconstruction*. Unpublished paper.

Reynolds, W. (1983). *Reconceptualist curriculum theory, epistemes, formula, and familiarity: A critique of the present discourse in curriculum theory*. Unpublished paper.

Reynolds, W. (1982). *The self and the curriculum*. Unpublished paper.

Rickover, H. G. (1963). *American education - A national failure: The problem of our schools and what we can learn from England*. New York: E. P. Dutton & Co., Inc.

Rickover, H. G. (1959). *Education and freedom*. New York: E. P. Dutton & Co., Inc.

Ricoeur, P. (1974). *The conflict of interpretations: essays in hermeneutics*. Evanston: Northwestern University Press.

Ricoeur, P. (1973). Creativity in language: Word, polysemy, metaphor. *Philosophy Today, 17*, 97-112.

Ricoeur, P. (1970). *Freud and philosophy: An essay on interpretation* (D. Savage, Trans.). New Haven: Yale University Press.

Ricoeur, P. (1973). The hermeneutical function of distanciation. *Philosophy Today, 17*, 129-141.

Ricoeur, P. (1965). *History and truth* (C. A. Kelbley, Trans.). Evanston: Northwestern University Press.

Ricoeur, P. (1976). *Interpretation theory: Discourse and the surplus of meaning*. Fort Worth: Texas Christian University Press.

Ricoeur, P. (1973). The model of the text: Meaningful action considered as text. *Social Research, 38*,(3), 529-562.

Ricoeur, P. (1977). *The rule of metaphor: Multi- disciplinary studies of the creation of meaning in language*. Toronto: University of Toronto Press.

Ricoeur, P. (1973). The task of hermeneutics. *Philosophy Today, 17,* 113-128.

Roszak, T. (1969). *The making of a counter culture: Reflections on the technocratic society and its youthful opposition.* New York: Doubleday and Company.

Ryan, M. (1982). *Marxism and deconstruction: A critical articulation.* Baltimore: The Johns Hopkins University Press.

Sahakian, W. S. (1968). *History of philosophy.* New York: Harper and Row.

Sartre, J. P. (1968). *Search for a method.* New York: Alfred A. Knopf.

Sartre, J. P. (1978). *What is literature* (B. Frechtman, Trans.). New York: Random House. (Original work published 1964).

Sartre, J. P. (1964). *The words* (B. Frechtman, Trans.). New York: Random House. (Original work published 1964).

Saussure, F. (1968). *Course in general linguistics* (P. Owens, Trans.). New York: Philosophic Library.

Scholes, R. (1974). *Structuralism in literature: An introduction.* New Haven: Yale University Press.

Scholes, R. (1982). *Semiotics and interpretation.* New Haven: Yale University Press.

Schwartz, S. (1983). Hermeneutics and the productive imagination: Paul Ricoeur in the 1970's. *The Journal of Religion, 63,* 290-300.

Scott, A. F. (1979). *Current literary terms: A concise dictionary.* New York: St. Martins Press.

Sheridan, A. (1981). *Michael Foucault: The will to truth.* New York: Tavistock Publications.

Spiegellberg, H. (1982). *The phenomenological movement: An historical introduction.* Boston: Martinus Nijoff.

Spring, J. (1972). *Education and the rise of the corporate state.* Boston: Beacon Press.

Spring, J. (1976). *The sorting machine: National educational policy since 1945.* New York: Longman.

Stewart, D. & Bien, J. (Eds.). (1974). *Political andy social essays.* Athens: Ohio University Press.

Sturrock, J. (Ed.). (1979). *Structuralism and since: From Levi-Strauss to Derrida.* Oxford: Oxford University Press.

Van Doren, M. (1943). *Liberal education.* New York: Henry Hold and Company.

van Manen, M. (1985) Hope means commitment. *The history and social science teacher.* pp. 42-44

Weigert, A. J. (1981). *Sociology of everyday life.* New York: Longman and Company.

Wexler, P. (1983). *Critical social psychology.* London: Routledge and Kegan Paul Ltd.

Wexler, P. (1982). *Ideology and education: From critique to class.* Unpublished paper.

Wexler, P. (1977). *The sociology of education: Beyond equality.* Indiana: Bobbs-Merrill Publisher.

Wexler, P. (1981). Structure, text, and subject: A critical sociology of school knowledge. In Michael Apple (Ed.), *Cultural and economic reproduction in education.* London: Routledge and Kegan Paul Ltd.

Wheelwright, P. (1968). *Metaphor and reality.* Bloomington: Indiana University Press.

Wingo, G. M. (1974). *Philosophies of education: An introduction.* Lexington: D. C. Health and Company.

Woolf, V. (1920). *The voyage out.* New York: Harcourt Brace Jovanovich.

Young, M. F. D. (Ed.). (1971). *Knowledge and control: New directions for the sociology of education.* London: Collier-Macmillan.

Young, R. (Ed.). (1981). *Untying the text: A post-structuralist reader.* London: Routledge and Kegan Paul Ltd.

Name Index

Subject Index